8/15

Schmitt

MAKE
SELL
REPEAT

MAKE
SELL
REPEAT

The Ultimate Business Guide for **Artists**, **Crafters**, and **Makers**

Emily Worden

Filament Press • Cambridge, Massachusetts

For more creative business advice and insider tips, visit the website www.makesellrepeat.com.

First printing 2014

ISBN-10: 0990592901
ISBN-13: 978-0-9905929-0-7

Library of Congress Control Number: 2014914316

Crafts, Business, Career

ATTENTION CORPORATIONS, UNIVERSITIES, COLLEGES, AND PROFESSIONAL ORGANIZATIONS: Quantity discounts on bulk purchases of this book are available for educational, gifting, or fundraising purposes. Special books or book excerpts can also be created to fit specific needs. For information, please contact Filament Press, PO Box 400451, Cambridge, MA 02140; (617) 433-8882, contact@filamentpress.com.

This book is dedicated to all the intrepid **Artists**, **Crafters**, and **Makers** who dare to create, think, and dream.

May you build a thriving career doing what you love.

CONTENTS

Chapter 5: BUILD A BRAND.

Chapter 6: LAUNCH A WEBSITE.

Chapter 7: MAKE HAPPY CUSTOMERS.

Chapter 8: BE AN EXPERT.

Chapter 9: SELL CONFIDENTLY.

Chapter 15: WOO VIPS.

Chapter 16: GET PRESS.

Chapter 17: GROW.

INTRODUCTION

"Build your own dreams, or someone else will hire you to build theirs."

Hello fellow creative person! Good to meet you. Thanks for reading this book - there's a lot of options out there and I'm glad you found this one. Thank *yourself* too because you just made a very smart decision for your burgeoning business.

If you're reading this book, you're either a creative person who wants to start a business or you've already been in business a few years. Either way, I'm sure you're feeling stuck. If you're new to this, you might feel overwhelmed and don't know where to start. If you've been in business awhile, you might feel burned out or stumped for new ideas.

I know exactly how you're feeling because I've been there myself. I started my custom handbag business eThreads.com in 2006. I was working three jobs, getting my MBA at night, and decided to start eThreads on top of that. I had just worked an awful catering shift and decided I had enough - I put down my serving tray, picked up my bag, and swore I would start making money doing what I love.

I have been sewing since I was a kid and I liked making bags, so I decided to sell custom-made bags. I sold at craft shows, in stores, and online. I finished business school in 2008 and quit my jobs to run eThreads full-time.

Since then I've moved studios, hired employees, started several businesses, and have proudly served thousands of customers. I've also made lots of mistakes, spent way too much money, and have endured many nights in a puddle of tears and fabric scraps.

Dear reader - avoid my mistakes! I wrote this book to give you all the answers I wish I had when I was starting out. Whether you're starting a business at Day 1 or entering Year 5, you'll find all the information you need to succeed in a language that's easy to understand.

This book is meant as a reference tool - something you can highlight, underline, and pull off the shelf again and again. Each chapter stands independently but all the chapters cross-reference each other. If you're a new business owner, read the entire book sequentially because each chapter builds on the previous chapter's lessons. Even if you've been in business awhile I recommend reading the entire book because it might give you a fresh perspective and new ideas for the business.

Watch out for the *Pro Tips* - they're insider tips I've cultivated through the years, many of which have never been published before. You'll find tricks for marketing, sales, and getting press that the professionals don't want you to know. There's also a glossary in the back of the book and a handy index for your perusing needs, plus appendixes full of resources for your creative business. Please note, I have not been paid to endorse any of the products listed in this book. I just find them really useful and I know you will too.

If you have questions after reading this book, please contact me. I have coached many Artists, Crafters, and Makers to be more efficient with their business and I love to help; I'm known as "the Maker Maker" for a reason. If you have any tips or resources you'd like to share, let me know and it might be included in the next edition of this book!

It is truly my pleasure to help other people succeed. Yes, running a business takes a lot of work, but anyone can do it if they're using the right tools. I'm here to give you the tools and teach you how to use them to build a thriving, profitable business. Everyone deserves to make money doing what they love, and I'm happy to help you do it.

Here's to your success!

Emily Worden
emily@emilyworden.com
Twitter: @eMakeitHappen
www.emilyworden.com
www.makesellrepeat.com

"The important thing is not being afraid to take a chance. Remember, the greatest failure is to not try. Once you find something you love to do, be the best at doing it." - **Debbi Fields, founder of Mrs. Fields**

Chapter 1: **SET GOALS.**

"Nobody ever wrote down a plan to be broke, fat, lazy, or stupid. Those things are what happen when you don't have a plan." - **Larry Winget**

So you want to start a business? That's pretty cool. You're creative, people want to buy your stuff, so you might as well start a business and make money doing what you love, right?

Sure! It's possible, but it doesn't happen overnight. Businesses require strategy, planning, and relentless commitment. I'm sorry to start off the book with such a somber tone, but this chapter is a reality check. Do you have what it takes to be a business owner? Do you have the time and resources available to make it happen?

TOP TEN QUALITIES NEEDED TO RUN A BUSINESS

I used to think the world of crafting was a pretty glamorous place - you make something and people pay for it - how great is that? Now that I'm on the other side of the table, I see it's really a world of long nights, aching backs, and unpredictable paydays.

Starting your own creative business is tough; there's more to it than being artistic. There's serious things to consider like taxes, registration, paperwork, and liabilities. If you want to make money doing this, start thinking of yourself like a business owner. Here's the top 10 qualities needed to run a successful business:

(1) Determination: You must absolutely believe you're destined to share your talent with the world and you're going to kick ass doing it. Your attitude determines your latitude, so you've got to be utterly determined to succeed. I mean it - this is a really tough lifestyle filled with setbacks. Be prepared to hurdle over disappointments and keep your eyes on the prize.

Don't let fear of rejection hold you back. I know it's really scary to create something you love then put it out there for the world to criticize. My advice? Get over it. You're not a $100 bill - not everyone is going to like you. In fact, it's better to appeal to a smaller niche market than a larger general market - we'll get into that in Chapter 3. Besides, criticism is good - it's a chance to improve your products and create happy customers.

(2) Excellent Time Management: Every teacher I ever had complained about my time management. One high school teacher even wrote on my report card, "Emily would be a great student if she got out of her own way." I was the worst with deadlines and the queen of all-nighters.

Now? I'm a time management machine. It happened in my mid-twenties when I was in grad school at night, working a full-time job and two part-time jobs ... then decided to start eThreads on top of that. Yeah, I had to learn time management pretty fast. Now I love it. Give me "to do" lists and I'll give you the world. You have to be this excited about time management too or you'll never be able to work on a business with everything else going on in your life.

(3) Discipline: You're the boss now; you don't have to report to anyone else. I know this isn't shocking news - it's probably one of the reasons you wanted to start a business in the first place. Stop to consider though if you really have the discipline to set a schedule and stick with it.

I am the worst boss I've ever had. I'm very demanding, work really long days, and set impossible deadlines. I don't advocate treating actual employees like this (seriously, don't) but the rules are different for you. This is your baby, your business, and you need to be 1,000% committed to it.

Set a schedule and stick to it. If you're scheduled to work Friday night and all your friends are headed to the movies, you can't go. Sorry, you have to work. Not only do you need to understand that, but your friends have to respect it too. They'll say, "But you're the boss! You can take time off!" No, no you can't. This is your job and you're committed to the schedule.

(4) Organization: Design a system to organize the bills, receipts, and invoices for your business. Remember the bank account paperwork, tax information, and inventory too. We'll discuss paperwork in Chapter 2.

For now, understand there's a lot that goes into your business and you need a filing system to keep on top of it.

Use Evernote and Google Docs for online organization. Evernote (www.evernote.com) gathers all your pictures, files, notes, and web pages in one easily accessible place from a computer, tablet, or smartphone. I love it because I no longer keep dozens of search tabs open for days just to remember one little thing.

Google Docs (www.docs.google.com) is Google's version of Microsoft Office and it's free with a Gmail account. Create documents, spreadsheets, forms, and presentations that are automatically saved to the cloud. Access it anywhere there's internet, and you can even download files to work offline if internet isn't available. I wrote this book with Google Docs because it automatically saves every keystroke so you can't lose information if the computer unexpectedly shuts down. Plus, since it's Google, all your Docs are easily searchable. (Trust me, you'll use that feature all the time.)

(5) Focus: If you're anything like me, you're pretty excited to start new projects and then try to sell everything you can. Fellow maker, resist the temptation. You're a businessperson now and you need to make smart business decisions. Each new product requires an investment of time, money, and energy and you don't have a lot of that to spare. Let me be clear - keep adding new products to your line, but they must compliment your existing products.

For example, eThreads sells custom bags. I've also been experimenting with custom lanyards, which is a product expansion that fits with my line. However, if I wanted to make custom dog collars it would be too much of a distraction from the eThreads brand. Stay focused on your main product line and how to continuously improve it. This will be discussed extensively in Chapter 3.

(6) Hard Working: Not only will you be the manufacturer of your product, but also the customer service agent, shipping coordinator, website operator, content writer, photographer, marketing department, sales team, and secretary. Oh and ... you most likely won't be getting paid for *a while*. Yeah, I'm telling you - this is hard work people! It's not glamorous. You'll have late nights, emotional fits, and depleted bank accounts. Are you capable of this madness?

(7) Patient: You most likely won't see a profit the first year, and even possibly the second year. It takes most businesses three years to make a profit. Other things will happen too - you're promised some press that never happens, your website takes longer to make than expected, there's ridiculously long lines at the post office every.time.you.go. This is not an overnight success story here.

(8) Efficient: There are three steps to completing a task: (1) preparing to do the task, (2) doing the task, and (3) cleaning up after the task. Every time you stop a task before it's complete, you're creating two-thirds more work for yourself. If you're in the middle of something and get interrupted, you have to go back through steps one and two all over again. Not only that, but gears shift in your head when you're distracted and they take time to adjust back to the task.

Be more efficient with these simple steps:

Eliminate distractions whenever possible. For example, I put my phone in another room when I need to get serious work done. Then I'm not tempted to check it every time I hear the bell like Pavlov's dog. Likewise, don't answer phone calls from numbers you don't recognize. Let it go to voicemail and check later.

Commit to checking email only once or twice a day. Even though I run several businesses, I only check email twice a day. If I stopped what I was doing to answer emails every time they came in, I'd never get any real work done. I know today's society expects you to answer everything within minutes, but trust me, the world won't end if you only respond to emails at 11:00 am and 7:00 pm. Speaking of ...

Don't answer emails first thing in the morning. If you start your day answering emails, you'll waste hours catering to other needs before taking care of your own. Start your day on your terms and get your own work done. Leave the distractions for later. Speaking of distractions...

Don't ever go on social media in the morning. Same reason as above. Nothing productive ever happens on social media unless you're promoting your business (check out Chapter 14 for juicy tips).

Apply the 80/20 rule. We'll discuss this in the next chapter, but for now understand that 20% of your activities lead to 80% of the results. What activities get you closer to your goals or provide the most profit? Focus exclusively on those.

Batch your activities. Set aside chunks of time to do one thing exclusively. For example, pay all your bills at once for the entire month. Answer all emails in one session. Do your laundry in one day. Run all your errands in one day, and plan your route to avoid left turns. (If it's efficient enough for UPS drivers, it's efficient enough for you too.) Remember, starting and stopping tasks adds two-thirds to your time, so batch activities and focus on one batch at a time.

Make lists. Keep a running list of everything you need to get done. Each night, review the list and create a smaller list of tasks to accomplish the next day. Prioritize those tasks in order of importance - consider labeling each task "A," "B," and "C." It is important to prioritize tasks because you're probably not going to get everything done. Tackle the "A" tasks first and move on to the "B" tasks only when everything that's "A" is complete. In a pinch, just highlight the most pressing tasks and don't stop until those highlighted tasks are done.

Feeling overwhelmed by big tasks? The list will be your best friend. Take the big tasks and break them down into small, bite-sized chunks. If you just write "clean out house" on your to-do list, you'll never get it done and those words will mock you forever. Instead, list each room of your house, then break down items in that room that need cleaning. For example, "Kitchen: Clean out junk drawer. Clean oven. Polish floors. Empty refrigerator. Bathroom: Clean toilet. Wash shower curtains. Scrub tub."

This may seem crazy, but trust me - your big tasks are suddenly less overwhelming when they're broken down into smaller pieces. For example, you might find yourself cleaning out the junk drawer while gabbing on the phone with Aunt Matilda. Voila! You're one step closer to a clean house and you get to scratch something off your list. Oh it feels so good.

(9) Goal Oriented: Set SMART Goals. I'm talking **S**pecific, **M**easurable, **A**ttainable, **R**ealistic and **T**imely goals. Determine how much you want to sell by the end of this quarter, this year, and 2-3 years from now. Decide which sales channels you'll enter this year and how many customers you'll have by the end of the year. Define your top three marketing goals for the next six months. Make your goals very specific and define how you'll measure success - sales numbers, customer acquisition, followers on Facebook, reduced costs, etc...

The key here is *specific and measurable*. If your goals are precise they're more attainable. Why? Goals keep you motivated and focused. They give you specific steps to success. Detailed goals help your brain analyze the necessary steps to achieve them. Remember, a goal is only a dream until you write it down.

Set some crazy, wild, and seemingly unattainable goals too. Want Oprah to endorse your business? Go for it; figure out the steps to make it happen. Nothing is impossible if you've got the hustle and drive. Besides, your wild and crazy goals will keep you going those late nights when a mental breakdown is on the horizon. I'm serious. Imagining Oprah gushing about your product will keep the stamina up when you feel like you're just ready to cry.

(10) Frugal: Listen up … you're not getting paid from this business for a long, long time. If you want to run the business full-time, you've got to save up at least a year's worth of expenses (more on that later). Even when you're making money it's mostly reinvested back into the business. You have to say no to take-out food, coffee on the run, and movie nights. You might have to reduce your cable or cell phone package too. Not only must you save, but you're also going to have to work ridiculously long hours and not get paid for some time. Cool with you? OK, moving on...

QUESTIONS TO ASK YOURSELF BEFORE STARTING A BUSINESS

It's time to think long and hard about what you want from this business. For example, what are your financial goals - do you just want extra grocery money or do you want to quit your day job? Those two options require very different strategies and levels of effort.

Also, realistically consider your schedule. How many hours per week can you devote to the business? Obviously you won't hit $100,000 in sales without a little effort. Can you carve out extra time by eliminating other activities or becoming more efficient?

Think about your quality of life too - the business is going to affect your family and those closest to you. You're going to be largely unavailable for a while - will they be ok with that? Will they be happy for you? Do you have a support system who can give you help when you need it?

Finally, consider your workspace. You must have a dedicated spot for your business (more on that later in this chapter). Find a quiet, private place in your house to clean out and use exclusively. Ask your family or roommates if they're ok with it.

PLANNING YOUR BUSINESS

You have to plan the business and finances. I talk about both topics extensively in the next chapter, but I'll mention the bullet points here.

Business Plan: Outline your entire business strategy before selling anything. I'm talking market research, production strategy, pricing structure, marketing plan, and all the proper paperwork filed. Don't worry! I've got it all covered in this book and it's actually pretty fun to do.

Financial Plan: You're likely paying for this business yourself so you need a lot of savings. I recommend saving at least six months of operating expenses before opening shop. If you want to quit your job and create full-time, you'll need one year of personal expenses in savings plus startup funds for the business plus no personal debt (and a 700+ credit score doesn't hurt either). Yes I'm serious! Operating a business takes money - don't run out before you even start.

BUSINESS RESOURCES

Lucky for you, today's environment is very welcome to creative businesses. Not only is there demand for your product, but there's a lot of support opportunities too. It's important to seek business advice from professionals and network with fellow crafters who are business owners. They'll have tremendous insight and help you avoid common mistakes. Here's some resources to get started:

SCORE (www.score.org): Free business mentoring advice provided by over 1,500 volunteers in the United States. SCORE is an excellent resource for indie artists because they offer advice on business plans, marketing, finance - and did I mention it's *free?* I know several business owners who've had great experiences with SCORE's mentoring services. Trust me, use this resource and you'll achieve profitability faster and easier than going it alone.

U.S. Small Business Administration (www.sba.gov): The SBA is an excellent resource for small businesses across the nation. They have advice on starting and managing your business plus information on loans and grants.

Women- and minority-owned businesses: If you're a minority or a woman, there are additional resources available to you. Check out www.MWBE.com to start, it's packed with tips about starting a business and special grants. There are lots of blogs and networking sites for women business owners too, like www.indiebizchicks.com, www.theswitchboards.com, and www.sheownsit.com.

Craftster (www.craftster.com): This is a *huge* online community for DIY and crafts. You'll find free craft projects, advice, inspiration, and city guides listing events in your area. The forum is excellent too. You're not allowed to post projects that you're selling, but you are allowed to buy ad space.

Makezine (www.makezine.com): You creative nuts are going to love this site from the publishers of *Make: Magazine* and pioneers of the Maker Movement. It's filled with DIY projects in all genres, including crafts and electronics. The blog is a fun resource and you can even write an article for tons of exposure.

The Society of Arts and Crafts (www.societyofcrafts.org): Founded in 1897 in my beloved Boston, the SAC is a national non-profit and the country's oldest craft organization. They encourage crafters and artists with educational resources, awards programs, and the opportunity to show your work in their galleries.

The Craft Mafia (www.craftmafia.com): Founded in 2003 by nine women in Austin, TX who formed a group around the shared love of craft. It has since grown into an active forum for networking and support for all crafters. Many cities even have their own Craft Mafia chapter, check out their site to see if you're one of the lucky ones.

Meetups (www.meetup.com): A fantastic website allowing local people with all sorts of interests to meet, socialize, and experience together. You'll find groups on nearly everything - volunteering, business, technology, movies, Frisbee, hikers ... even crafting. I just searched "Craft" within 5 miles of my city and found over 40 creative groups, including "Etsy Artists of Boston."

Hello Craft (www.hellocraft.com): The fine folks behind Hello Craft are dedicated to empowering indie artists and advancing the handmade movement. Become a member for $35/year to support their mission and receive exclusive access to handy resources. Check out their fantastic book *Handmade to Sell* too.

Etsy Forums (www.etsy.com/forums): If you have a question about running an indie business, I bet it has already been asked and answered in an Etsy forum. People are very willing to share tips and tricks here, it's excellent insider information.

Handmadeology (www.handmadeology.com): A valuable resource that teaches creative people how to successfully sell their handmade goods. Find excellent articles about pricing, creating tutorials, improving your Etsy shop, product photography tips, and so much more.

Ravelry (www.ravelry.com): A massive online support community focused entirely on fiber arts. Ravelry's four million members share projects, ideas, and materials for the love of knitting, crocheting, weaving, and spinning.

Indiemade (www.indiemade.com): An excellent resource for building your artist website cheaply and easily, Indiemade is also packed with resources for indie artists. Browse their articles about marketing, packaging, pricing, craft shows, and a host of other topics.

Library: Me and the library … we have a special connection. Hello, you can get books on any topic you've ever imagined, all for free. Want to learn how to crochet better? There's several books about it. Want to learn accounting for your business? Oh yeah, books on that too. Want to learn how to be a more confident salesperson? BOOM - entire shelves dedicated to this stuff! Seriously, don't overlook this valuable resource. (The free movies and CDs aren't bad either. Come on! Do you need any more convincing?)

WORK/LIFE BALANCE

Everyone has a hard time finding balance between work and play. This is especially difficult when you're running an indie business. First, you're probably selling something you love to make, so it's already a mix of work and play. Plus, your workstation is most likely in your home, so there's blurred lines there too. You need boundaries my friend.

First, separate everything between your business and personal life. For example, set up separate bank accounts, maintain separate email addresses, and use separate phone lines (we'll cover this in Chapter 2). When you're working you need to be 100% focused and not distracted by temptations in your personal life.

Next, set specific times for work and stick to it. If you're scheduled to check business email at 11:00 am and 7:00 pm, only do it at those times. If you know Wednesday nights are the only time in the week you have to work on the business, then nothing else stands in your way on Wednesday nights.

Likewise, set specific family time and stick to it. If you have a Thursday night pizza date with your family, don't miss that because of the business. You're asking the family to respect your work time so you must respect their time too.

Also, have a workstation in your house that's dedicated to business only. Try to keep business out of other areas of your house. When you go to work, personal distractions should disappear. Likewise, when you emerge from the studio you must leave work behind.

It took me years to master work/life balance, and I still have some improving to do. I remember one Thanksgiving awhile back I got a nasty email from a customer just as we were sitting down to eat. I was in the other room frantically emailing the customer because I was so upset. Meanwhile everyone else was upset with me because they were waiting to eat. Ugh, I cringe when I think about that now. Listen, I'm all about 5-star service and wowing customers. But it's just the same to people if they hear back in 30 minutes or 24 hours. Heck, I've even gotten back to customers two days later and they said, "Thanks for responding so quickly."

Seriously, I can't emphasize enough you don't have to be at customers' beck-and-call 24 hours a day. People understand you need to take evenings and weekends off. Provide excellent customer service by being courteous, generous, and thoughtful. They'll remember small gestures more than response time.

SETTING UP YOUR WORKSPACE

I've mentioned a workspace several times already because it's so important. It's your studio. Your headquarters. Your home base. It's where you design, create, and ship your products. When you're setting up a home-based studio, follow these tips to get it right:

(1) *Make a list of everything you'll need to work:* I'm talking storage, lights, chairs, tables (bedspreads, couches, or living room floors don't count). You'll also ideally fit a computer and printer in there. Your packing supplies too. Oh, and don't forget about a place to actually *make* your work. And all the supplies that come with it. Write it all down and figure out a place in the house that could feasibly work.

(2) *Once you've found the space, give it a thorough cleaning:* Get rid of the clutter, wipe down the shelves, add a coat of paint. You're going to be spending a lot of time in there so make it your own.

(3) *Get creative with materials:* My first sewing station was a hollow-core door over two filing cabinets. I only got rid of it because it didn't fit in my new apartment. My second sewing station (and still standing 12 years later) is a reinforced piece of plywood on 4 cheap shelving units. (Storage bonus!) Other inexpensive ideas: Use shoe boxes for storage. Find baskets at the dollar store. Look around on Craigslist, I've found great office chairs there. Use recycled cardboard boxes for storage and write the contents on the outside for easy identification.

(4) *Go vertical:* You're quickly going to run out of room, so build up. Shelves are you best friend here, make the most of them. Nail screw-top jars to the bottom of shelves to store small things or just add hooks for hanging. Do an internet search for "DIY storage ideas" and spend days in a storage vortex.

(5) *Set up an inspiration corkboard:* An excellent place to pin fabric samples, sketches, photographs, random notes … you get the idea. Trust me, it'll fill up fast.

(6) *Clean your station every night:* Even if you're elbow-deep in a serious project, I'm sure there are a few spare things to pick up. Reserve a space to store works-in-progress. I have a series of stacking shelves that store eThreads' works-in-progress. This way, the main cutting station is cleaned off each night with all the scissors and thread put away. Your productivity will increase in a cleaner room, trust me.

... Oh hi there! You're still reading. Good, that means you're not scared off yet. If you feel undaunted by these Herculean requests, then welcome to the proud team of creative business owners. Great to have you. Now flip the page to learn everything you need to know about running a business. It gets really fun, I promise!

Chapter 2: **GO LEGIT.**

"There's no scarcity of opportunity to make a living at what you love. There is only a scarcity of resolve to make it happen." - **Wayne Dyer**

Confession time: I went to business school and didn't learn a thing about starting a business. Sure, I learned tons of stuff about *running* a business, but never learned how to *start* a business. Entrepreneurship just wasn't a thing then.

Here I was in business school learning everything I could ever want to know about business except - duh - where do I start? I knew I wanted to make custom handbags, but I didn't know anything about business paperwork or finance or regulations. I learned it all the hard way and made several mistakes.

Dear reader, don't repeat my errors! I wrote this chapter just for you and packed it with every bit of information I wish someone told me when I was starting out.

This isn't the sexiest chapter in the book but it's really important. It's like we're building a house - I know you want to start picking out paint colors and bathroom fixtures, but we have to pour the foundation first. This chapter is your concrete foundation.

THE FOUR BIG QUESTIONS TO ASK ABOUT YOUR BUSINESS

(1) *What product(s) am I selling?*
(2) *What type of customer is buying?*
(3) *How am I making the product and selling it?*
(4) *How am I going to finance the business?*

(1) Product: What product(s) are you selling?

This topic is so important I've dedicated an entire chapter to it (coming up next). I will mention the basic points here:

(1) *Your product has to satisfy a need, want, or desire for your customer:* People buy products to solve problems. How does your product do this? Sometimes it's obvious - like heating pads for sore backs. Sometimes it's more subtle - like cufflinks to enhance a suit.

(2) *Study the market.* If you have a product idea, examine the market to gauge popularity. Start with Etsy (www.etsy.com) because it's easily searchable and filled with handmade goods. Refer to Chapter 3 and "How to Find a Niche" for more tips and detailed information.

(3) *Identify the competition.* As you're studying the market, notice the competition. It can be anywhere, from fellow crafters to big box stores. Every product has direct and indirect competition. Direct competition comes from those business selling the *same* product to the same target market. Indirect competition comes from any business selling a *substitute* product to the same market. For example, candle makers experience direct competition with other candle makers, but they also have indirect competition with potpourri, flameless candles, room spray, and essential oil diffusers.

After you've identified the competition, study them. How long have they been in business? How are their prices compared to yours? Examine their website, products, branding, and photographs - what do they do well? What can you do better? Look for opportunities, like offering products they don't.

(2) Customers: Who are they and what do they want?

You might be tempted to say, "Everyone is my customer" because frankly, anyone who wants to give you money is welcome, right? True, but let me share a favorite expression: "If you're selling to everyone, then you're selling to no one." That means if you don't have a clear vision of your ideal customer and what they want, you're chasing everyone and appealing to no one. What a waste of time and energy.

It's absolutely critical to identify your type(s) of customer. Everything about your branding, marketing, and sales strategy revolves around your ideal customers. We're going to talk about this a lot in the book, so it's important to address now. Ask yourself, "Who is my customer?" "How old are they?" "Where do they live?" "Why are they buying my products?"

Create *customer personas* around those types of customers who might shop with you for different reasons. For example, furniture makers have several potential customer personas: interior decorators looking for custom projects, upscale furniture stores wanting to showcase indie products, and individuals shopping for their home. Each of these personas buy furniture for different reasons and therefore have different needs and require different information.

For excellent examples of customer personas including a Customer Profiling Worksheet, see "Profiling Your Most Valuable Customers" in the book *The Crafty Superstar Ultimate Craft Business Guide* by Grace Dobush.

Not all customers are created equal: Are you familiar with the Pareto Principle? Also known as the "80/20 rule," it dictates that 80% of outcomes result from 20% of the effort. Economist Vilfredo Pareto (1848-1923) first observed that 80% of society's wealth was produced and possessed by 20% of its population. Pareto even observed this phenomenon in his garden peas - 20% of his pods produced 80% of the peas. Ever since, the Pareto Principle has been a guidepost for economists and sociologists alike.

What does this have to do with you? EVERYTHING! I could write an entire chapter on how to apply the 80/20 rule to your life to achieve maximum effectiveness. Let's just stick with one example for now, and it involves your customers.

As you develop a roster of customers, you'll notice that some are very easy to work with and others suck up precious time. Look at your sales sheet and identify which types of customers provide the most profit for the least effort. Examine those specific customers and try to identify a pattern - where did they come from? Are they buying your products for a specific purpose? Why do they buy from you and not a competitor? Identify patterns in your top customers to find more like them.

(3) Production: How are you making the product and where is it sold?

There's an in-depth discussion about this in Chapter 3, but it's an important question for your business and thus worth mentioning here.

Obviously you're quite familiar with the process for making your own products, but it's important to really examine the steps here. For example, let's talk supplies. Gone are the days of purchasing supplies in craft stores, that's too expensive now. Buy in bulk or wholesale instead (see Chapter 3 for tips).

Also, streamline the creative process. Are there steps you can batch together or skip altogether? Can you teach anyone to do certain tasks? Can you make steps more efficient? I have examples in Chapter 4, and I'll offer one here from eThreads:

Our bag patterns used to be made of paper and we'd have to cut fabric slowly for fear of cutting the pattern. Today, our patterns are made with thick plastic sheets and we can move a lot faster. Find opportunities to streamline your process too.

Finally, where is your product sold? Today's creative entrepreneurs have a lot of options. You can sell online on Etsy or your own website. You can sell to retail stores and wholesalers. What about craft shows and local art fairs? Some products are excellent for museum gift shops. What about making "blank label" products that companies can order as gifts for their clients? I love partnering up with other businesses that don't compete with me but have similar customers, there are so many opportunities there (more on that in Chapter 13).

Find people willing to pay for your talent too. Many people have custom projects like lawn sculptures, pet portraits, and unique engagement rings. List your products or services on Craigslist (www.craigslist.org) under "For sale" or "Services." Try your luck at CustomMade (www.custommade.com) too; they connect thousands of artists with consumers who are looking for one-of-a-kind custom projects. See Chapter 17 for more information.

There's lots of "sales channels" or "revenue streams" for your craft. To learn more about these options, see Chapter 6 (Website), Chapter 10 (Craft Shows), Chapter 11 (Etsy), and Chapter 12 (Stores).

(4) Finance: How are you going to pay for the business?

Here's the good news about starting a creative business: you don't need a lot of start-up capital. ("Capital" includes money and other items needed to make your craft, like machinery and property.) You likely already own the necessary tools and hopefully can work out of your own home and not a rented studio. Since you're starting small, you'll need to purchase very little raw materials too.

That said, you do need to spend money to start the business and keep it running. Your financing options are personal finances, savings, credit cards, getting a loan from a bank or from a family member/friend.

Obviously the best options are personal finances and savings. If you're really responsible with credit cards and pay off the full amount each month, you can use credit cards too, but I don't recommend it. It's difficult to get a bank loan these days for small businesses, so loans from friends or family members might be your next best option.

If you borrow money from a friend, get the agreement in writing. Spell out exactly how much is being loaned, at what interest rate, the expected life of your loan, and payment plans. Also discuss penalties for not paying on time. These types of arrangements can ruin relationships, so treat it professionally and responsibly.

The best way to fund the business is with your own finances, otherwise known as "bootstrapping." You must show restraint here. I went crazy when I started eThreads because I love fabric and suddenly I had an excuse to buy it all the time. Oh, what a mistake. I'm still carrying fabrics I first bought over eight years ago. I thought the fabric was pretty at the time, but my inexperience proved it wasn't what my customers wanted. Over the years I've become much smarter at buying fabrics, and if I could go back eight years and tell myself to stop buying everything I'd be in a much better position now.

If you bootstrap the business, put financial boundaries in place. Know your spending limits. Keep separate accounts for business and personal finances. If you want to quit your job and run the craft business full-time, save enough money to cover at least a year of expenses (because you won't be getting a paycheck for a while.) Pay off all your personal debt first too. Budget yourself with less visits to the coffee shop and less take-out food. Soon you'll be reinvesting everything you make back into the business, so it's important to learn financial discipline now.

A quick note on business loans: Most banks make loans when you've been in business 2-3 years and show strong profits. They examine your "Six Cs" - Credit (your credit score), Capacity (your ability to repay the loan), Condition (your loan's specific terms and conditions), Capital (how much you need and how you'll use the funds), Collateral (your assets), and Character (your reputation). Even if you pass all these hurdles, banks are still stingier today with small business loans. You may have better luck at your local small bank, credit union, or an institution that specializes in small business lending.

PROPER BOOKKEEPING

It's really important to maintain good business records. Keep copies of everything - receipts, invoices, bills, checks - and file them in an organized system. Did you get gas driving to a craft show? Keep the receipt (and record the miles). Did you get a parking receipt at that craft show? Keep it. Did you buy food at the craft show? Get a receipt and file it away too.

The ink on receipts usually fades, so write over the important information (date, location, purchase amount) in pen. Also label each receipt with the purpose of the purchase and the category to which it belongs. For example, if you have coffee with your accountant, label the receipt, "Meals & Entertainment, with accountant, reviewed bookkeeping." Buy a divided folder and label the sections like "Meals," "Gas," "Shipping," "Office supplies," and "Inventory" and file receipts in the appropriate section. After you've filed taxes for that year, scoop out all the receipts and put them in a big envelope labeled with the appropriate year. Keep these envelopes for seven years, because the IRS can audit up to six years past.

Update your sales and expenses every month. (Remember to record your driving miles too - the IRS will want to know your mileage at the beginning of the year, the end of the year, and how many miles were for business. Keep a small notebook in your car and record the mileage when driving for business.) It's not that exciting, but it will make your life a lot easier come tax time. Plus, you'll be up to date on the profits or losses for your business each month.

I use a simple Excel sheet to do this, but you can always use professional accounting software like QuickBooks or Mint (www.mint.com), which is free. You could also attend a bookkeeping, QuickBooks, or accounting class at your local community college or adult learning center. If you're really confused, talk to an accountant or professional bookkeeper. (We'll talk about hiring accountants and other professionals later in the chapter.)

Monthly Income & Expenditures: I mentioned this above, and it's really important. Record all the money going in and out of your business each month. Track sales, purchases, and anything else that affects the money in your business account. It's important to update statements every month to take a temperature of your business and gauge its health.

Profit & Loss Statement: (Also known as a "P&L," "Earnings statement," or "Income statement.") This is a condensed version of your monthly income and expenditures. It has a running total of your income and expenditures for information at a glance. P&Ls are usually categorized monthly or quarterly.

Balance Sheet: This is a relatively simple form listing your business' assets and liabilities. Assets are anything you *own* that has value, like cash, machinery, and raw inventory. Liabilities are anything that you *owe* such as credit card debts, advertising bills, or pending wholesale orders. It's the snapshot for your business, an easy way to understand its financial health.

Taxes: I'm not a tax expert but I can offer some advice here. First, if your business makes more than $400 a year, the federal government requires that you pay a self-employment tax. The self-employment tax is the freelancer's equivalent of Social Security and Medicare tax that would be automatically deducted from a regular paycheck.

In addition, if you owe the federal government more than $1,000 on tax day (April 15), they'll charge you interest and penalties for not making estimated tax payments during the year. In my state of Massachusetts, that minimum number is $400, but it varies by state.

To avoid penalties, send money every quarter to the federal government and your state government. How much should you send? That's tough to say because it depends on your income. Those just starting their business will probably be ok sending 15% of income, but to be really safe try to keep it around 25%. (Don't worry, you'll be credited if you overpay.) For example, if you sell $5,000 worth of art in a quarter, send $1,000 to the federal government and $250 to your state when the next quarterly estimated tax payment is due. To see the current federal tax rate and filing instructions, check out form 1040 at www.irs.gov. For my friends in Massachusetts, you'll also want form

1-ES "Massachusetts Estimated Income Tax" from www.mass.gov. For those in the other 49 states, search for a similar document on your own state's website or ask an accountant in your state.

You can deduct more expenses than you probably thought possible. For example, did you know you can deduct a home office? If 5% of your home is used for the business, then you can deduct 5% of the mortgage insurance, real estate taxes, insurance, etc... If you're renting, you can even deduct part of the renter's insurance. A good accountant can outline all the deductions for you - it's a big help, especially when you're starting out.

For more information from a tax expert, I highly recommend the book *Etsy-preneurship* by Jason Malinak. He is a CPA and Certified Treasury Professional who specializes in taxes for creative entrepreneurs like yourself. *The Craft Artist's Legal Guide* by Attorney Richard Stim has an extensive chapter about taxes too.

Inventory List: Keep a running tally of your finished inventory and raw materials because you'll need this information at tax time. You'll likely be filling out a Schedule C (Profit or Loss from Business) and you must note how much in raw materials you had at the beginning of the year and how much you had at the end.

Calculate raw materials with inventory and product costs. For example, if you sell 50 necklaces in a year and you know each necklace takes 2 beads and 36" of leather at a cost of $2.50 per necklace, you can calculate (50 necklaces x $2.50 raw materials) = $125 in raw materials used during the year; that's what you enter on your Schedule C.

LEGAL STRUCTURE

Your business must be registered in your state as a certain entity type, business structure, or legal structure. "But Emily," you're thinking, "I'm just a small indie artist. Why do I need to know about legal structures?" Well, you must file as *something* when you're doing paperwork, so it's important. As an indie artist, you will most likely be a Sole Proprietor, Partnership, or Limited Liability Company (LLC).

Sole Proprietorship: This is the most common legal structure for indie artists. You don't have to sign any formal paperwork to be a sole proprietor. It doesn't cost anything nor do you need to renew your status annually. You and your business are considered linked, there is no separation. The downside is that you're 100% liable for any legal or financial issues from the business. If someone sues your business, then your personal assets are at risk; they're not separate from the business.

That's ok for most sole proprietors working out of their home - there isn't a storefront where customers can get hurt, and the products sold are usually harmless. However, if you sell baby products, food, candles, body care, or if customers come into your home, you have a higher liability risk (we'll talk about this later in the chapter when we discuss insurance). If the idea of having your personal assets at risk makes you nervous, consider an LLC (see below).

Partnership: If your business has two or more owners, file as a general partnership. Just like a sole proprietorship, each partner's personal assets are at risk. However, it's a little trickier with partnerships. Because both partners are liable for business debts, if one partner is unable to cover their portion of the debt creditors can pursue the other partner, even if the latter has already paid their debt. That is, if you've paid your half of the debt but your partner hasn't, you're still liable for their half of the debt.

There is a little more paperwork involved with partnerships too. Unlike sole proprietorships, partnerships must get an EIN (a federal tax ID number, more on that below). Also, partners should draft a partnership agreement outlining each person's specific contributions and duties. The agreement should also determine allocation of profits and losses, voting rules, and how to proceed when a partner wishes to withdraw from the business or there's a change of ownership. See *The Craft Artist's Legal Guide* by Attorney Richard Stim for an excellent example of a partnership agreement.

Limited Liability Company (LLC): A favorite among small business owners, LLCs can be owned by an individual or group of people and personal assets are not at risk. In an LLC, your personal identity is separate from your business, meaning only your business can be sued if something goes wrong. You're not completely free of responsibility (thus *limited* liability), but you're only on the hook for the amount you put into the business. For example, if you've invested $2,000 into the business and someone sues you, the most they can get is $2,000 - your home, car, and personal finances are not at risk.

Sounds great, right? Well, here's the downside: LLCs are costly and time-consuming, especially for indie artists. Though you don't need an attorney or accountant to file, it involves a lot of paperwork and hundreds of dollars in fees. For example, in my state of Massachusetts, it costs $500 to file LLC paperwork, plus an extra $500 each year to file an annual report with the Secretary of State. Fees for each state vary, get more information at your state's *.gov* site (e.g., www.mass.gov).

There's other legal structures like Cooperatives, S Corporations, and C Corporations, but you don't need to worry about those now or likely ever. Your state's *.gov* site has information about those too if you're curious.

REQUIRED PAPERWORK

Here's a list of paperwork you must file when starting any type of business in the USA:

Registering Your Business/DBA ("Doing Business As"): A DBA is also known as a "trade name," "assumed name," or "fictitious business name." Choosing a name for your business is a big deal; we'll talk about it in Chapter 5. If the name of your business is different than your own name, you must register in the state where you plan to do business. For example, if your name is John Smith but you want to operate as Smith Photography, then you need a DBA filed in your town, city, or county clerk as Smith Photography. This applies to all types of businesses including sole proprietorships, partnerships, and LLCs. There is a small fee to register the business name and you must renew every 1-4 years, depending on the laws in your state. Visit the website for your town or state for more information. Please note - registering a DBA does not give you the exclusive rights to use the name. That requires trademarks or copyrights, and you'll learn more about that in Chapter 3.

Zoning: When registering the business, town officials will verify your zoning allows for your type of business. In most cases it's no problem as long as you don't post signs outside your home advertising the business or make a lot of loud noises. If zoning doesn't allow your type of business in the neighborhood, apply for a special use permit.

Sales Tax License: Also known as a "certificate of resale," "sellers permit," or "certificate of authority." In some states it's a criminal offense to operate without a sellers permit, so listen up: *if you sell taxable goods you need a sales tax license.* The definition of "taxable" varies by state, but you're most likely selling a taxable product. This certificate allows you to charge and collect sales tax for the state in which you're selling.

Now here's where it gets tricky. If you sell items online, you only need to collect sales tax for the state in which you're registered. (For example, I operate out of Massachusetts, so only Massachusetts residents are charged sales tax when they buy eThreads products online.) If you sell at craft shows, art fairs, and expos in your state you need the sales tax license for that. If you sell at shows outside of your state, you need sales tax licenses for those states too. I know crafters who sell at craft shows full-time all over the country and have a dozen sales tax licenses. They're responsible for filing taxes with each of those states every year.

Go through your state agency responsible for collecting sales tax, it's usually the Department of Revenue. The first time you'll likely have to file and pay once at the end of year. After that, the state might increase your filing schedule to quarterly or even monthly, depending on your sales volume.

Federal Tax ID: Also known as "EIN" for "Employer Identification Number," it's like a social security number for your business. If you're a sole proprietor and don't have any employees, you don't need a Federal Tax ID because your social security number is sufficient. If your business is an LLC or partnership OR if you hire employees (even as a sole proprietor), you'll need a Federal Tax ID. Get one either way, it's free through the Internal Revenue Service. Go to www.irs.gov and enter "EIN" in the search box for step-by-step instructions for filing online. You'll complete form SS-4 and receive an EIN immediately.

Health Department Permits: If you sell food, either directly to customers or as a wholesaler to other retailers, you need a health department permit from your town or county. If you're selling food at craft shows, you'll likely need a permit from those towns as well. This costs about $25, depending on the size of your business and type of equipment you have. The health department will also want to inspect your facilities (and home-based facilities are usually verboten).

Insurance: There's several types of insurance to consider for your small business:

(1) *Home insurance:* If you're working out of the home, consider home insurance that covers your business as well. Talk with your insurance agent about covering any tools, equipment, inventory, or materials stored in your home. If you have customers coming into your house I especially urge you to have extra home insurance. If you work outside of the home, consider property insurance for your studio to cover fire, theft, vandalism, and other damage.

(2) *Health insurance:* Hopefully you're lucky enough to get health insurance through your employer or partner's employer. Otherwise, you might be able to get a group discount through an artist guild or similar association. Check out membership organizations like the American Craft Council (www.craftcouncil.org/membership/join), the Craft and Hobby Association (www.craftandhobby.org), and the Freelancers Union (www.freelancersunion.org). The Artists' Health Insurance Resource Center (www.ahirc.org) is filled with helpful advice too.

(3) *Product Liability Insurance:* This insurance covers damages caused by someone getting hurt using your product. If you sell something like headbands this might not be necessary, but if you sell candles, electronics, food, body products, or anything for children, I urge you to consider it. General liability insurance could also cover your products; talk to an insurance agent for more details.

Phone Line: Legally speaking, your home line can't be your business line; the two must be separate. Your cell phone number is fine for business, but it's better (and more professional) to have a dedicated phone line. You can get phone numbers for cheap nowadays. Try Kall8 (www.kall8.com), where toll-free numbers start at $2/month. Thousands of businesses rely on MagicJack (www.magicjack.com), after you buy the $50 adapter plans start at $3/month. If you use Gmail you can get a free phone number from Google Voice (www.google.com/voice) and make calls with their cell phone app. Of course there's always Skype (www.skype.com) and Vonage (www.vonage.com) too.

Business Account: I know I mentioned this earlier, but it's worth repeating again. You must set up a separate bank account for your business. Not only is bookkeeping easier, but the IRS will want to see it if they ever come a-knocking.

HOW TO HIRE PROFESSIONALS

A knowledgeable accountant is valuable, especially during your first year of business. Here's my tips on hiring a good accountant and attorney:

Accountants: Find an accountant who has experience with creative businesses. Ask fellow crafters and artists for accountant suggestions or start an internet search. Once you find potential candidates, ask them questions like, "Do you work with many indie artists?" "Can you provide three small business references?" "In what industries do you specialize?" "What is your hourly rate?" "How about a set monthly fee?" "Do you also prepare business taxes?" "Do you also do bookkeeping?"

Accounting vs. bookkeeping: A bookkeeper records the transactions of your business, all the sales and expenses. An accountant uses that information to prepare your taxes and other financial documents. I do eThreads' bookkeeping and quarterly tax filings but hire an accountant for April tax time.

Attorneys: You might need an attorney to help draft or review contracts, incorporate your business, and help with patents and copyrights. Find a lawyer who has experience with small business. Ask your local small business development center if they have references or partnerships with local bar associations (maybe you can get pro-bono advice).

Lawyers don't have to be expensive either. You might find an attorney for free through SCORE (www.score.org) as we discussed in the previous chapter. Communities usually have a law library at the local university that offers free legal days or legal aid clinics. Local law schools often offer free legal clinics to the community too. You'll find easy-to-understand legal advice at Nolo (www.nolo.com). Finally, check out Volunteer Lawyers for the Arts (www.vlany.org). This organization specializes in pro bono legal advice for artists and crafters; they are very familiar with the challenges creative businesses face.

Ask fellow small business owners for lawyer referrals too. Once you find potential candidates, review their credentials on your state bar's website (confirm they're licensed in your state). Just like your accountant, ask for three referrals from other small business owners. Other great questions include, "What's your retainer?" "What's your fee schedule?" "What's your typical response time?" "Have you worked with others in my industry?"

WRITING A BUSINESS PLAN

Did I just hear you gulp? Whenever I mention the words "business plan" people seem to go into a tizzy. I get it, I really do. I've written a few myself and they're no walk in the park. Here's the deal with business plans though - unless you're going for funding (and therefore need to show it to banks or investors), the business plan is mostly for your eyes only. So why do it? Because it's a valuable tool for setting strategic goals for your business. Remember - if you fail to plan, you plan to fail.

Write your business plan *after* reading this book. These chapters cover every question you will face as a new business owner, and the answers are the foundation of your business plan. As you move through the chapters on product, pricing, and selling, you'll have a much better direction for the business plan.

The average business plan is 15-30 pages and includes 10-15 items like Executive Summary, Operations Plan, and Financial Projections. There's hundreds of resources on writing business plans and I won't go into gruesome detail here. Instead, I'm highlighting just the parts that are necessary for you. The items are summarized below, pick up any book about writing business plans for more details about each section. I recommend Kari Chapin's book *Grow Your Handmade Business* because she discusses business plans from a creative perspective, especially in Chapters 11-20. I especially love Jennifer

Lee's book *The Right-Brain Business Plan* because she makes business plans approachable and fun for creative people.

Remember, unless you're going for funding this is mostly for your eyes only, so your business plan might end up being incomplete sentences stretching over just three pages. That's ok, as long as you're doing the strategic thinking required.

Mission statement: This one is dreamy. It's the equivalent of, "What do I want to be when I grow up?" and "I'm having a midlife crisis." It involves existential questions like, "Why am I starting a business?" and "What do I want to accomplish?" Obviously you want to make money, so that's not an acceptable answer. Think more along the lines of, "What impact do I want to make with this business?"

For example, I started eThreads with the Triple Bottom Line in mind: People, Planet, and Profit. I wanted to create a socially responsible business that was so successful it influenced other businesses to do the same. I designed eThreads with charitable donations, eco-friendly fabrics, and recycling programs in mind. The Triple Bottom Line is in eThreads' mission statement.

Whatever beautiful thing you want to do with your business - from making the perfect bike messenger bag to creating wearable works of art - should be written in your mission statement too.

Product description: Describe exactly what you're selling. Go into detail about each product including prices and the process for making them. Talk about the procedure and whether you're hiring anyone to help. Mention how your product is unique or different from anything else that's on the market. Discuss the benefits your products provide to customers, more than the competition. *How does your product solve problems or improve lives?* (We'll explore this in the next chapter.)

Market analysis & Marketing plan: I grouped these two together for the purpose of brevity, though they should be separate in your business plan.

Market analysis includes the size of your potential market, the competitive landscape, and the sense of urgent need for your product.

Marketing plan discusses your position in the market and why your product is superior to the competition. It outlines your marketing strategy including advertising, social media, and press opportunities. You could include sales channels here, (e.g., craft shows, stores, and Etsy) or write a separate section for your sales strategy.

For in-depth details about researching your market, read *How to Start a Creative Business: The Jargon-Free Guide for Creative Entrepreneurs* by Doug Richard. He devotes an entire chapter to identifying your target market and it's packed with helpful tips.

Operations plan: Discuss how you'll run the business day-to-day. Outline the process for manufacturing, shipping, and customer service. Identify how you're getting raw materials. Outline the equipment and materials. Detail all the necessary paperwork and business permits including insurance and zoning requirements. In other words, cover all the nuts and bolts of your business here.

Management team: Highlight your expertise, special skills, and background. Explain your knowledge of the industry and why you have the skills to run the business. If you have a partner, explain what each person contributes to the business and exact responsibilities moving forward.

Financial plan & Financial projections: I grouped these two together, but in actual business plans they're separate. The *financial plan* concerns *today* - e.g.: your budget in the first year and how you'll finance the business. *Financial projections* are about *tomorrow* - educated guesses about your profits and losses at the end of Year 1, Year 2, Year 3, etc... usually up to Year 5.

Whew! You made it through the business chapter! I know it was dry as toast but you persevered. I promise the rest of the book is really fun. Look out for my *Pro Tips* too ... they're exclusive tricks I've developed over the years that I'm sharing for the first time with you, the intrepid indie artist. Here's to your success!

Chapter 3: **REFINE PRODUCTS.**

"Hell, there are no rules here - we're trying to accomplish something."

- Thomas A. Edison

There's a long-standing business principle called *The 7Ps of Marketing*. Don't let the title fool you - it's not just about marketing. Yes, the *7Ps* help with marketing strategy, but they're also regularly used to evaluate business activities and set objectives. The *7Ps of Marketing* include:

Product: What you sell
Price: For how much
Promotion: Spreading the word
Place: Where you sell your stuff
Positioning: How people think about your product
Packaging: How your product is physically presented
People: Who your customers are

The 7Ps cover *everything* about your business - they're essential for planning. I mention the 7Ps of Marketing a lot in this book. The two Ps we're talking about in this chapter are **Product** and **Packaging**.

Product: What is your product and what problem does it solve for your customers?
Packaging: How is your product presented and shipped?

DEFINING YOUR PRODUCT

I bet a lot of you already know what you want to sell - pottery, cuff links, lip balm, wooden bowls, screen-printed t-shirts, fused glass, terrariums ... therefore you're thinking, "Emily, I already know what

I'm selling, so why should I read this?" Because my friends, if you say, "I sell widgets" and start making widgets without doing research, you're doomed to fail before you start.

Solve a problem: Customers are teeming with wants, needs, and desires. The most common needs are primal: survival, protection, freedom, comfort, and pleasure. Other common needs are often more subtle: success, popularity, style, beauty, convenience, efficiency, cleanliness, and individuality.

Does your product fulfill a need or solve a problem? For example, if you craft leather bracelets, make one that doubles as a coffee cup cover (fulfilling comfort, beauty, and efficiency needs). If you make electronic kits, specialize in bicycle kits that attach to wheels or handlebars (fulfilling survival, protection, and individuality needs). If you make furniture, create innovative storage solutions that look beautiful too (fulfilling style, convenience, and cleanliness needs).

Successful businesses solve problems for their customers. Sometimes it's obvious, like making heat pads to soothe sore backs. Other times it's more subtle, like making candles to create an inviting home.

Are you racking your brain and can't find an obvious benefit for your product? People in jewelry and fashion accessories often have this problem. Since these items are considered decorative, their benefits are not as urgent as hunger, thirst, or comfort.

However, people have been adorning themselves since the dawn of time. Accessories, jewelry, makeup … all have been used for centuries to help people feel more attractive, stylish, sexually appealing, popular, and self-assured. If your product can't fulfill a need, it should fulfill a desire.

Find your niche: I like to say, "If you're selling to everyone, you're selling to no one." You can't be everything to everyone, so don't even try. Find your niche group(s) and develop products to satisfy their wants, needs, and desires.

Take the furniture example above - a niche group for "storage solution" furniture is people living in small spaces. Two potential customer groups from that niche are urbanites living in cramped apartments and college students living in compact dorms.

How to find a niche: There isn't an easy way to do this unless you're a keyword and SEO wizard (more on that in Chapter 6). Here's a few resources to get your wheels spinning:

eBay Popular (popular.ebay.com): View the most popular items selling on eBay. Everything is organized by category and some will be particularly useful for you: Antiques, Jewelry, Toys, Art, Craft, etc... This gives you an idea of what people really want and hopefully you'll find a way for your products to fit in there.

Amazon Best Sellers (www.amazon.com/Best-Sellers/zgbs): Just like eBay, you can view the most popular items on Amazon to get a good idea of what people are really buying. You'll find all the great categories here too: Children, Clothing, Jewelry, Pet Supplies, etc...

CraftCount (www.craftcount.com): This site lists the top performing Etsy shops by category and it's updated every 24 hours. These shop owners are making thousands of dollars a month on Etsy. Study what they're doing and try to get a piece of that action yourself.

Etsy search (www.Etsy.com): Since you'll likely be selling products on this handmade marketplace, you might as well see what's happening now. On the homepage you'll find curated content and top picks from best sellers. Search your category (i.e. "crochet") and marvel at what's out there. Examine different shops' numbers - are there a lot purchases in your category? Study the most popular items, including photographs, descriptions, and prices.

> **•PRO TIP•** Find Etsy shops in your category and examine their "Feedback." Customers evaluate their purchases here, and it's an excellent research tool for two reasons. First, you can see what items *actually* sell (as opposed to the items on a shop's home page which haven't sold yet). Second, customer feedback for your category - even when it's not about your own products - illuminates your target market's general product and price expectations. Same deal applies for eBay and Amazon stores.

Google Trends (www.google.com/trends): An excellent tool from Google that observes trends over time. You can search any word, term, or phrase (up to 5 per search) and see how popular it's been over 30 days or several years. Add words to narrow your search or see how they compete with each other (e.g., crochet vs. knitting). Use Google Trends to study the seasonality of products. For example, baby shower searches peak in January, so that's a good time to be showcasing baby products.

Google Analytics (www.google.com/analytics): After your website is set up, take advantage of Google Analytics. This free service gives you in-depth analysis of your website's performance. It tells you which pages are most popular, which items are viewed the most, how long people stay on the site, and the search terms they used to get there. This type of information may help define your niche. See Chapter 6 for more information about Google Analytics.

•PRO TIP• *Be a niche multiplier.* Now that you've researched niche markets, think about creative ways to combine them together. Blend old-school and new-school techniques in unique and thoughtful ways. For example, utilize laser technology to recreate Victorian lace patterns. Carve an iPhone charging dock out of reclaimed wood. Create a watercolor painting of graffiti.

The most viral, popular, and media-friendly concepts combine old crafting skills with current trends, like crocheted Super Mario Brothers bike helmet covers and cross-stitched quotes said by famous musicians and celebrities. Combine two unrelated concepts together to create a new (and highly marketable) niche.

New technologies: Everyday there are new advances in materials science and manufacturing processes. No matter what field you're in, there's something new that's happening that can be applied to your craft. I've seen visual artists utilize laser-cut metal, jewelers print 3D earrings, and furniture makers design custom upholstery fabric.

Experiment with new ways to incorporate advanced materials and techniques into your products. One of my favorite sites is Ponoko (www.ponoko.com) which can cut any shape out of nearly any material. Wood, plastic, felt, metal, acrylic, 2D, 3D - they do it all. You can buy the materials through Ponoko then sell the finished items right on their site. Similarly, Thingiverse (www.thingiverse.com) by

MakerBot prints an unbelievable array of 3D objects designed by people like you and sold directly on their site.

HOW TO GET INSPIRED

Finding your niche is great place to start, but there are lots of other ways to get inspired about your product line.

Carry a notebook wherever you go. You never know when inspiration will hit you so always be prepared with a paper and pen. Draw pictures, take notes ... record whatever you're thinking.

Observe the world around you. You might have a product idea after observing someone on the street. Maybe your next collection will be inspired by the color palette of a house. Browse store windows for display ideas. Inspiration will hit you when you least expect it.

Join a group. Ever heard of a "Stitch and Bitch?" Think of it like a book club for crafters - people get together, bring their DIY projects, and socialize. There's also tons of opportunities on www.MeetUp.com and professional networks (like www.theswitchboards.com). Ask your local craft store if there's any groups in your area too. Not only will it be a good time, but you'll also get helpful tips, words of encouragement, and product feedback.

Follow the trends. Do you see a trend on the streets or in magazines that your product could be a part of? At the time of writing this book I've noticed owls, bicycles, mustaches, and head wraps are popular - can you do anything with this information? Crochet an owl hat? Make a bag out of bicycle fabric?

Consider what's popular in today's culture too. For example, a lot of people buy anything with the Super Mario Brothers on it. I've seen quilts, key chains, t-shirts, and even bathing suits all based on the Nintendo game. The HBO show *Game of Thrones* (based on the novels by George R.R. Martin) has been really popular lately too ... I recently ran into a jeweler who specializes in chainmail jewelry and suggested she make a *GoT*-inspired piece.

Note on trends While it's always good for businesses to have a few trend-worthy items, it's also important to create products that are true to yourself and stand the test of time. You'll burn out trying to make new products for changing trends, plus your stuff will look dated in a short time.

Visit Etsy, Pinterest, craft shows, and regular stores. Look at what hit the front page of Etsy. Study what's most popularly shared on Pinterest. Notice which booths are packed at craft shows. Examine the best sellers in stores. Search your category and elsewhere - inspiration could you hit you anywhere.

Note on copying I hope it goes without saying it's never cool to copy someone else's work, but here it is: copying someone else's work is forbidden, especially in the tight-knit creative community. People notice this kind of stuff and you could get virtually blacklisted in the community and on the internet.

It's ok to be inspired by someone else's work. However - find a way to make it your own. Change the pattern, the materials, the assembly ... put your own original spin on it. Copying someone else's work is not only karmically wretched, but you could be violating copyright or patent law and perhaps contacted by someone's angry attorney. The exception to this rule is if the seller explicitly states you can use their original pattern ... that usually happens under a *Creative Commons* license and you usually have to give credit to the seller. See more on protecting your work later in this chapter.

FOUR REASONS TO LIMIT SELECTION

Before diving into the wonderful world of product development, I urge you to start small and limit choices. Don't offer tons of styles, shapes, and different types of product. For example, don't sell silver necklaces and knit scarves and ceramic bowls at the same time. Why? Here's four reasons to carefully curate your products:

(1) *Save money:* Every product you develop costs time and materials. Limiting your selection saves precious time and expenses. This is especially important if you're starting out or developing a new product line.

(2) *Test the market:* Start small and see how customers respond. They may tell you they like one item over another or give you entirely new product ideas. Having less invested makes it easier to switch gears.

(3) *Make it easy on customers:* It's a proven fact too many choices paralyze customers. People become overwhelmed with options and choose not to buy anything at all instead of dealing with the stress

of making a decision. A limited selection is actually more attractive to potential customers.

(4) *Create exclusivity:* Consider making a handful of products in limited quantities. This is an especially great tip for high-end products or the "red bag in the window" (see Chapter 4 for more information). People pay a premium for exclusive items. Think about ways to make your product more exclusive - how about a high-end limited edition product line or a collaboration with another artist?

The good news about limiting selection is you can easily experiment with different products. Drop the worst ones and focus on your best sellers - remember, you don't want the *most* inventory, just the *most profitable* inventory.

ASK FOR CUSTOMER FEEDBACK

I love getting real-time feedback from customers at craft shows. I talk with them, ask questions, and observe which items attract the most interest. You can do this too, even if your customers are online.

Ask for feedback and product ideas over email, social media, or through surveys. I do this all the time on Facebook. Recently I asked our Facebook fans what they want in a diaper bag. We were designing our first one and I had no idea where to start. They had such great insight about wet clothes, leaky bottles, and massive diapers that I knew exactly how to design the perfect diaper bag. Our customers were really into it too, they love giving feedback.

I talk about customer feedback a lot in this book because it's so important for business development and customer service. See Chapter 13 for more information about email management and Chapter 17 for more information about using surveys.

HOW TO ATTRACT MORE BUYERS WITH ONE PRODUCT

If you make women's handbags and wallets, can you tweak the design and make a men's messenger bag or billfold wallet? What if you make body creams - can you make a men's after-shave lotion? Apply the same idea to kids and infants ... if you make fashionable headbands, can you make soft, velvety ones with big flowers for children? How about pets too ... can you make bow ties for humans *and* pets?

The point is - consider how to tweak your existing products and cater to a whole new type of buyer including men, women, children, and pets. Also consider making specialty products for holidays, special events, or sports fans. Sports is a HUGE market - can you incorporate different teams or sports into your craft? For example, we've bought fabric with team names on it and made bags for tailgating season. Those are always a hit.

Children's Products: The Consumer Products Safety Improvement Act of 2013 imposes strict guidelines for producing children's products ("children" is defined as anyone 12 years old or younger). There are also new requirements for manufacturers of apparel, shoes, personal care products, jewelry, accessories, toys, and probably anything else you'd want to make. It's worth checking out, especially if you're going to make products for children (www.cpsc.gov/en/Regulations-Laws--Standards/Statutes/The-Consumer-Product-Safety-Improvement-Act/).

PROTECTING YOUR WORK

You might have heard about copyrights, trademarks, and patents before. They're weighty topics deserving an entire chapter. I'll provide the highlights here, but if you're interested in pursuing one of these I urge you to get further information and talk with someone like a patent attorney. See Chapter 2 in this book for legal aid suggestions. Also check out *The Craft Artist's Legal Guide* by Richard Stim for in-depth advice about copyrights, trademarks, and patents.

Copyrights protect original works of authorship like books, art, music, plays, movies, advertisements, illustrations, patterns, and photographs. Copyrights don't protect the idea itself, just the way the idea is *expressed* (in music, on paper, performed out loud, etc...) The moment you draw a line, write a sentence, or snap a photograph your work is technically copyrighted. Put a ©, the year of creation, name of business or person, and "All rights reserved" at the bottom of your work (e.g., © 2014 Emily Worden. All rights reserved).

Officially register with the US Copyright Office for greater legal protection. It currently costs $35 to file online for copyright registration, check out www.copyright.gov for fees and more information. Once you complete the application and pay the fee, send a physical copy of your work to the Library of Congress' Copyright Office in Washington, D.C. (they receive about 2,400 submissions a day). They'll process your fee, review your application, and if all requirements are met you're approved. You'll get a registration number, a certificate of registration, and they'll put your registration in the public record. The entire process takes about four months. Registered copyrights last a long time - your lifespan plus 70 years.

"All rights reserved" says that you're not interested in sharing any piece of your work without written permission. Many people want to be more lenient with their copyrights (e.g., to share DIY projects or get quoted in articles). In this case, don't include "All rights reserved" or consider a Creative Commons license which is a free, easy way to protect your work.

Creative Commons (www.creativecommons.org) is an organization that created a more flexible copyright model. As an alternative to "All rights reserved," publishers of content can choose which rights to reserve and waive.

For example, Creative Commons' *Attribution* license is the most accommodating - people can distribute, copy, or sell your work as long as they credit you. The *Attribution NonCommercial NoDerivs* license is the most strict and only allows people to share your work if they don't use it commercially and credit you as the source. Creative Commons licenses are free to acquire and provide some level of protection for your work.

Trademarks protect words, phrases, symbols, or pictures that distinguish you from another company. Examples include business name, tag line, product name, and logo. Trademarks prevent someone else from operating or selling products with the same name as your own.

You can use ™ now and that's perfectly acceptable. It's not legally enforceable however, nor will your name show up in any trademark searches. If you'd like some recognition and legal protection, go ahead and file for trademark protection.

Do some research on availability first. You can do it on your own, hire a legal service, or hire a patent attorney. For those who are doing it themselves, you have two options: do everything yourself or pay an online legal service like LegalZoom (www.legalzoom.com) to research and apply for you.

If you're doing it completely on your own, check out the US Patent and Trademark Office's TESS tool first. TESS stands for "Trademark Electronic Search System" - start an internet search for "USPTO TESS" to find the latest version. Search TESS and confirm availability for the word, phrase, or image you want to trademark. Your state will also have a trademark search tool - use it. It's important to do a thorough search because the USPTO will deny applications that are too similar to already-existing trademarks.

File for a trademark directly with the USPTO using TEAS - the Trademark Electronic Application System. The application will cost $275-$325 and take months to process. During this time, an attorney from the USPTO will review your application and do some federal, state, and common law research to see if your trademark is unique enough to be approved. If so, you'll receive notice from the USPTO and gain the rights to use a ® instead of ™ and the ability to take legal action against anyone using your registered trademark. Trademark protection lasts 10 years before you have to renew.

Patents protect inventions and discoveries and are awarded by the US Patent and Trademark Office (USPTO). If you've developed a new product or updated an existing product, you might qualify for a patent.

There are two types of patents: a *utility patent* lasts 20 years and is meant for machines or processes. A *design patent* lasts 14 years and is meant for ornamental (as opposed to useful) design. Patents are generally not helpful for the average indie artist unless you come up with something truly extraordinary to patent. There is extensive time and money involved; a patent application can take over $20,000 and several years to complete.

International protection: All copyrights, trademarks, and patents must be registered in each country where you seek protection. Seek a patent attorney for more information about international protection.

MANUFACTURING

How will you manufacture your product? Decide where you'll get supplies, how the product will be made, and how to expand should you get a massive order overnight.

First, figure out your suppliers. Your days of shopping at the craft or art supply store are over - that's way too expensive now. Buy wholesale to take advantage of bulk discounts. If your materials are easy to source, like jewelry clasps, then you'll have no problem starting an internet search for jewelry clasps and finding dozens of vendors who sell them in bulk. If your materials are a bit more specific, like a certain type of pottery clay, you might need to do some more snooping.

Don't ask other crafters where they get their supplies. Everyone in the crafting world is friendly, but great vendors are hard to find so we don't like to share that information easily.

Start your search on Etsy (www.etsy.com) and look for "suppliers." Many sellers on Etsy buy supplies in bulk then break them up into smaller orders for resale. For example, if you want to buy necklace clasps from a real wholesaler, they'll likely want a minimum order of 1,000 pieces. Instead, suppliers on Etsy purchase 1,000 necklace clasps wholesale, repackage them into smaller groups, and resell to crafters like you.

You'll find great suppliers at trade shows. I've been to fabric shows where all the big-name fabric vendors sell. Friends of mine have gone to bead shows and brought back the most beautiful items. Wholesalers' minimums are usually waived at trade shows too. For example, I've opened accounts with vendors at trade shows with a $75 order when there's usually a $750 minimum for new accounts.

There's trade shows for everything, from soap-making to special gems. Whatever you need, there's probably a trade show for it. Check out the Trade Show News Network (www.tsnn.com) for listings. Can't attend a show? Find the sales reps from the shows and contact them directly. Also browse the Thomas Register of American Manufacturers (www.thomasnet.com) for more options.

When you find a potential vendor, check their customer reviews and ask for referrals. Inquire about payment terms, delivery schedule, and product availability. Whenever I find new vendors, I ask how long they've had the product in stock and whether it will continue to be in stock for a while.

If you use non-traditional materials like necklaces made with seashells lovingly collected at the beach, think about what you'll do if you suddenly get an order for 100 necklaces and it's February and the beach is closed.

Speaking of big orders ... you might get one at a moment's notice so it's important to streamline your manufacturing process now. Examine your steps to find anything you can knock out for efficiency. Try batching items together (see Chapter 4 for tips). Are there steps that require less skill that you could teach someone else? Could you ultimately train someone to make everything so you could focus on marketing and sales?

Speaking of hiring other people ... figure out how to do that now. How would you teach the process to someone else? Could they work with you or would they have to work at home? Who would you hire, how would you find them?

Here's my top seven tips for hiring people:

(1) *Do not hire friends:* Oh, this seems like such a good idea at first, but trust me it's a bad one. It's really awkward being the boss or talking about money with friends. I've seen too many friendships combust over indie businesses - don't be another statistic.

(2) *Send out inquiries:* Since you're not hiring friends, you have to find some other people to hire. First, send out a Craigslist ad (www.craigslist.org) for your area - that works nearly every time. Also, send out inquiries in your local community. For example, if you are looking for seamstresses, post an ad at your fabric or craft store. Look for students at your local college too. Be specific about the pay and skill level to find qualified applicants. See Chapter 17 for more information about hiring employees and interns.

(3) *Ask for samples:* Ask applicants to bring samples of their work to the interview. Have them work a little bit in front of you too so you can observe their skill level. Remember, they'll be nervous and probably a little slower than usual.

(4) *Hire on skill AND personality:* Technical skills can be taught; a good personality cannot. Hire people who are enthusiastic, self-starters, and seem to make good judgments. Ask yourself: "Would

I feel comfortable delegating a task to this person and letting them work independently?"

(5) *Contact referrals:* Ask for three referrals if it's not already included on their résumé. Ask the referrals if the candidate is on time, able to work independently, and honest.

(6) *Probationary period:* Avoid making a bad hiring decision by hiring on a "probationary period" for three weeks and assessing the situation after that.

(7) *Build the cost of labor in your price:* I talk about this a lot in Chapter 4 but I'll mention it here: anticipate hiring people and paying them. Add that cost into your price now so you have the funds when you need to start hiring.

PACKAGING

Ah, we've come full circle and back to the *7Ps of Marketing*. *Product* is well covered, so let's talk *Packaging*.

How will you present your products to customers? How will they be shipped? How will you wrap at craft shows? What will it look like on a store shelf? Customers are very visual; your packaging must be appealing. Good packaging can increase your product's value and justify the cost in your customers' eye.

You don't have to get fancy with it, just thoughtful. There's a lot of charm to a package wrapped in brown paper, bakers' twine, and rubber-stamped with your logo. How about using remnants from your craft? What about just really nice inkjet labels? I love the effect of typewriters myself. Start an internet search for "Etsy packaging ideas" to find some of the best examples from indie artists.

I'll give you an example with eThreads. Our bags are wrapped in recycled scented paper with our postcard and a small personalized note. The package is sealed with a sticker emblazoned with eThreads' logo. It's simple but we consistently get compliments on our packaging. One customer even said "it's like opening a Christmas present."

Seven Packaging Rules

(1) Include information about how to care for your product (keep wick trimmed ¼", keep away from heat, hand wash only, etc…)

(2) Include a little story and some information about your business and its products (handmade in Boston, sourced from recycled materials, etc…)

(3) Always include extra business cards with the order so people can spread the word about your business.

(4) Think of it like wrapping a gift. Use tissue paper, twine, ribbons, tape, stickers … people enjoy unwrapping gifts, it makes your product more exciting. If you sell plush toys, handbags, or other items made of fabric, consider wrapping them in plastic bags to ensure they don't get damaged in transport if the box gets wet.

(5) Just don't make the process so elaborate it takes a half hour to pack up one order. You don't have time like that to waste.

(6) You must include a handwritten notecard, or at the very least a small message on the invoice. Personalize the note with your customer's name and thank them for supporting your business.

(7) Factor in packaging costs ahead of time. For example, I get large boxes for $1.25 each, but it costs $50 to ship 25 boxes, so they're really closer to $2.50 each. I build that cost into the larger items that need those expensive boxes.

> •PRO TIP• If you ship small items, get free boxes and envelopes at www.USPS.com. The Postal Service gives away free Priority Mail and Express Mail packaging and it's delivered right to your door.

SHIPPING

Speaking of the Postal Service, let's talk shipping options. If you sell small, light, or inexpensive items, ship with the United States Postal Service. They have an easy-to-use website, you can print labels at home, they offer free packaging, they pick up at your front door, and they're the cheapest when you're starting out.

For example, I've shipped items that cost $8 with USPS that would have cost $15 with UPS and $25 with FedEx. The latter two options are awesome when you're mailing large heavy items, expensive items that require extra insurance, sending overseas, or shipping so often you can open up a business account and save big. For all the newbies and smaller operators, stick with USPS.

Save time by shipping at home. You'll need a postage scale ($30) and shipping labels. I use USPS's Click-N-Ship and get my shipping labels from Online Labels (www.onlinelabels.com), they're half the cost of anything at office supply stores. I know a lot of people love using Stamps.com (www.stamps.com) and Endicia (www.endicia.com) too. Get a tracking number for every package (it should be free with any shipping service) and share it with your customers.

Should you ship internationally? I say yes if you're comfortable with it. Not only is it a great way to increase your fan base, but it feels really cool when you're shipping something off to Paris. It's not easy to ship internationally though. As I discuss in Chapter 7, you have to create a shipping chart that lists estimated costs and times for shipping to different countries. USPS, UPS, FedEx, and DHL all have shipping calculators on their websites to help with this.

As much as I love USPS, they're not great with international shipments. You can't get tracking once the package has left the US and I've seen packages take up to three weeks to arrive in Europe. In this case, it might be worth checking out UPS, FedEx, or DHL for international rates. These companies all specialize in international shipping and can provide accurate tracking and estimated shipping times. The rates get cheaper once you open an account and ship a large volume of packages.

EVALUATE

Now that you've designed your products and packaging, it's time to evaluate. Take a hard look - would *you* buy it? Pass out samples to friends, family, and acquaintances to see what they think. If you can, don't tell anyone they're your products - you'll get honest feedback that way. For example, if you make a wearable product, just put it on, wear it around town, and see how people react - do you get compliments? Do people ask where you got it?

Test your products too - if you say it's machine washable, wash it several times and see how it stands up. If you claim to have the world's best foot cream, test it against store-bought creams. I test eThreads' bag prototypes for months before they go into production. Take your time designing products that truly satisfy the wants, needs, and desires of your customers.

Chapter 4: **PRICE HIGH.**

"Price is what you pay. Value is what you get." - **Warren Buffett**

"Emily, how do I price my products?!" I'm asked this question all the time, usually by a nervous-looking artist, crafter, or maker. I think people are uncomfortable with pricing because talking about money is often awkward, never mind when it's about your own work.

I get it, I really do. It took me *years* to stop feeling guilty every time I quoted a project. Here's the thing though - you started a business to sell your stuff, so it's time to get over any anxiety about it. I'm going to show you how to price products and then *own it*. Never apologize for making a sale again.

DETERMINING YOUR COGS

What does COGS mean? It's fancy accounting speak for *Cost of Goods Sold*. It accounts for everything - and I mean *everything* - that goes into making and selling your product.

Materials + Labor + Overhead = COGS (Cost of Goods Sold)

Materials: Write a list of the materials used in making your product and the cost per material. Let's say you're a candle maker creating a small jar candle. Your materials list might include a glass jar, wax, wick, and scent. List the cost per material and total it up for your materials cost. For example, a small jar candle's list might look like the chart on the next page. Repeat this process for all your products:

SMALL JAR CANDLE	
List of Materials	*Cost of Materials*
1 small jar	$1.50
1 oz wax	$1.00
1 short wick	$0.25
2 tsp scent	$0.14
TOTAL MATERIALS COST FOR SMALL JAR CANDLE	**$2.89**

Labor: How long does it take to make the product? Multiply that by your hourly wage and add it to COGS. (For example, if your hourly wage is $20/hour and it takes 15 minutes to make the product, the labor cost for that product is $5.)

How to calculate hourly wage: This one is really up to you. I think $15 is an acceptable minimum wage for labor. Keep in mind however, you're a skilled artisan. You've spent years perfecting your craft and should be compensated as such. I think you should start at a minimum of $20/hour, but move closer to $30, $40, or more if you can. Before you clutch your pearls and call me crazy, let me tell you a story about the artist Pablo Picasso.

A woman asked Picasso to sketch something on a piece of paper (it was a picture of her or a bird depending on the storyteller). He obliged, quickly sketched on the paper, handed it to her and said, "That will cost you $10,000."

Are you shocked? The woman was too. She said, "It took you *five minutes* to do the sketch. Isn't $10,000 a lot for five minutes work?" Picasso smiled and replied, "Madame, the sketch may have taken me five minutes, but the learning took me a lifetime."

There's several variations of the story, but the point is always the same - charge for your expertise and don't penalize yourself for working quickly. It took you *years* to figure out how to make your product beautifully and efficiently, so charge accordingly.

Overhead costs: This is the hardest number to quantify. Studio rental, craft show fees, office supplies, utilities, business cards, advertising fees, and anything else needed to make, market, ship, and sell your products should be included here. Start by writing down your monthly expenses. For example, if you work in your home and the electric bill is about

$60/month and you estimate 20% of that is for your craft, then overhead utilities cost for your business is $12/month. Calculate how often you make miscellaneous purchases like mailing envelopes, labels, or printer cartridges. It's ok to get a rough estimate here, just realize how much extra money goes into running your business and tally accordingly.

Accountants divide overhead costs into two categories - those costs directly involved with making your product, and those costs directly involved with running your business. For example: labor, materials, and electricity to run your tools are direct costs. Advertising, interest, and rent are indirect costs. Technically the COGS equation only involves direct overhead costs, but I want you to consider all your indirect overhead costs as well when planning your prices (the average indirect overhead cost for a business is 10-15%).

> •**PRO TIP**• When calculating costs (or "guesstimating" as I'm sure a lot of you are doing), always over-estimate. Round up to the nearest dollar, add $1-2 to overhead, or even simply fudge the final COGS figure by a few bucks. It's better to make a little more money in the end than realize you've been undercharging the whole time.

Congratulations! You've figured out the first step in pricing, your COGS. We're not done yet though. Now we need to calculate your wholesale and retail pricing. For that we need the pricing formula.

PRICING FORMULA

This is the closest you'll ever find to a magic pricing formula:

COGS x 2 = Wholesale Price
Wholesale Price x 2 = Retail Price

What?! Stay with me. Let's talk about candles again. Let's say your COGS for a small candle is $5. Plug $5 into the equations above and you'll get the retail and wholesale prices:

$5 x 2 = $10 Wholesale Price
$10 x 2 = $20 Retail Price

WHOLESALE VS. RETAIL PRICING

Wholesale is a great sales channel for artists, crafters, and makers. It means selling your items in bulk to one person - a store owner, gallery owner, corporate client, etc... The minimum order size is up to you. When I first started out, my minimum was $500 to qualify for wholesale pricing. I quickly raised it to $750, then $1,000, and continued from there. Remember, wholesale prices are generally 50% off retail prices so confirm the order is big enough to be worth your time.

Retail means selling individual items directly to customers from your website, Etsy, at a craft show, or wherever else you interact with the final consumer. It's naturally more work to deal with customers directly, but I like retail because the profit margins are a lot better than wholesale and it's fun to get to know your customers.

Once you've priced COGS and calculated wholesale and retail pricing, what do you think about the prices? Look around at similar products on Etsy and at craft shows - are your prices comparable?

If your prices are cheaper than average, consider raising them a bit so your products don't look inferior. If your prices are higher than average, why? Are you using more expensive materials? Is your work higher quality? Is your idea more original? It's ok if your prices are higher as long as you prove the value to customers.

I believe in charging higher prices because hardworking indie artists deserve every penny. However, if you think your product prices are too high for your target market here's a few possible remedies:

(1) *Consider two product lines;* one wholesale and one retail. The retail line has more details and higher quality materials, while the wholesale line is easier to make with cheaper materials. Alternatively, choose to sell one type of product retail and an entirely different, cheaper product wholesale.

(2) *Consider the materials.* Can you use cheaper materials without sacrificing quality? Can you reduce costs by buying bulk or wholesale? Find different suppliers and have them compete against one another for your business.

(3) *Consider your product design.* Try to remove time-consuming details or redesign products to use less materials.

(4) *Consider your process.* Can you work more efficiently - maybe something to do with your tools or machinery? For example, our

patterns used to be made of paper and we had to move slowly to avoid cutting the edges. Now, our patterns are made with heavy-duty plastic and it's a breeze to cut fabrics. Same thing with grommets - they used to be installed by hand until I bought a grommet press. Can you do something similar to increase your speed?

PRICING PSYCHOLOGY

We humans are a lot more predictable than we'd like to admit. Below are some classic psychological concepts that marketers and advertisers have been using for years to lure your interest:

Anchoring: When we encounter a new product, we accept the first price we see and that price anchors our long-term perception about what the item should cost. It happens every time someone experiences "sticker shock" and it's the primary pricing rule working against indie artists, crafters, and makers.

Take eThreads for example. I sell tote bags for $150, but people can get tote bags for $20 at Target. That means customers are looking at my bags, seeing the $150 price tag, and thinking they can get a similar bag at Target for $20.

This will be your #1 problem too. As I said in Chapter 2, you have direct and indirect competition everywhere and it's not just the handmade market. Unless you're selling something that is so wildly unusual no one has ever seen it before, you have competitors. Even if no one has seen your product before, it's likely serving the same purpose as something that's cheaper in a big store.

"But wait," you're saying, "my stuff is handmade and that stuff is made in China! It's not a fair comparison!" You're right, it's not. But that doesn't stop people from thinking this way anyway. Of course your product is better than anything at Target - it's handmade, one of a kind, guaranteed for life, and your attention to detail is exquisite. Tell your customers that! Justify the higher price tag that comes with handmade. (Don't ever try to compete on prices with big stores, it's a losing game.)

Since people have preconceived ideas about what your item should cost, your pricing job is to find the happy medium between what they think they should pay and what you think it's really worth.

•**PRO TIP**• **Pricing Tricks:** Here's some great pricing tricks based on basic consumer psychology:

(1) *BOGO ("Buy One Get One Free") is more attractive than 50% off.* Even though it's the same discount, people are more attracted to the word "free."

(2) *Percent is more attractive than dollars.* For example, if the price is $100 and you're putting it on sale, say "20% off" rather than "$20 off." In this case, the percentage sounds like more value.

(3) *Use 7s in your pricing.* Humans are really attracted to the number 7. You see a lot of "7 Ways to ..." and "How to ... in 7 days" for this reason. Same deal with pricing. Items that are $57 will sell better than $55. I can't tell you why, they just do. Try it yourself and tell me I'm crazy.

(4) *However, if you're selling high-end products, price in even whole numbers ($200, $320, $540).* This makes your products look more exclusive and luxe.

TO PRICE HIGH OR TO PRICE LOW? THAT IS THE QUESTION

In the battle between high and low prices, I'm always on Team High Prices. Yup, I'm telling you to *raise your prices.* I guarantee whatever price you've settled on, you could charge more. Think I'm crazy? Remember the Picasso Principle. You're very good at what you do and very talented. You make high quality, original products that are guaranteed for life. Your customer service is excellent and you're a reliable vendor. Why wouldn't you charge more money and be damn proud doing it? This is what you've been working for, might as well make maximum profits.

Not convinced by my pep talk? Here's a few more reasons to charge higher prices:

(1) *Customer expectations:* People expect a better experience with more expensive products. Higher prices indicate better quality, so people value a product more when it's expensive. Think about how much people value expensive designer jeans over a cheap pair from

Target. People covet expensive jeans ... don't you want customers to covet your work too?

(2) *Less effort for you:* If you want to make $500, it's a lot easier to sell to 10 customers at $50 than 50 customers at $10. Higher prices = less customers = higher revenue. Oh it sounds so counterintuitive I know, but trust me - you want less customers for more money. It's not about how many customers you have, it's about how much profit you make per customer.

Plus, the less time you spend in production, the more time you have to diversify sales channels, create new designs, and build the business by teaching, blogging, and collaborating with other businesses.

(3) *Higher prices = lower-maintenance customers:* This is another counterintuitive point but it's true. Every waitressing and retail job I've ever had has proven this over and over again - the people who spend the least money are the most hassle. (Anyone who has ever worked those jobs is nodding their head in agreement right now.) Even my sister, who is a lawyer, experiences this. Of course, there are exceptions to every rule, but for the most part higher prices attract lower-maintenance customers.

(4) *You'll never compete on price - so don't even try:* You may survey the competition and realize your prices are higher than most people. That's ok, you can work with that (see Chapter 9 for more info). Don't you ever, EVER, lower prices and cut into margins to compete with the next guy. I guarantee that no matter how low you go, there is someone else who can make the same product cheaper and faster and will eventually put you out of business. Name your price and don't apologize for it.

THE COST OF DISCOUNTS

Discounted prices can actually reduce sales. It's all about customer expectations - people see cheap prices and assume it's a cheap product. You don't want anyone thinking your product is cheap, right?

Plus, if you offer discounts often, customers learn to wait until the next sale before making a purchase - then you're training customers to avoid full retail price altogether! I actually have a supplier who does this - they send out coupons every month so when I need to restock I just wait until the next coupon. One of my main competitors sends out a coupon at least every month too – and that's a bad sign ...

Why? Well, regular coupons tell your customers business isn't doing well. After all, you usually offer sales when business is slow, right? Therefore, if you offer lots of discounts then customers assume you don't have a lot of business. Remember, customer expectations are everything and coupons say your product is not very desirable.

Here's one more story about discounts: in Dr. Robert Cialdini's fascinating book *Influence: The Psychology of Persuasion*, he shares a story about a jewelry store owner in Arizona who wanted to move a bunch of turquoise jewelry that wasn't selling well. So the store owner left an exasperated note for an employee to put all the turquoise jewelry 50% off. The employee misread the note and actually *increased* prices 50% ... and sold out of the stock in days! This is what I'm telling you guys – higher prices really are good for business.

RED BAG IN THE WINDOW

This pricing trick combines *anchoring with perception*. I call it the "Red bag in the window" but it's also called "Red dress in the window," "Red shoes in the window," and whatever you're selling can be the "Red ____ in the window." The point is, create some eye-catching and high-priced items that grab people's attention, just like a red item in a shop window would.

Create a few products that are much more glamorous and expensive than the rest of your inventory. They must get people's attention. They must be showstoppers. They must be ridiculously priced and probably no one will ever buy them. So why make them? Three reasons:

(1) Duh - they're showstoppers. Red bags in the window stop people in their tracks; they're attention-getting. Use pictures of these high-end products to drive people to your website and display the actual items prominently in your craft show booth.

(2) Remember anchoring? If someone sees your expensive red bag in the window it becomes an anchor for the rest of your products, and everything else will look like a steal in comparison.

In sales, this is also called the *Contrast Principle* and it's a trick car salesmen use all the time. They'll show you the highest-priced model before an entry-level model. When you compare the two, the entry-level car feels like a deal. Restaurants also use this technique with food and wine - you likely won't buy the most expensive dish or bottle of wine, but you're ok buying the second most expensive.

(3) Your red bag in the window is so awesomely detailed and so outrageously stunning and so crazy expensive that everything around it looks beautiful too. Showcasing the best of your work makes customers realize what they're really getting when they buy something from you.

SALES TIPS

I have an entire chapter dedicated to sales (Chapter 9), but I wanted to mention a little something here because it's so appropriate.

As you know, there's a difference between the *actual* value of your product and the *perceived* value. It's the reason indie artists feel squeamish quoting prices to customers - we can't get past charging more than the actual value. The actual value is based on COGS, but the perceived value is all about talent - design, craftsmanship, experience, quality, exclusivity, uniqueness ... *that's* what customers can't buy at Target. Help remind people why they're buying from you and not somewhere else:

(1) *Tell people what they're getting with your product.* Tell them why it's unique or about the special skill that went into making it. Were you trained by a master crafter? Are your products made with a special machine? Are your materials from an exotic location or certified organic? Will your products perform better than anything in stores? Think of special details that set you apart from competition *and* benefit your customers.

(2) *Help people imagine already owning your product.* Tell them what it's like to feel it, smell it, hear it ... whatever your product is, help potential customers visualize using it. If you sell necklaces, talk about different ways to wear it with a turtleneck or camisole. If you sell wooden bowls, suggest salad recipes. At craft shows, I invite people to put their stuff in the bags to "see how everything fits." Eight times out of ten, they'll purchase the bag once their stuff is already in it.

(3) *Use logic.* People *want* to buy your stuff but they're having a hard time justifying the purchase (especially when they can get it

cheaper elsewhere). Use logic to explain why they're making a smart purchase with you. Explain how they're getting a great deal because your product lasts years. Talk about your warranty or repair policy. Emphasize how your product makes lives better or easier. Share a story about another customer who benefitted from using your product. Use logic and reason to convince potential customers they're making a smart decision purchasing from you.

(4) *Use data.* Customers love numbers and statistics to justify their purchase. Can you say your candle burns 20% longer than average? Do your ceramic mugs hold heat for three hours? Are your photographs printed on archival paper that lasts 75 years? Do your recycled felted pins save two sweaters from the landfill? Customers LOVE these kind of details - it's what makes them buy the product and tell their friends.

A FINAL NOTE ON PRICES

Remember, your prices are never set in stone. Experiment a little. Most customers won't notice if you add or subtract a few dollars from your prices occasionally. Try it and see what happens - do purchases increase or decrease with the price change?

I love testing prices at craft shows and observing reactions. I've seen people pick up a price tag and mutter, "That's too much," and I've seen people look at the same price tag and say, "That's really reasonable for the quality you're getting." You can't please all the people all the time – just aim to please your target market. Experiment to find the happy medium between you and your customers. You'll find the sweet spot over time.

Chapter 5: **BUILD A BRAND.**

"What makes you weird, makes you unique, and therefore makes you stand out."
                                                            - Dan Schawbel

Branding is much more than a logo - it's an entire business philosophy. Branding is the identity of a business. It involves mission statements, goals, and competitive advantages. Branding is about behavior too - how to interact with customers, wrap packages, and organize a website. With branding, what you say is just as important as what you do.

ELEMENTS OF A BRAND

Branding is a broad concept that includes many elements, including the 7Ps of Marketing from Chapter 3:

Product: What you sell
Price: For how much
Promotion: Spreading the word
Place: Where you sell your stuff
Positioning: How people think about your product
Packaging: How your product is physically presented
People: Who your customers are

All these items combined make up a brand, especially *Positioning.* Once people have an impression of your brand, it sticks. Therefore it's critical to shape the narrative of your brand before someone else does it for you.

So, I ask you - what do you want people saying about your business? Do you want them talking about price, selection, quality, guarantees, customer service, uniqueness ... what's important to you?

I want eThreads to be known for quality and customer service. Everything we do is driven towards those two goals and our customers love us for it. What is the value in *your* brand?

Unique Selling Proposition (USP): Also known as the Unique Value Proposition (UVP), this is what sets you apart from the competition. It's something you do that is different from everyone else. In Chapter 3 we talked about solving a problem and finding your niche. Whatever problem you're solving or niche you're serving, *that's* your USP. Another USP could be better service, faster delivery, or expert knowledge. Think about Avis Car Rental - they're the second biggest car rental company, so their USP for 50 years was "We try harder" (suggesting they provide better service because they want the #1 spot).

Personality of your business: This part is pretty fun. In Chapter 2 we talked about picturing your ideal customer and asking a series of questions about them. This is the same exercise, but for your business.

If your business were an actual person, describe what they'd be like. What's their name? Where do they live, in the city or suburbs? How old are they? What are their favorite books, movies, and TV shows? How do they dress - comfy casual or business professional? Do they have pets? What are their favorite activities?

This exercise is a fun way to shape the branding of your business. For example, the content for a bubble-gum-popping-ponytail-twirling teenage girl is much different than a business-suit-wearing-frequent-flying middle-aged woman.

BRANDING INSPIRATION

So far we've covered the 7Ps of Marketing, USP, and business personality. Now let's turn outward and look at other sources for branding inspiration:

(1) *Your customers:* Study your target demographic - what's important to them? What grabs their attention? Where do they like to shop? Research your target customers for branding inspiration since you ultimately want your brand to appeal to them.

(2) *Your competition:* What do they do well and what can you do better? Purchase something from your competition to experience their sales, customer service, and packaging strategies first-hand.

(3) *Your idols:* Are there other artists, crafters, makers, businesses, organizations, or websites that you admire and want to emulate? Take notes on whatever grabs your attention - a witty headline, cool logo, or neat packaging trick.

(4) *Your keywords:* We'll talk about keywords in-depth in Chapter 6 so I'll just mention it here. Keywords are those words associated with your business. For example, some of eThreads' keywords are *custom, bags, DIY, fabric,* and *vegan.* In this case, I'd type into Google "custom vegan bags" and "DIY fabric bags" for branding inspiration.

APPEALING TO CUSTOMERS

Design your brand for maximum customer appeal. Think about what's important to them - information, price, speed, selection, quality, value, trust, exclusivity - and build it into your process. Deliver a compelling experience for customers, from advertising your product to post-purchase support. Remember, people aren't just buying your products, they're buying your brand. Make the experience amazing.

There are three compelling ways to appeal to customers

(1) *Make their lives better:* Everyone has problems, wants, needs, and desires. Meet your customers' needs in a friendly and efficient way.

(2) *Build a strong emotional connection:* The grocery store chain Trader Joe's has a rabid customer following who rave about the store (I'm included in this group, I love TJ's). Help customers get emotional about your brand too through stellar customer service, unique branding, and high-quality products.

(3) *Communicate your trustworthiness:* Demonstrate to customers you have their best interests at heart. Build relationships and treat them like family (see Chapter 7 for more information).

Help people personally connect with your brand. It's easier to do than you think:

Tell stories. People love stories, it's very engaging. Talk about why you started a business or what motivates you to create. Discuss your struggles starting the business or a challenge you've overcome.

Share customer experiences and testimonials too. Not only to demonstrate how your products make lives better, but also for credibility. You can talk about your awesomeness 'til you're blue in the face, but it's a lot more effective when someone else does it for you. Plus, talking about satisfied customers helps potential customers imagine feeling the same thing. Testimonials are a persuasive sales tool.

Finally, *be personal when building your brand.* Be the face of the business. Share goofy stories about your daily life or behind-the-scenes pictures of works in progress. Customers want to know the person behind the business; it's usually the reason why they buy from indie artists.

•PRO TIP• Have you ever heard of *K.I.S.S. - Keep it Simple, Stupid?* Anytime you're talking or writing, keep it short and easy to understand. Don't overcomplicate things. Drop technical jargon and confusing acronyms. Likewise, be brief - never use three sentences when only one will do.

For example, long-winded artist statements are *the worst.* Yes, customers want to know all about your credentials and expertise, but they won't read three pages about it. They likely won't read one page either. Most people won't get past the first three sentences, so put your most important information there.

NAMING YOUR BUSINESS

This is one of the hardest things you'll do, so do it last. Figure out the *7Ps of Marketing and most of your business plan* before thinking of names. I know this sounds counterintuitive because most people think of names before anything else. That's the wrong order of operations and I'll tell you why.

First, fleshing out a business plan gives you future direction. For example, you might start off thinking you're just selling chocolates, but after doing a business plan you realize cupcakes might also be possible. Aren't you glad you didn't waste precious time and money investing in the name "Posh Chocolates" before completing the rest of your plan? Choosing a name first might pigeonhole you later.

Also, the *7Ps* identify what kind of customer you're after and how to appeal to them. Your business name is a big part of marketing appeal; it has to resonate with potential customers.

Elements of a good name: A great business name is catchy, memorable, and easy to say. You want customers telling all their friends about your business so the name can't be difficult to pronounce, recall, or spell. Likewise, people will be typing this into a URL so it should be short. Don't use fake words or misspell real ones. Don't use common names either or you'll be impossible to find on Google.

A good business name also hints at what you do. "Green Ribbon" is ok, "Green Ribbon Designs" is better, "Green Ribbon Fashions" is best. If you sell clothing and accessories, consider "Green Ribbon Fashions" and the tagline "Fine Clothing, Accessories, and Design."

Name inspiration is all around you. Is there anything distinctive in your product line, packaging, or branding that you could use? Notice the words often used on your favorite blogs. Name the qualities of your brand and look them up in the dictionary and thesaurus. Plug your keywords into Google. Once you have a few options, test them with friends and family. Ask coworkers and neighbors then see what people remember most. You're going to be stuck with this name for a long time so choose wisely my friends.

> **•PRO TIP•** When comparing possible names, consider how it will spell out as a URL. Often double words like "Sally's Sweaters" are harder to read in URLs: www.sallyssweaters.com. Sometimes the domain name is downright graphic. For example, there is a company called Pen Island. I'll let you imagine what their URL looks like.

Researching and registering a name: Is your business name also available as a domain name (e.g., www.eThreads.com)? Search available domain names with Network Solutions (www.networksolutions.com) or WhoIs (www.whois.net).

Your ideal name will most likely not be available as a domain name. It happens a lot because the best domain names are already taken. If your ideal name is not available, make it more specific (e.g., "GreenRibbonDesigns.com" instead of "GreenRibbon.com.") Or, move down the list of possible business names until you find a matching domain name available. Do not use hyphens in your domain name, it's too difficult to explain or remember.

If your domain name is available then register it, even if you don't plan on having a website right now. You may want a website in the future and it's wise to reserve the domain name before someone else snaps it up. It costs about $10-$15 annually to register a domain name, I do it though Network Solutions.

If you want a website, you'll also need a web host. Most domain name registrars also provide hosting services. If you go with one of the DIY website resources in Chapter 6, the hosting is done for you.

For those hosting on their own, I like Media Temple (www.mediatemple.com) but they're a little more expensive because they're very reliable and can handle a lot of traffic. When you're starting out you can go with cheaper options. Do an internet search for "Top 10 cheapest web hosts" and read the customer reviews. I bet you'll find something for $7-$10/month.

After registering the domain name, reserve it on every social media site (see Chapter 14 for more about this). Even if you're not using social media now, it's smart to hold your spot before someone else takes it. If your ideal name is already taken, consider adding another word to make it your own. For example, I was able to reserve "eThreads" on Twitter (www.twitter.com/eThreads) but it was already taken on Instagram. Instead, our Instagram account is "eThreadsBags" (www.instagram.com/eThreadsBags) which I actually prefer because it better explains what we do.

Search the US Patent and Trademark Office's TESS tool (Trademark Electronic Search System) too (www.uspto.gov). The USPTO registers all trademarks, so if anyone has already legally registered the name you can't use it. (For information on how to trademark your name, go back to Chapter 3.) A simple Google search is also necessary. Type in several variations of your name to see if it's being used elsewhere.

NOTE: During the domain name search you might see your desired name unavailable as a .com but available as a .co, .biz, .us, and other combinations. Should you buy one of those instead? People have different opinions on this topic and I'll give you mine - I don't buy the domain name unless I can get the .com. Customers only really use .com (unless it's .org or .gov, and you don't qualify for those). I think the other extensions are useless unless you're buying them to protect your name or you're absolutely dead-set on a name and the .com isn't available or ridiculously expensive. I usually do buy the .co only to protect my business name, but I'll likely never use it.

DESIGNING YOUR LOGO

It's hard to design a logo, that's why most people hire professionals. (Check out Appendix A in the back of the book for tips about hiring professional designers.) That said, it's possible to make your own logo, particularly when starting out on a shoestring budget. Do you know anyone who is an artist, designer, or has computer skills? They can help with logo design. Local art students are a good resource too. The logo for a business I started in college was drawn by an artist friend and I loved it. You can even design a logo for free with Logo Garden (www.logogarden.com) and it takes zero professional skills.

If you're DIY here's a few basic logo guidelines to follow:

(1) *The logo has to work in a variety of sizes.* Your logo is going to be printed on large banners and small postcards alike, and it must be flexible enough to work on both. Don't make the logo so intricate that details will get lost on a small business card.

(2) *Keep it simple.* Think about the logos for Nike and Target - they're simple and effective. Aim for that - avoid too many details and complicated fonts.

(3) *Design with your target customer in mind.* What grabs their attention? Consider which fonts, colors, or images are most appealing to your target demographic; more about that below.

(4) *Design your logo in vector format.* Adobe Illustrator is best or use the free vector application Inkscape (www.inkscape.org/en). Why is vector format important? Vector images can be resized and used in lots of different mediums without losing quality. If a logo is not in vector format, the designer or printer will have to edit a pixelated image

or recreate a new one from scratch and that will cost time, money, and image quality.

Logotype/Wordmark: A logotype (a.k.a. "wordmark") is simply your business or brand name in a stylized font, like the logos for CNN, Dell, Disney, and IBM.

The font is the foundation for your logo and brand; every font suggests a different meaning. Thick, bold fonts imply power. Italicized or slanted fonts express movement. Hand-written fonts signal friendliness. Script fonts indicate elegance. You can use fonts already available on a computer, but I prefer paying for premium fonts. Why? Three reasons:

(1) A lot more options - we're talking thousands.

(2) It makes your brand unique and stand out from the crowd.

(3) Most premium fonts have a variety of weights like black, bold, regular, light, extra light, italic, etc. and this helps tremendously with logo design. Using the same font in a different weight makes your branding interesting without looking sloppy. For example, the words "Make," "Sell," and "Repeat" on the cover of this book were made with three different weights of the same font.

I like to use FontShop (www.FontShop.com) to find fonts because they have an excellent selection. Though fonts start at $20, you can expect to pay at least $100 for a font with multiple weights. I understand this is pricey, especially for beginners, so go ahead and use something from your computer if this isn't in your budget right now.

Don't use more than two types of fonts in a logo. Ideally stick with only one and use different weights to achieve design depth. Stay away from fonts that are excessively curly or cursive. I know they're pretty, but they're hard to read. You want a font that is easy to read at a distance but has a little bit of personality too.

Logomark/Icon/Symbol: This is the image in a logo. Popular brands are recognized by their icon alone, like the Nike "swoosh" or NBC's rainbow peacock.

Logomark options are limitless. You could forgo an icon and just play around with fonts. Or the icon could be your initials, a popular product, or something that plays off your name. Brainstorm icons that represent the personality of your business and product selection.

When designing a logomark, keep these tips in mind:

(1) *Keep it simple.* Just like your font, keep the icon simple and easy to recognize at a distance. Remember, this needs to work on small business cards *and* large banners alike. Likewise, design the icon in vector format.

(2) If someone is drawing the logomark for you, they should draw it rather large, at least an 8.5" x 11" sheet. It's easier to shrink an image and maintain good quality rather than the other way around.

(3) Don't use gradients. No matter how cool gradients look on your computer, they won't translate well through different mediums (especially embroidery or low-scale print jobs).

(4) Don't use photographs for your icon. Just like gradients, a photograph is hard to translate into different mediums.

(5) Don't use clip art. They're not appropriate for a logo; they're too common and you want something distinctive.

Color: Limit the logo to two colors for two reasons. First, printing costs are cheaper - since you're charged by the color, four-color business cards can get quite expensive. Also, less colors make your logo simpler and easier to read. Design the logo first in black and white. Once you like the overall image, play around with color options.

What are your brand's emotions? The colors of your logo play a large part in that. For example, blue is the color of dependability and strength. Red evokes passion, excitement, and youthfulness. (It also stimulates hunger, which is why so many restaurants use it in their logos.) Yellow and orange suggest warmth, friendliness, and humor. Purple invokes royalty and creativity. Green represents health, wealth, and nature.

Background: Most people choose white for logo backgrounds and I think that's a safe bet; it looks crisp and prints well on a variety of media. If you want color in the background, ensure the logotype and logomark are both still clearly visible. Remember, this should be easy to read very small or from a far distance.

While you're looking at the background, consider negative space. Have you ever noticed the arrow in the FedEx logo? It's in the negative space between the "Ex." It's simple, but it reinforces the FedEx brand. Can you do something similar with your logo?

Test several variations: Make 3-6 versions of your logo and show them around. Ask friends, family, coworkers, and even passersby on the street for their opinion. You want a logo that appeals to a broad group of people, so ask as many people as you can.

It's ok if your logo evolves over time. Your business name, domain name, and social media names can't change, but your logo can be updated if needed. Don't do it all the time because brand consistency is important. However, I don't want you stuck with an outdated logo if your business evolves into something more.

NOTE: We've talked about design a lot in this chapter. Once your materials are designed, read Chapter 13 for detailed information about printing business cards, postcards, banners, and other types of marketing materials.

A NOTE ON BRAND CONSISTENCY

Make your branding consistent across all media and communications. Use a consistent font, icon, and color pattern. Maintain the same voice on your business cards and product descriptions. Ensure the photography style is consistent too.

Anyone should be able to pick up any piece of media about your business (postcard, website, photograph, advertisement, logo, product description, packaging) and recognize they're all from the same place. Apple is famous for their white products on white backgrounds with simple fonts and copy. You could pick up any piece of Apple marketing and the consistency is apparent. Do the same with your brand.

Chapter 6: **LAUNCH A WEBSITE.**

"Too often, feeling intimidated becomes our excuse not to be awesome."

- Scott Stratten

If you're serious about your business, you need a website - an Etsy shop alone won't cut it. Etsy is a great sales channel (we'll talk about it in Chapter 11), but nothing replaces your own website.

Why? Because a website makes it easy for customers to find you. Instead of searching Etsy for your shop, they can just type your name into a web browser. Websites are more professional-looking too. A domain name is also easier to remember than a whole Etsy link.

Plus, websites improve your search engine ranking which helps land you on the first page of Google. Potential customers usually don't look past the first page of Google, so you want to be right at the top. (More about this later in the chapter.)

Finally, a website is the online storefront and social hub of your business. Hopefully you'll be blogging on there, uploading pictures, providing tips, and sharing testimonials. Read on to learn about everything you'll want on your website plus tips for improving your Google ranking.

HOW TO MAKE A WEBSITE (THE EASY WAY)

This is an amazing time to be an artist, crafter, maker, and entrepreneur because there are so many resources available that were unthinkable even a few years ago. For example, making websites at home used to be nearly impossible unless you were a web developer fluent in HTML. Today, several companies help small business owners just like you set up a whole website in an afternoon - no web developing skills required.

First, read this entire chapter to plot out your website. Once you've figured out the basic structure, check out these resources to build your own website from user-friendly templates:

(1) *Squarespace* (www.squarespace.com): If you're selling more than 1 item, you'll want the "Professional" plan ($16/month for 20 items) or the "Business" plan ($24/month for unlimited items).

(2) *IndieMade* (www.indiemade.com): Starts at $4.95/month to sell 10 items. These fine folks really support indie artists, there's tons of great resources on their site too.

(3) *Big Cartel* (www.bigcartel.com): You'll likely want the "Platinum" ($9.99/month for 25 products) or "Diamond" plan ($19.99/month for 100 products).

(4) *Storenvy* (www.storenvy.com): Build an online store and sell in the Storenvy marketplace at the same time. There are no monthly costs, however once you open a shop you can choose to add $5/month options like a custom domain name or super discount codes.

(5) *Weebly* (www.weebly.com): You'll want the "Business" plan for $25/month, it's the only plan that services e-commerce.

(6) *Wix* (www.wix.com): It's free to create a website with Wix. However, if you want a shopping cart, you'll have to choose the "eCommerce" plan starting at $16.17/month.

(7) *Goodsie* (www.goodsie.com): Prices change depending if you're a monthly, bi-annual, or annual subscriber. You can probably get away with the cheapest options ($25-$30/month), you likely won't need the other add-on features.

(8) *Carbonmade* (www.carbonmade.com): Strictly a portfolio site for visual artists, no shopping cart support. It's free to join up to 35 images. Then it's $12/month for 500 images and 10 videos.

As you're evaluating these options, read customer reviews and take notes on the various features available. Make a list of the features you'll need, like the ability to offer coupons or gift certificates, linking with social media, "share" buttons, website analytics, image gallery, SEO optimization, mobile-friendly, accepting credit cards, and a custom domain name (don't worry, we'll talk about all of this later in the chapter).

NOTE: *"Can I hire someone to build my website?"* Sure you can. I don't recommend it though. It's costly, time consuming, and you might not get exactly what you want. For small businesses, it's best to DIY with one of the resources above. However, if you're a sucker for punishment and want to hire someone else, you'll want two types of people: (1) graphic designer and (2) web developer. The former designs the site while the latter makes it happen. These are two different skill sets, it's rare to find one person who does both. Check out Appendix A in the back of the book for more info about hiring designers and developers.

WEBSITE CONTENT

Your website only has *one second* to capture someone's attention before they click away - that's it. In fact, the average website's *bounce rate* is 50%, meaning half the people visiting the website go away before clicking anything. Don't be discouraged by these statistics; just understand you have to work hard to grab people's attention.

How do you capture attention? By defining your target audience and providing content that is relevant to them.

Remember back in Chapter 3 we talked about defining your customers and finding a niche? Your website should appeal specifically to those niche customers. For example, transcribe your customers' frequently asked questions and answer them on your website. Write product descriptions that appeal to your target demographic. Use images that grab their attention. Keep everything cohesive like we discussed in Chapter 5.

Next, define your goals for the site. Is it portfolio-only? Does it have a shopping cart? Will you be blogging? Also, think about the sections you'll want like: Portfolio, Store, Blog, Contact, About, FAQs, Etsy Shop, Calendar, and News/Press section. Don't use more than seven sections (also known as "Pages,") otherwise the site becomes too overwhelming.

Contact: People will want to contact you. Customers need to know they're dealing with a real person, so include as much contact information as you can. List your name, business address (PO boxes are fine), business telephone, email address, and picture if possible.

Email: Always have an email sign-up form on your website. Email addresses are marketing gold. As we'll discuss in Chapter 13, email marketing has a 50:1 return over traditional marketing.

When you're writing content for the website, appeal to your target demographic while differentiating yourself from competitors. What makes your business better than any other? It could be your helpful customer service, generous return policy, or sourcing of quality materials. This type of information increases customer confidence and the likelihood they'll purchase from you.

Storyboarding your website

You might have heard the term "storyboarding" before in the context of movies, television, or animation. "Storyboarding" is the process of breaking down a story into a series of sequential images. It helps visualize a project before it's complete.

Professional designers go through this process to map out a website before it's created. Storyboarding allows you to imagine the entire project and ensure all objectives are met in the most efficient way possible. Simplicity is important because websites should be easy to navigate.

The goal here is to make things easy for your customers. You want them to be able to find relevant information effortlessly, contact you simply, and purchase an item painlessly. The more steps between your customer and purchasing, the more likely you'll lose the sale. Try taking customers from homepage to purchase in three steps or less.

While you're storyboarding, make a list of everything needed to complete each web page - product descriptions, photographs, headlines ... things like that. When you're finished, you should have layouts for every page on your website (e.g., Store, About, FAQ, Blog) and the navigation confirmed as well.

Product descriptions

Product descriptions are a powerful sales tool, almost as much as pictures. The best descriptions are concise, detailed, and persuasive. You should read Chapter 9 before writing product descriptions because that chapter is packed with sales techniques to enhance descriptions. For those who can't wait, here's a little information to get started. Also, put some variety in each product description so search engines don't think you're spammy, more on that below.

Dimensions: Include the specific measurements of your products, both inside and out (if interior measurement is much different than exterior). Not only that, but suggest real-life uses too. For example, not everyone can picture an 8" x 5" bag, so mention it can hold sunglasses, wallet, and keys. This is especially important for jewelers - your customers might not understand what earrings with a 2" drop length looks like, but if you say the earring hits mid-neck they can visualize it better.

Materials: List all the materials used in making the item. Not only does Etsy require it, but your website customers want to know too. Get descriptive with materials. Instead of listing, "cotton, wool, and thread" try "cotton broadcloth, Merino wool, and waxed thread."

Descriptions should be informative and entertaining too. Do you have a story about creating the product, or has a customer gotten great enjoyment from it? Include anything noteworthy or interesting in your description. Mention benefits like "Machine washable" or "Burn time 20 hours." Utilize senses too - does your product feel especially soft? Does it smell lovely? Is there a sound when you open it? Not only does sensory language capture the reader's attention, but it helps potential customers imagine already owning your product.

TAKING GOOD PICTURES

When I'm shopping in a store and see something I like, I immediately touch it. We all do this; touch is an important part of the product experience. Unfortunately this sensation is lost for online shoppers, so you have to make up for it with amazing visuals. Create photographs that command attention, inform, and educate.

Customers need to feel confident about their purchase and photographs build confidence by providing information. Great pictures clearly represent the product and help potential customers imagine using it. Product shots can be your best sales tool.

What makes a great product shot? Three elements:
(1) Lighting
(2) Background
(3) Composition

(1) *Lighting:* Natural daylight is your best friend. It's easy to use, free, and illuminates products beautifully. Try photographing

outside if you can, but avoid harsh direct sunlight that casts shadows and glares. Photograph in the shade or around sunrise and sunset. Overcast days are great for photographing; clouds act like a natural diffuser.

For those who never have time to photograph during the day, fear not - artificial light can work very well too. Use daylight bulbs (not incandescent, which will turn your images yellow) and try filtering them through tissue paper. Make your own light box for easy, consistent shots. What's a light box? It's a box with filters on the sides to diffuse light. You can make your own with a cardboard box and tissue paper or purchase them online starting at $35. Also check out Hello Craft's book *Handmade to Sell* for excellent photography and light box tips.

> •PRO TIP• You know those big silver reflectors professionals use for photography and video shoots? Those things take advantage of limited light while reducing shadows and increasing highlights. You can do the same with white foam core from an art or craft store. Whether outside or in your light box, experiment moving the foam core and bouncing around light for really vibrant product shots.

(2) *Background:* The background should be clean and simple, void of anything distracting. I'm an advocate for plain white backgrounds for five reasons: (1) it's easy to do, (2) it keeps your product shots consistent, (3) it best highlights your products, (4) it's not distracting, and (5) most editors and press require your images to have a white background. Some merchants like Amazon.com demand it too.

The exception to this rule: I've seen glass blowers photograph with a black background because glass shows better on black than white. It's one of the few times black backgrounds are accepted.

(3) *Composition:* Keep your product clearly the center of attention - don't confuse customers with distractions. Also, experiment with turning the camera horizontally and vertically (landscape vs. portrait). Finally, experiment with the *Rule of Thirds*. Imagine your photograph split into three vertical sections and try placing your product in the first or third section. In the Rule of Thirds, products are photographed off-center. This might sound counterintuitive, but it produces more engaging images.

The photographs you need

Customers crave information so they appreciate a lot of photographs. Use 3-5 pictures for each product, including these shots:

(1) *General product shot:* White background, shows your full product. Clean and simple shot, no distractions.

(2) *Detail product shot:* White background, zoomed in pictures of anything that showcases your quality handiwork or materials. Show the interior of handbags, the grain of your wooden bowls, or the smooth tops of soy candles. No detail is too small for your customers.

(3) *Lifestyle shot:* A picture of your product used in everyday life (no white background required). A woman wearing your scarf. Your ceramic mugs with steaming tea and cookies. Your prints hanging in a living room. These images are not only editorial, but they help potential customers imagine using your product. Plus, it gives them an idea of the actual size and shape of your product.

Take 100 shots per product and expect 5 perfect ones. Experiment with different angles and compositions to find what works for you. Note the set up so you can recreate it in the future.

A word on props: Keep the background of your lifestyle shots interesting but simple. Use one or two statement props and place them in the background with your product in the foreground. Don't use props that take away attention from your products. Any props that help convey the size of your product are great, especially people. Customers respond best to any pictures featuring real people using your stuff.

Photo editing

If you have great lighting, simple backgrounds, and excellent composition, you don't need to rely on photo editing too much. For the rest of us, editing is your best friend.

You don't have to be a graphic designer to edit great photographs either. Yes, crazy Photoshop skills are preferred, but don't let that hold you back. Today it's easy to edit pictures in minutes with minimal skills.

I basically use two editing tools with my photographs: *cropping* (cutting out portions of the image) and *contrast* (making the picture lighter or darker). That's it, that's all I do. You could play with color correction and brightness too, check it out with these photo editing resources:

(1) For those with zero photo editing skills, head over to PicMonkey (www.picmonkey.com). They make photo editing really intuitive and there's tons of great features. It's free to use (there's paid options too) and you don't have to create an account. Plus, I think their branding is really great.

(2) Photoscape (www.photoscape.org) is another free photo editing software that has cool features like combining photographs, splitting images, and batch processing groups of photos.

(3) If you have a Mac, try iPhoto. It's similar to PicMonkey and Photoscape but for fancy Mac users.

(4) If you want to step up a skill level, try Photoshop online (www.photoshop.com/tools). Not only is this version free, but it's easier to use than the full professional application. It's a level up from PicMonkey or iPhoto because you can get into serious photo editing that's similar to what the pros use.

Photography tips

(1) Research great photographs on Etsy, particularly those items that make the front page. Check out Pinterest (www.pinterest.com) too and observe the most popular pictures in your category.

(2) Use a tripod whenever possible. Not only does it reduce blurriness, but it's easier to recreate photographs later. I mark my floor with tape to remember where to place the tripod legs.

(3) Don't ever use the flash. It will wash out products and all your beautiful little details will be lost.

(4) Be consistent with photographs. You're going to be doing a lot of "photo sessions" so make your setup easy to recreate, especially if you're photographing similar products in the future.

Three things to look for in a camera

You don't need a fancy camera with a big lens to take awesome product shots. Today's smartphones have surprisingly excellent camera functions. Your point-and-shoot digital camera will work great too, particularly if it has these three options:

(1) *Macro setting:* You will be taking a lot of close up detail shots and you'll need the macro setting to do it (the icon looks like a flower on most cameras).

(2) *White balance/daylight setting:* I have done multiple photoshoots forgetting to white balance first and paid the price in post-production. White balance ensures that whatever white you see in person will also be white in the camera (as opposed to yellow or blue, which has happened to me more times than I care to admit).

(3) *Depth of field/aperture setting/bokeh:* This is the cool effect that makes your foreground in focus and background all blurry (often called "bokeh.") It's technically known as depth of field which is accomplished through adjusting the aperture. Lens aperture is given an f-number (for the focal ratio) and the lower the number, the wider the aperture. That is, a low f-number (like f/2.8) makes your products in the foreground focused and the background blurry. I use f/2.8 to achieve this effect, but you might like f/4 or higher.

SEO: SEARCH ENGINE OPTIMIZATION

SEO is about optimizing your website to attract search engines. The better your SEO, the higher your search engine ranking (i.e., ability to appear on the front page of Google). This is a beefy topic worth its own book and there are thousands of resources focused on SEO - there are even companies dedicated exclusively to it.

SEO is a dark art. It's largely based on Google's algorithm (their mathematical equation that ranks websites), which is a highly-guarded secret. There isn't a magic formula for improving SEO, but there are loads of tips and tricks. You don't have to be a professional with HTML skills either - here's some SEO tips you can do right now with no technical experience.

First, understand that Google cannot be tricked. Sure, there are some evil SEO practitioners who buy links or stuff keywords for short-term gains, but in the long term Google can't be fooled. The best way to reach the front page of Google and stay there is to consistently generate quality content.

There's three key ingredients to great content:
(1) Post regularly
(2) Use links, both incoming and reciprocal
(3) Use keywords strategically

(1) *Post regularly:* Search engines love it when your website is updated regularly. If your site hasn't been touched in a long time, it looks outdated and thus ranks lower in searches. Try updating your site at least once a month with blog posts, new products, testimonials, special announcements, and whatever else might be relevant or interesting to your customers.

(2) *Use links:* Search engines put a lot of emphasis on links, especially incoming ones. When another website writes about you, they'll provide a link to your site. This "legitimizes" your site in the eyes of Google. Incoming links from popular websites help more than unpopular ones. For example, if the *New York Times* links to your website, Google puts more importance on that link than say, your mom's blog (no offense to your mother, but she's not the *NYT*).

If you do get an incoming link on your site, go ahead and link back - it's called a *reciprocal link* and Google likes it. For example, if your website gets written up in a furniture blog, write your own blog post about it and link back to the furniture blog's article. Not only is this good for SEO, but it's great for networking and providing good content too.

Get creative with links. Try linking between different pages on your site, perhaps in product descriptions and blog posts. Also link to third-party sites that contain interesting or relevant information for your customers. Link to your social media accounts too and be sure they link back. Contribute articles to popular websites and include links to your website there. See Chapter 13 for tips on partnering with other businesses for promotions and you can get loads of links from that.

(3) *Use keywords strategically:* This topic is so important I've dedicated an entire section to it on the next page. Your keywords should be used everywhere - in product descriptions, blog posts, product titles, About page, FAQs, and social media.

You'll become more comfortable with SEO over time. After mastering the techniques above, read more about SEO and learn how to further improve your website's ranking. You might learn about things like "Title Tags" and "<h1> & <h2> Tags" which sound overwhelming but they're not too bad and they're very beneficial for your site's SEO. Plus, many of the DIY website resources mentioned above do a lot of the SEO legwork for you, so you can learn how to maximize their potential.

There are lot of opportunities to improve SEO. Experiment with the site. Tweak it a little. Have patience. You don't reach the front page of Google overnight and once you do, it takes work to stay there.

KEYWORDS

Have you ever typed something into Google and seen those words in bold in the links below? Those are keywords. In fact, the phrase you typed into Google is all about keywords too.

Keywords are those phrases that people type into search engines. Keywords are important - they help consumers find your products and help search engines rank your website (and get you closer to the first page of Google). Keywords are critical on Etsy too; that's how potential customers find you.

Keywords are words that describe your product or business. They might not always be obvious either. For example, one of eThreads' keywords is "vegan" because we don't use animal products in our bags. Though it's not as evident as "custom" or "tote bag," it is a search term our customers use. Use keywords to mark your products for special holidays too like "Christmas ornaments" or "Valentine's card."

How to find keywords

First, think like a customer - what search terms would they use to describe your product? "Monogrammed cuff links." "Reclaimed wood bench." "Wrought iron cabinet hardware." Also, if your product has alternate spellings, use them as keywords. For example, "chainmail" is traditionally spelled like "chainmaille" - with an "le" at the end, and some people even write "chain mail." In this case, use all three versions as your keywords.

Next, head over to Etsy's search bar. Start typing your keywords and the search bar automatically populates common terms. Here's excellent insight into the keywords people really use.

Visit Google next and try the same thing. For serious insight, check out the Google Adwords Keyword Tool (https://adwords. google.com/keywordtool). It requires a Google Adwords account, but if you have a Gmail account you can set it up for free in minutes (if you don't have a Gmail account, you have to create one first, which is also free and easy to do). Google's Keyword Tool provides in-depth analysis about popular keywords, including historical and comparative data.

Google Analytics (www.google.com/analytics): We talked about Google Analytics in Chapter 3 to help define your niche. It's also tremendously helpful for identifying keywords. Since Google Analytics shows the search terms people use to find your website, it automatically lists the most popular keywords for your business.

Etsy Shop Stats: If you have an Etsy shop, check out the Shop Stats. See how many people visit your Etsy shop, which items are most viewed, and the keywords people use to find your shop. Plug Google Analytics into your Etsy Shop for more in-depth details.

What to do with keywords:

Your keywords should be used wherever reasonably possible. Use keywords in product descriptions, artist bio, FAQs, press releases, marketing materials, blog posts, advertisements … everywhere.

Why? Because search engines like it when you have multiple pages of content with important keywords sprinkled throughout. Select your top 15 keywords and use them regularly. Do not repeat keywords over and over again mindlessly, search engines consider that spammy and might punish you with a lower search ranking. Just sprinkle your top 15 keywords naturally throughout the website.

This goes for product descriptions too. Don't repeat the same phrase for every item's product description or search engines will consider the site a "bot" and punish you with a lower search ranking. Even if you sell the same product in four different colors, switch up the title and description of each color: "Brown felted hat," "Red hat made with felt," "Blue hat made with recycled felt," and "Eco-friendly purple felt hat." Tweak each listing slightly to vary keywords and improve search engine ranking.

BLOGGING

Blogs have been mentioned a lot in this chapter; everyone should have a blog for their business. Most people think of blogs as something frivolous, but in truth they're very important for business strategy.

For those scratching their heads, let me take a step back and say that "blog" is short for "weblog" and it's a website that is updated regularly by one author or a group of authors. Blogs are usually published through Wordpress (my favorite - www.wordpress.com), Tumblr (www.tumblr.com), Blogger (www.blogger.com/features), or Typepad (www.typepad.com), among others. The DIY website services listed at the beginning of the chapter have blog capabilities too.

People blog for business and pleasure. You can find blogs on any topic you'd ever imagine, from entertainment to finance to crafting to aging to everything in between. To find other blogs that might interest or inspire you, do an internet search for your topic of interest plus "blog" (e.g., "metalsmithing blog"). This type of research is helpful when planning your own blog.

Blogs are great for business in numerous ways. First, they're beneficial for SEO as we discussed above. Also, they're a useful way to update your site without redesigning anything. Finally, blogs are an easy way for customers to get to know you and engage with your brand.

Content of your blog:

It's important to write about things that are relevant or engaging to your customers. Whatever they're interested in, that's what you should be blogging about. We'll talk about this a lot in Chapter 14 so I'll just briefly mention a few items here:

(1) *Photographs of you, your work, or your studio:* People love to see who they're dealing with and what happens behind the scenes.

(2) *Personal stories that are funny or engaging:* It helps customers connect with your business on a personal level.

(3) *Articles and resources your customers would find interesting:* It doesn't have to be directly related to your business, it could just be topical, newsworthy, or poignant.

(4) *Tips and tricks about your industry:* "Top 10" or "Top 5" lists are especially effective. For example, candle makers might have a blog post, "10 Ways to Keep Your Home Smelling Fresh" or jewelers could write, "5 New Fashion Trends in Accessories."

(5) *Features and interviews:* Find other makers or people who inspire you and interview them for the blog. Feature their artwork and creative process. Encourage them to share the blog post for increased exposure and improved SEO.

(6) *News and events:* Talk about the exciting things happening in your career too. Did you win an award or do you have an upcoming event? Did you just finish an especially difficult piece of work? Are you introducing new products on the website? Blog about it!

Writing style is important too. In Chapter 5 we talked about the personality of your business. Channel that personality when blogging, it's more engaging and strengthens your brand. Keep it simple. Make your entries short (600 words or less) with short paragraphs and bulleted lists. Use photographs or illustrations in your posts - they're attention-grabbers. Speaking of grabbing attention ... put a lot of thought into blog post titles. Not only should they be snappy and engaging, they should include keywords. See Chapter 16 for tips about writing good headlines.

Post on your blog regularly. It's best to post something 3-4 times a week but I know you probably don't have time for that. At least once a week is best. If your schedule doesn't allow that, than write 1-2 blog posts a month - you won't have regular readers but at least SEO will remain intact. Make it easier on yourself - write multiple blog posts at once then schedule them to publish over time.

Include keywords and links in your blog posts too. Don't mindlessly stuff keywords into a blog post or search engines will punish you; just write conversationally and include keywords when you can.

•PRO TIP• When comparing the DIY website options listed at the top of this chapter, look for ones that help readers subscribe to an RSS feed. RSS means "Really Simple Syndication" and allows users to stay updated on their favorite websites without having to check each one. What does this mean to you? RSS helps SEO. It's all about SEO.

WEB ANALYTICS

You can't manage what you don't measure - that's why you need analytics. As we've discussed, services like Google Analytics and Etsy Shop Stats let you track how many people are coming to your site, where they're coming from, what they're looking at, how long they're staying ... it's remarkable. (*Facebook Insights* does the same for your Facebook page, we'll get to that in Chapter 14.)

There are several analytics services but the most popular (and clearly my favorite) is Google Analytics (www.google.com/analytics). It's free, easy to sign up, and most of the DIY websites sources listed at the beginning of this chapter have Google Analytics capabilities.

Google Analytics gives you amazing insight about your business. For example, *Traffic Sources* and *Visitor Flow* list how people found your site. I love the *Geo* feature - it tells you where in the world your website is being viewed. *In-Page Analytics* shows where customers are clicking - thus telling you what's popular on the site. Remember we talked about keywords? There's a tool in Google Analytics that lists which keywords your customers use most.

There are two other key measurements that are very important. The *Bounce Rate* tells you how many people click away from your site before clicking anything on the site. If your bounce rate is higher than 50%, you've got a problem. Examine the pages with the highest bounce rate and figure out why people are leaving your site before clicking anything. It's usually because something on the page is broken or they can't find relevant information easily.

Average Visit Duration/Time on Site is also important. You'd be surprised how low this number is - usually 30 seconds or less. If you have 1:00 as time on site you're in good shape. eThreads has varied from 3:00 - 6:00 minutes for time on site, and that means our website is "sticky" - people "stick" around and click from link to link. If your time on site is low, think about ways to make your website more appealing and engaging.

There are entire companies dedicated to analyzing this kind of data and creating action plans. You can do the same with your site. Notice what products are viewed most often, where in the world you're most popular, and what kind of customer demographics you have. This type of information should guide your product development, advertising strategies, and marketing plan. Plus it's really fun to boot.

You survived the website chapter! This is one of the meatier chapters in the book, so don't worry if you feel overwhelmed. Just go back and re-read the chapter and take it one section at a time.

Also, don't let perfection get in the way of action - build your site then throw it up on the web. As people begin to use the site, study your analytics and make improvements from there. I have launched 3 versions of eThreads' site - 1.0, 2.0, 2.5 - and we're currently developing the 3.0 version. Websites evolve - yours will shift and change over time, and as you learn more about what's important to your customers, each version will be more effective than the last.

Chapter 7:
MAKE HAPPY CUSTOMERS.

"If you are not taking care of your customer, your competitor will." - **Bob Hooey**

Sam Walton (the founder of Walmart) once said, "We all have one boss, the customer. And she can fire us anytime she wants by simply deciding to shop somewhere else."

Mr. Walton is 100% correct - your customer is the boss, and you should do everything possible to please them. *If you don't have happy customers, you don't have a business.* Make customer service a top priority.

ABOUT YOUR CUSTOMER

People buy stuff to improve their lives in some way. As we'll discuss in detail in Chapter 9, customers are driven to satisfy *wants, needs, and desires.* Your job is to convince customers you satisfy their needs better than any competitor.

Today's consumers are pretty tough though. They're more well-informed and skeptical than ever before. Thanks to an "on demand" society, people want better, faster, cheaper, more, and they want it now. Plus, the competitive landscape is overpopulated and your customer's attention span is getting shorter.

But you're just an indie artist, looking to sell some handmade goods. You don't have a marketing department to compete with all the big boys, so what are you supposed to do?

It's easy - focus on the customer and do everything possible to please them.

Here's the good news - consumers are not as brand-loyal as they were decades ago. This means you, the solo artist, can capture someone's business just as easily as the big guys and keep them from going to competitors. All you need is great customer service.

TOP 10 WAYS TO PROVIDE STELLAR CUSTOMER SERVICE

What defines great customer service? It's anything that makes someone say, "Wow!" and run off to tell everybody about your business. Want to get there yourself? Here's 10 ways to master the art of superb customer service:

(1) Provide information: Customers want to be well-informed before making a purchase, especially today's hyper-vigilant buyers. Write thorough descriptions of your products and how they're made (types of materials, your process, etc...). Talk about texture and how it feels in your hand. Showcase a lot of photos with tons of details. Be very clear with your return, exchange, and sales policies. Write an FAQ page. Describe how to use and care for your products on the website and product labels.

Every potential customer experiences tension when they want to buy something. They're thinking, "What's in it for me?" "Is it a good value?" "Is this business trustworthy?" Customers want to be confident about their purchase. The best way to build confidence is to provide information and prove your products are a smart decision for the buyer.

(2) Create a personalized experience: One of the reasons people buy indie-made is for the personal touch that comes from dealing directly with an artist. Make your customers feel special with an individualized experience. Include a handwritten note with their order. Follow up after purchase. Track birthdays, anniversaries, or special events and send a personalized card with a coupon. These extra touches help your business stand out and remind your customers to come back again.

(3) Ask questions and listen to customers: There are three easy ways to interact with your customers: (1) email, (2) survey, and (3) social media. Always send an email one week after customers received their purchase and ask for feedback - see Chapter 13 for more tips about sending emails. I love to send periodic surveys as well, we'll talk about this in

Chapter 17. Social media is the best way to converse with your customers because you can involve a lot of people and receive immediate feedback. We'll talk about social media in Chapter 14.

Don't limit yourself to post-purchase feedback either. Talk with customers often and get their opinions. I love chatting with eThreads customers on social media about new bag designs and fabric choices. I often post pictures of design prototypes and ask for feedback. Not only is their insight invaluable, but customers love getting involved with the design process too.

I know it's scary to get customer feedback, but trust me you'll win either way. If customers love your stuff, it feels great. If they don't like it, you can figure out how to make it better. Not only are you improving products, but you're building customer relationships too. Plus, people are going to talk about your products whether you like or not - wouldn't you rather they said good things?

(4) Exceed expectations: All customers have unwritten expectations about your business - find out what they are and exceed them. For example, all customers expect a certain level of quality and service - go beyond that. Include something unexpected like a small sample. Use really creative packaging. Write a personalized note. Upgrade their shipping option. Include a 20% coupon for their next purchase. Send a gift voucher on their birthday.

This is the sort of stuff that makes customers sing about your business to all their friends. You want them saying, "This is a GREAT product!" "What an AWESOME business!" "I have to tell EVERYONE about this!" Be super generous with your customers and they'll repay you tenfold.

(5) Make it easy: Today's consumers are distracted easily; extra steps are a hassle for them. Make everything about your business very easy ... how to use the website, how to order, how to contact, how to make returns ... The less steps in your sales process, the higher the response.

Speaking of making it easy ... make it easy to spread the word about your business. Have social media buttons like "Share" (for Facebook), "Retweet" (for Twitter), and "Pin this" (for Pinterest) all over your website. Also include links to your social media accounts so people can follow you easily. Include five extra business cards in each order so customers can pass it out to friends (maybe with a $5 gift certificate attached). Create a referral system where customers get free stuff when their friends make a purchase.

(6) Treat each customer like they're your mom: Be courteous, respectful, and timely in your responses. I don't care if a customer says something nasty and you're upset - always give them the same kindly attention you would your mother. Not only is it professional, but you don't want to add fuel to the fire. If a customer ever rattles your chains, take a deep breath and imagine you're talking with your mom. Believe me, when cooler heads prevail you'll always be the winner.

(7) Be reliable and predictable: I'm talking about personality *and* inventory. Respond to customer inquiries within 24 hours and try to get their packages out that quickly too.

Also, keep your inventory reliable. If you're known for making floral headbands, don't suddenly stop selling those and start making leather key chains. Please, introduce new products occasionally but keep the bestsellers around forever. Think like the clothing store The Gap - even though they update offerings every season, you can still get basic staples like button-downs and blazers no matter what.

Finally, keep your inventory well-stocked, especially around peak times. For example, we start planning our Christmas season in September. Also, May is graduation season and a very busy time for us so we stock up on supplies in March. You'll notice your seasonal patterns too and will be able to plan accordingly.

(8) Be responsive: Today's consumers expect you're available 24 hours a day, 7 days a week, on every available outlet - social media, email, phone, Etsy conversations … I'm not advocating you actually *are* available that much, just be aware of customer expectations.

I check eThreads' email and social media twice a day - once in the morning and once in the evening. Then I'm done. This way I can answer customer inquiries in a timely way but also maintain my sanity. I suggest you do the same.

(9) Ship quickly: Don't you get excited when you're waiting for something to come in the mail? Your customers have that same feeling and will love you more if you get orders shipped quickly. Ready-to-wear items should ship within 24 hours and custom orders should take no longer than 2 weeks. The faster you get an order in your customer's hands, the better your business looks.

(10) Build trust: Remember, customers are skeptical. They're aching to do business with someone they can trust. Prove your worth and have their business for life. How? Provide tons of information about you, your business, and your products. Add your bio and picture to the website - people love knowing they're working with a real person. Add customer testimonials too and any awards or press you've received.

Finally, be honest with your customers. If you've made a mistake, own up to it. Tell them what happened, why it happened, and what you're going to do to fix it. Trust me, I've made countless mistakes with eThreads customers and it's never been the end of the world. People appreciate honesty more than anything else - start with that and the rest is easy.

> **•PRO TIP•** Since 80% of a household's purchasing decisions are made by women, I'm going to go out on a limb and say the majority of your customers will be women. In this case, it's especially important to note that women notice small details - they'll appreciate your thoughtful wrapping or handwritten card. Women also remember everything - good and bad - and are the most likely to tell their friends about your business. Finally, women appreciate when you ask for feedback - they love being asked for opinions and can readily tell you what they think.

SHOP POLICIES: PAYMENT, SHIPPING, RETURNS, AND EXCHANGES

Define your shop policies now, display them clearly wherever your customer shops, and include them in order confirmation emails. Be clear about policies now to avoid hassles later.

Payment Options: What forms of payment do you accept? If you're selling from a website, accept credit cards with PayPal, Amazon Checkout, or other similar online payment options. If you use one of the website builders mentioned in Chapter 6, they have payment gateways available. If you're selling at craft shows, accept credit cards with mobile card readers like Square Up (www.squareup.com). If you accept checks or money orders online, tell them where to send it and to whom it should be written, also explain the order will be delayed while you're waiting for the check to clear. If you accept checks at craft shows, get their driver license number and telephone number in case there are problems.

Shipping Policy: How do you send orders, with USPS, UPS, DHL, or FedEx? Do you ship internationally? How long does an order take to ship? When will it arrive? These are questions your customers will be asking, so figure it out now. I talked about shipping in Chapter 3, flip back there for more advice.

If you offer ready-to-wear as well as custom orders, be very clear about those different shipping times. Ready-to-wear items are from your inventory and should ship within 1-2 days of receiving the order. Custom orders will take longer - be specific with your customers to avoid confusion. Provide a shipping timetable so people know when to expect their package, and add a tracking number if possible (you get those free with FedEx, UPS, DHL, and USPS Priority shipping).

International shipping: If you ship internationally, provide a chart with shipping fees for different countries. (Every package carrier has a shipping calculator on their website to assist with this.) Also tell your customers they are responsible for additional taxes or tariffs imposed by their country. Finally, estimate shipping time if possible. I've found USPS international packages usually arrive within two or three weeks (yikes). Also, their tracking number is only as good as the US border; as soon as the package leaves the border the tracking number is useless.

FedEx, UPS, and DHL offer more accurate timetables and tracking numbers for international shipments, but their services are often two or three times as expensive as USPS. Offer both options to your customers - some might prefer paying more to have a tracking number and specific arrival date.

Returns & Exchanges Policy: Should you accept returned merchandise? YES! Absolutely, it's good for business. Remember the #1 tip for great customer service at the beginning of this chapter - every potential customer experiences tension when they want to buy something. Customers need to feel confident about their purchase and the ability to return increases confidence.

It's going to happen - someone at some point is going to want to return one of your products. It's a little crushing at first, but don't take it personally. I've had people return products for many reasons - the color wasn't right, the size too small … I just had someone return a bag they bought on Amazon because it was a gift for a friend who "just bought a bag for herself."

Returns are no big deal - if you state the policy up front. I've heard horror stories of customers wanting to return something a year after purchasing it. They got away with it because the business didn't state a clear return policy at the time of purchase! Don't let this happen to you - decide how you'll accept returns and announce it to the world.

I think a fair return policy is, "We accept returns of unused merchandise within 14 days of receipt." This gives the customer two weeks to decide if the product is right for them. Remember shipping time - give them 14 days to get the product in the mail and provide you with a tracking number. They are responsible for return shipping costs.

Ready-to-wear orders are easy to return - you're just restocking inventory. But what about custom orders? That one is a lot tougher. Today's business consultants would tell you to accept returns on anything, even custom items. I agree, but I also understand you're probably a new business and accepting returns on customer orders could hurt your burgeoning bottom line. When you're first starting out it's ok to say, "Custom orders are non-returnable." As your business grows and you see how few returns you actually receive, I urge you to consider accepting returns on custom orders as well. Trust me, this will help your bottom line more than hurt it.

HOW TO DEAL WITH IRATE CUSTOMERS

Winston Churchill once said, "A lie gets halfway around the world before the truth has a chance to get its pants on."

He speaks the truth - negative information spreads a lot faster than positive information. It's because people remember negative experiences more than positive ones. What does this mean to you? One unhappy customer can make your life reaaaallly difficult. Let's discuss how to turn their frown upside down.

First, determine why your customer is unhappy. Remember, they're likely distressed when they're contacting you and therefore not entirely clear or pleasant. Your job is to stay calm, determine the exact reason they're unhappy, and don't take it personally.

Listen to complaints then apologize. An irate customer relaxes significantly after some encouraging words. Tell them you're here to help and want to make it right.

Most customer complaints come from misunderstanding - the package was lost in the mail, it arrived too late, the wrong product was delivered, or it was damaged upon delivery. There's no simple way to deal with these situations, other than to do whatever you can to make it right and still feel good about yourself.

Sometimes you're going to take a hit, and that's ok. Even though you might clearly state, "No returns, no exceptions," someone will still want to return something. In that case, it's better to accept the return and lose a little money than gain an irate customer.

Why? Two reasons. One, negative information spreads quickly and lingers awhile, so it will cost your reputation more than just the sale in the long run. Two, turning a negative experience into a positive one builds customer relationships for life.

Allow me to share a quick story as an example. In 2012 I was getting married and looking for earrings to wear to the wedding. I went to Etsy and quickly found a pair I loved. I purchased the earrings, anxiously awaited their arrival, tore off the packaging, slipped them in my ear ... and winced in pain. Even though the posts were sterling silver, something about them was not agreeing with my earlobe. I've been wearing earrings a long time and never experienced this before. I asked my friend to try on the pair and she had the same experience. I visited the seller's Etsy shop and saw they had a "No returns, no exceptions" policy. I wrote them anyway and explained my story and asked if I could return the earrings. They said no. I wrote back and explained I was also a crafter and normally would follow the return policy but these really hurt and clearly something must be wrong and please make an exception. They said no, and their temper was starting to flair. In no uncertain terms I was told I couldn't return the earrings.

Lucky for them I didn't want the bad karma of leaving a negative review but boy was I tempted. It's a shame too - I found several other earrings I wanted to buy as bridesmaid gifts, and if they took my one simple return they would have gotten five times more business in my next purchase. Don't let this happen to you friends. Make exceptions to your rules, I promise it's good for business.

When a customer complains, you must first understand what went wrong. Then figure out how to solve the problem and let them know how you're going to do it. Be clear about the steps you'll take and what they'll get in return (e.g., a full refund, an exchange, a new product, etc...) Apologize for the confusion - it might hurt, but just do it. Offer a free bonus too, like free shipping on the exchange or a 20% coupon for next time.

One last note on customer service - you'll occasionally meet unhappy customers who can't be pleased no matter what. Sometimes truly ungrateful customers are just unhappy people taking it out on you. It happens, but not often. We've had thousands of customers and I could count on one hand the number of truly bad people we've ever experienced. Just forget about it and let them go bother someone else. You have a bunch of other great customers who are thrilled to do business with you - spend your time making *them* happy.

Chapter 8: **BE AN EXPERT.**

"We are what we pretend to be, so we must be careful about what we pretend to be." - **Kurt Vonnegut**

I bet a lot of you are cringing at the word "expert." I used to be uncomfortable with it too until I realized how great it is for business. I wrote this chapter to convince you that you're already an expert about something and it's time to tell the world about it. Share everything you know about your craft, art, talent, hobby, or special skill and people will be flocking to do business with you.

WHY IT'S IMPORTANT TO BE AN EXPERT

Here's the deal - potential customers want to give you money, but confidence is holding them back. Remember in Chapter 7 we talked about information and the customers who crave it? People want to make the right decision, but too often they don't have the information needed to feel confident about their purchase.

Your customers want information. They have questions about size, color, wearability, delivery, guarantees, return policies, price comparisons, customer service, warranty, and anything else necessary to make a well-informed purchase. They need to know they're buying the best product for the best price that best solves their problem.

Not only that, but customers want to know they're purchasing from someone who knows what they're talking about. People respect knowledge. They respect authority. Customers want to do business with an expert because it gives them confidence to make the purchase.

Be that expert. Educate people on your materials and why you chose them. Tell customers about your assembly techniques and why they're the best. Remind them about the product's durability or your repair-it-for-life guarantee. Talk about your experiences and accolades. Trust me, this isn't bragging, it's empowering your customers.

Not only do consumers love experts, but journalists love them too. Position yourself as an expert and journalists will call you when they need a quote. Call yourself an authority and the press will want to hear from you. People respect experts' opinions - enjoy it.

GET OVER THE FEAR OF CALLING YOURSELF AN EXPERT

"Gee Emily, that sounds great and all, but *I'm* not an expert." Stop it. I guarantee you are. Think about your art, craft, hobby, or skill. You've likely spent years nurturing that talent and learned a lot through mistakes and errors. Sure, there are some people who know more than you, but there are a heck of a lot of people who know a heck of a lot less.

Besides, there's lots of room in this world for experts. Trust me, there's space for you too. *All you have to do is share content that other people find helpful.* That's it. For example, I wrote this book to share all the knowledge I wish I had when I started eThreads. Are there other business experts out there? Sure. Lots and lots. But that didn't stop me from writing this book and it's not going to stop you from declaring yourself an expert either.

HOW TO BE AN EXPERT

Still not convinced you're an expert? This section is for you. It's easier to be an expert than you think. It really takes a few simple steps:

(1) *Network:* Be a popular player in your field. Be present at the right art shows and trade expos. Participate on Etsy forums. Leave comments on hobby blogs. Get to know the media people who cover your field (see Chapter 15 for more about this). Be thoughtful and engaging with your community and your status will elevate automatically.

(2) *Go niche:* We talked about niche products for niche customers earlier in the book and it's no different as an expert. Try narrowing your focus of expertise. It sounds counterintuitive I know, but trust me. You know the phrase, "Jack of all trades, master of none?" That's what's happening here. You're not going to have time to learn

everything there is to know about all your interests, so choose something specific and become an expert at it.

(3) *Join organizations:* Are there groups you could join that would elevate your professional status or crafting experience? How about professional organizations? For example, there's the Craft & Hobby Association (www.craftandhobby.org) which is great for networking and professional credentials. If you join an organization, put "Member of" and the organization's logo on your website. Check out Appendix A in the back of the book for more group ideas.

(4) *Never stop learning:* Read blogs and books about your medium to learn new techniques. Study upcoming trends and how to capitalize on them. Practice new styles on different materials. The more you know about your product and the industry, the more customers will want to do business with you.

WHAT TO DO AS AN EXPERT

It's your duty to share your knowledge with the world. Find out the information your customers want and become their go-to source for answers:

(1) *Contribute articles to relevant blogs and magazines:* An excellent way to get free advertising, unlimited exposure, and expert status all at once. You'd be surprised how easy it is to get an article published, see Chapter 13 for more information.

(2) *Leave comments on articles and blog posts:* Did you read a helpful article about your topic? Leave a comment with your business name and something useful for the audience.

(3) *Actively participate in forums:* Etsy forums (www.etsy.com/forums) is a great place to start. (See Chapter 13 for a list of more forums.) Be an active member of the community by answering questions and interacting with others to establish your expertise.

(4) *Make videos:* Create a short video of you working or explaining a particular part of your process. It doesn't have to be fancy, you can just attach a camera to a tripod and hit the record button. Post the video on YouTube (www.youtube.com) with your keywords in the description and a link to your website and/or Etsy store. See Chapter 13

for detailed information about making videos including creating content and useful editing tools.

(5) *Teach a class:* Not only can this be profitable, but it's great exposure for your business. Somewhere in your area classes are already happening and you could be part of the fun. Inquire at craft stores, art supply stores, fabric stores, and anywhere else appropriate for your medium. Think about community centers or adult education centers too. If your project is portable you could teach at home parties or local schools.

(6) *Write a blog:* Do you have a website (or plan on having one)? Good, because blogging is a great way to demonstrate expertise. Blogs were discussed in Chapter 6, flip back there for more information.

(7) *HARO:* Help a Reporter Out (www.helpareporter.com) is a service that pairs journalists with sources. I've gotten eThreads loads of press thanks to HARO and you can too. Check out Chapter 16 for tips.

We've talked a lot about sharing tips and tricks with the world, and you might be uncomfortable with it. After all, you've worked years perfecting your craft and they're your "trade secrets" - why would you want to give them away?

I get it, I used to feel like that too. Here's the thing though - have you ever heard of Martha Stewart? She built an empire giving away DIY secrets. Giving away free knowledge establishes expertise. Experts are in demand and command higher prices. Trust me, you'll make more money like this than keeping every tip to yourself. Besides, there are people out there who could really use your advice.

Chapter 9: **SELL CONFIDENTLY.**

"I have always said that everyone is in sales. Maybe you don't hold the title of salesperson, but if the business you are in requires you to deal with people, you, my friend, are in sales." - **Zig Ziglar**

Do you gulp when you think about sales? Do you have trouble approaching customers or closing deals? This chapter is for you. I used to be very uncomfortable as a salesperson - it was my least favorite part of the job. Now I'm a sales machine and you can be one too.

Think of salesmanship as helping people. Your products are solving problems and they're high-quality to boot. Be proud of what you're selling; consider how much people enjoy it. Your products make lives better so there's nothing to be nervous about.

WHY PEOPLE BUY

Why do people buy things? *To satisfy needs, wants, and desires.* People purchase goods and services to improve a situation or solve a problem: they want to save money or time; they yearn to be more comfortable or beautiful; they want better relationships or healthier lifestyles. People don't just buy *products*, they buy *solutions*.

Furthermore, *people purchase based on emotion and then justify with logic.* It usually takes seconds to make a purchasing decision, and dopamine (the feel-good neurochemical) rises in the presence of shiny new objects. Emotions rule, the credit card is swiped, dopamine recedes and buyer's remorse sets in. Then customers use logic to justify their emotional purchase. ("It was a great sale, I couldn't pass it up!" "Sure it was expensive, but I got it before anyone else!")

What does this mean to you? It's your job to figure out *why* customers are buying your products - what emotional need do you satisfy? Your products could help people be healthier, better care for families, support core values, provide comfort, feel secure, look more attractive, save time, express individuality, or belong to a group. Ask customers why they buy your products and you'll get some really insightful answers.

Learn what motivates your customers. Not only is it great salesmanship, but you'll identify how to satisfy their needs. You'll probably get new product ideas too.

HOW TO BE A GOOD SALESPERSON

Are you nervous thinking about sales? I meet many creative people who are anxious about selling for several reasons: they're uncomfortable discussing money and pricing their own products; others don't like striking up conversations with strangers; many people fear rejection too.

I felt this way when I started. I was really nervous at my first craft show; I sat at my booth and barely spoke to anyone. I worried about my prices too - even though they were totally reasonable, I felt guilty about charging people money. I was anxious. I didn't make a single sale. It was not a great experience.

That was in 2006. Now I'm really comfortable with sales … in fact, I actually enjoy it. I like talking with customers, discovering their needs, then finding products that make their lives better. Being a good salesperson can be easy and natural; read these tips to get started:

Nice appearance

Your clothes and demeanor make a difference in sales. Wear clean, tailored clothes. Shave and trim your hair. Clip your fingernails; people will notice. Always be smiling - not only to appear friendlier to others, but to brighten your mood as well.

Be an authority

No matter where you're selling - in store, online, or in person - portray your expertise. Share information. Answer questions. Explain your process. Why? Because people respect knowledge and authority; it gives them confidence. People want to know they're making the best decision in parting with their hard-earned money. Buying from an expert tells them they're making a great choice. This is an important topic; flip back to Chapter 8 to read more about it.

Practice your elevator speech

An "elevator speech" is the summary of your business delivered in the time span of an elevator ride. That is, if you suddenly found yourself in the elevator with a very important person, you'd have about 30 seconds to deliver the pitch for your business. Great salespeople have an elevator speech ready for any situation; it's a convincing sales tool.

The elevator speech should explain how your business *helps people and solves problems.* It should be tailored for each audience to highlight what's important to them. It must be clear, concrete, and concise - avoid technical jargon or complicated language.

Remember back in Chapter 5 we talked about USP - Unique Selling Proposition? It's what sets you apart from the competition; something you do that is different from everyone else. That's what your elevator speech should be about. For example, here's my pitch for eThreads: "We make custom bags. People go on our site, design their own bag, and we make it from scratch in our Boston, MA studio. Everything is lined in waterproof nylon and machine washable. I call it 'Emily-proof' because I'm a klutz."

Help people understand your business' unique value and make it sound intriguing enough that they ask for more details. Remember to keep it short - overselling information makes you look like an overzealous car salesman.

Determine the most important selling points for your product and practice saying them in front of family and friends. Ask for feedback and streamline the sales pitch. Feel confident about this so customers can feel confident in you.

SEVEN SALES TIPS TO GET YOU STARTED

Alright, this the fun stuff. What you see below is a list of insider sales tips that are so easy to do you'll wonder why you were nervous about selling in the first place. Revisit Chapter 4 and read Chapter 10 for even more selling tips.

(1) Scarcity

The *Scarcity Principle* is a psychological theory that says we value something more if we fear it will be taken away. The idea of potentially losing something suddenly makes it that much more attractive. Likewise, if something is difficult to possess, we value it more and want it more. What does it mean for you, dear indie artist?

(1) *Create a sense of urgency:* Make certain products available for a limited time or in limited quantities. For example, I only buy fabrics in limited quantities so they're selling out all the time. This gives customers incentive to order a bag quickly in case the fabric sells out. Can you do something similar with your business?

(2) *Consider special pricing:* Try bundling products together at a special discount (for a limited time of course). Occasionally offer 20% off for the entire weekend. Try one-day or exclusive sales too. For example, sometimes I offer a crazy 50% off coupon only to our Facebook and Twitter customers for one day only. Since we rarely offer discounts, this event is special and exclusive.

(2) Justify with logic

Because your products are indie-made they're going to be more expensive than anything in retail stores. That's ok, they should cost more than a cheap piece of junk from China. It's your job though to convince customers *why* your product is worth the price tag.

You'll never compete on price, so compete with logic. We've talked about being an expert and providing information - *that's* what your customers need to hear to justify their purchase. Tell them how your product makes lives easier or more pleasant. Talk about your quality materials and attention to detail. Explain your warranty and guarantees. Educating customers on the intrinsic value of your product helps them justify the cost in their minds, thus closing the sale.

(3) Give something away

Include a gift with purchase, even if it's something small like a branded notepad. Perhaps a tiny product sample? Or something that's cheap and easy to create just for this purpose, like a button or pin? This small gesture of goodwill means a lot to your customers. They'll appreciate the thought, trust me. There's a tad bit of guilt involved too. Ever wonder why nonprofit organizations send address labels with your name printed on them? Because of reciprocation; they're hoping you'll feel a little guilty and compelled to donate in return.

(4) Include testimonials

Customer testimonials are a very effective sales tool. Why? Because of *Social Proof,* which says that we determine what is correct by observing other people. If potential customers see you have a slew of satisfied customers, Social Proof tells them you're a safe bet.

Follow up with customers post-purchase to see how they like your products. (Send a survey for best results. See Chapter 17 for more information.) If you get a good quote, ask permission to use it as a testimonial. I've even had customers write "official" testimonials when they know it's going to be published. Happy customers are your best sales team, encourage them to spread the word too.

> •PRO TIP• Include the first name, last name initial, location, and picture of product in your testimonial (i.e., Emily W., Boston, MA; picture of bag). Why? Because detailed information makes a testimonial more credible.

(5) Tell stories

Customers love to hear the stories behind your business, your products, and how you've helped other people. Stories are powerful for two reasons: (1) they're memorable, and (2) they're emotional. Stories help people connect with your brand.

I tell stories about eThreads rePurpose, in which we take customers' old treasured clothing and recycle them into new bags. I have two favorite rePurpose stories. First, a woman's boyfriend was overseas in the Marines and she sent us one of his old jackets to be recycled into a large tote because she wanted to carry it with her every day. (*Sniff*) In another story, one of our regular customers sent us her daughter's 25-year-old pajama shirt to be recycled into a crossbody bag. The daughter had no idea her mom kept the pajama shirt, never mind turned it into a new bag!

Think of your own stories to share. For example, why did you start the business? Maybe you were unsatisfied with your job or wanted to create more things. Here's another story idea - how does your product help people? Share customer testimonials or stories about your evolving design process.

(6) Talk benefits, not features

Have you ever heard the phrase, "Sell the sizzle, not the steak?" That's a fancy way of saying, "Sell the benefits, not the features." Too many businesses make the mistake of talking about the great features of their products, but never mentioning *why* a customer should care. Remember, your customers want solutions, so give it to them:

Feature	Benefit
Made with titanium	Super tough yet lightweight
100% Merino wool	Antimicrobial and breathable
Printed on canvas	Sturdy with vivid color reproduction

(7) Take care of your customers

You want repeat customers. Yes, it's great to attract new ones, but it's actually cheaper and easier to sell to returning customers. Remember back in Chapter 7 we discussed the top 10 ways to provide stellar customer service? Follow those rules and you'll have a devoted group of repeat customers in no time.

Alright, we've pretty well covered the art of sales here. It's not so bad, is it? With a little time and practice you'll be an expert at this stuff. For those interested in learning more about sales and persuasion, check out Appendix B in the back of the book for a list of suggested reading. In the meantime, I think you're ready to sell at craft shows, fairs, and expos. Flip to the next chapter to learn all the information you need to conquer craft shows and other retail events.

Chapter 10:
CONQUER CRAFT & TRADE SHOWS.

"Pretend that every single person you meet has a sign around his or her neck that says, 'Make me feel important.' Not only will you succeed in sales, you will succeed in life." - **Mary Kay Ash**

This chapter covers craft shows, art fairs, expos, trade shows, and any other event where you're selling directly to the public. Artists, crafters, and makers alike all benefit from this chapter, just insert "art fair" or "expo" instead of "craft show."

WHY SHOWS ARE GREAT FOR BUSINESS

Craft shows range from big regional events in expo halls to small local events in high school gymnasiums. I started selling at craft shows in 2006 and stopped in 2012 when I got too busy to do them. At my peak I was selling at 30 shows a year. I have a love/hate relationship with craft and trade shows because they can be beneficial for business but - hello - they are a lot of work. You have to research the shows, apply, prepare your product and display, then the day of show is exhausting. You're up early, home late, and on your feet all day talking to a lot of people.

Why participate in craft and trade shows? They are just simply really good for business. Not only are you getting cash in hand (oh how we love that), you're also getting insane market research, valuable connections, and customers for life.

Market research: Big companies pay big money for the kind of market research you get at a craft show. Watch customers react to your products and get valuable information. What are they grabbing? What do they avoid? I've gotten incredible insight by standing away from the booth and eavesdropping while people look through my products.

If you get chatty with a customer, ask them questions. See how they like your product's shape, size, color, texture, price ... not only will they love sharing their opinion but they might give you some great product ideas.

Step out of the booth and walk around the show for more market research. Look at other items - is there anything similar to yours? See any trends you could be a part of? Look for displays that inspire you. Notice which booths have the largest crowd.

Customers for life: Some of the most devoted customers come from craft shows. Why? Because people go to craft shows to find unique items and meet artists. They love to touch products and hear the stories behind them. Craft shows are about personal connections and supporting indie artists, and those are the types of customers you want to have. The customers you meet at craft shows will become customers for life.

Sales channel: Ideally you're selling products through multiple sales channels like *online* (through your website or Etsy) and *in stores* (through wholesale or consignment agreements). Craft and trade shows are a great addition to this equation.

Network: Craft shows are mini-cities for the day, filled with the friendliest and most helpful people. Neighbors become fast friends watching each other's booths and competitors become co-conspirators sharing tips. I've worked two different shows where my neighbors also sold bags. (That's not supposed to happen, but sometimes it does.) Instead of warily giving each other the side eye all day, we chatted and shared tips on sewing machines, fabrics, display options - I even ended up partnering with some of them for the rest of the holiday season and sold three times more than I could have alone.

Walk around and talk with other vendors to learn about cheap suppliers, special artist opportunities, tips on accountants, other great shows in the area ... craft show people are really friendly and willing to help.

HOW TO CHOOSE, APPLY, AND PREPARE FOR SHOWS

How to find the right show

SEARCH: First, start an internet search for "indie craft shows" or "craft fairs." You'll likely find a website that lists dozens of shows in your area - many sites catalogue this type of information for free. Craftmaster News (www.craftmasternews.com) lists thousands of events by state. Buy an annual subscription (starting at $48.95/year) to get access to detailed information like organizer's contact information and estimated attendance. Try Sunshine Artists too. It's a popular magazine dedicated to art and craft shows and you can access their database via their website (www.sunshineartist.com/shows). Also check out Chapter 17 for more craft show suggestions.

Note: Your internet search may turn up random listings for church bazaars and craft shows on college campuses, especially around the holidays. Those are often good opportunities, especially if you're new to craft shows, because they're affordable and accessible.

RESEARCH: Once you've found some possible craft shows, get into the nitty gritty research. Examine the show's website - does the event look well-organized? Are there a lot of vendors? Has the event been around long? Is it getting bigger each year? Any news items about the event? Find the list of vendors and visit their websites to see what type of stuff is sold at the show. Are your products complementary? Are the price points similar?

> •**PRO TIP**• Contact other vendors and ask about their experience with the show. They can tell you if it's a good show, if the event organizers know what they're doing, if vendors have accessible parking, etc. You'll find most craft fair people are very willing to "talk shop" with other vendors, it's a great community like that.

ATTEND: If possible, go to the craft or trade show before you apply. Most shows are annual events, so you can research the big ones before laying down the big bucks. Walk the aisles and notice the types of products sold - do they complement your work? Are the prices similar? Are the customers similar? Look at the attendance - are there a lot of people walking around? Are they carrying shopping bags or just browsing? Talk to the artists - tell them you're thinking of applying next year and they'll be happy to talk about their experience. Don't be discouraged by one bad review - everyone has an off day. Talk to people in different mediums to get a well-rounded vision of the event.

EVALUATE: Once you've done the research, evaluate which shows are good for you:

Time of year: Are your products seasonally appropriate? For example, if you sell sundresses avoid shows in cold climates. Christmas ornaments probably don't sell too well in the summer either.

Type of products: Are your products appropriate for the show? For example, don't bring handmade doll clothes to a fine art fair.

Other vendors: Is there too much competition in your category already? Jewelers have an especially difficult time with this and many craft show organizers limit the number of jewelers allowed.

Vendor guidelines: Is it relatively convenient to get to? Is vendor parking available? Is there electricity or internet available? Are there volunteers to watch the booth or help unload the car?

Cost: Is it affordable? Most small shows at schools and organizations rarely cost more than $50. Larger events are usually $100-$200. Big, professional, expo-type events that last multiple days can start at $700 for 3 days and go for thousands of dollars more.

NOTE: *To share or not to share?* Sharing a booth is great for indie artists, especially when starting out. Not only are you splitting booth fees, but it helps fill up a booth when you don't have a lot of stuff to sell. Also, splitting the booth means you can help each other unload the car, set up, and watch over things when someone needs to take a break. Finally, sharing a booth brings in new customers because each of you should be advertising to a different group of people. If you do share a booth, ensure the items are complementary and displays cohesive. Also indicate you're sharing a booth on the show's application - not only to ensure you're both listed on the event's website, but some of the larger expo shows don't allow booth sharing or they charge an extra fee.

How to write a good application

#1 tip: *Follow the rules.* I mean follow them *exactly.* If they want three pictures sent in JPEG format, do exactly that. Don't send 10 pictures, don't send pdf files, and don't send a link to a website. Craft show organizers are usually volunteers working their hardest to put together a fantastic show. They're taking care of planning, permits, insurance, advertising ... and all they need from you is to follow a few simple rules. Make their lives easier and do exactly as they say.

> •PRO TIP• Thank organizers and volunteers for their hard work - they don't hear it nearly enough.

Show applications usually ask for your name, business name, contact information, a short description of your work, price range, and pictures. It's great to have a website too (not Facebook, not Etsy, a *website*) because the organizers see you're serious about your business and thus you're a serious vendor.

The pictures are everything in a show application; they should be well lit, in focus, and convey the products well. See Chapter 6 for more information about taking great pictures.

Art show applications: Pictures for juried art shows are especially important. During the jury process, most applicant's images are projected onto a wall for a few seconds each; consider how your images look flipped through quickly. Be consistent with picture orientation (horizontal vs. vertical), image color, and overall composition for the most pleasing "flipbook" effect.

How to deal with rejection

What?! They didn't accept you? Even though your products are perfect for the show and you submitted a winning application they *still* didn't accept you? Well, that stings. It's hard not to take rejection personally because this is your personal art - and someone flat out denied it. Here's a few reasons to get up, brush it off, and move on with your day:

(1) *There were more applicants than spots available.* This happens all the time because big shows often receive 3-5 times more applicants than they can accept. This happens a lot with jewelers too - organizers limit the amount of vendors in each category and jewelry is always the first to fill up.

(2) *Your products were not a good fit for the show.* Perhaps your items are too high- or low-end for the type of show. It's a good thing you got rejected because otherwise you would have wasted time and money trying to sell to the wrong audience.

(3) *Your application could have been stronger.* Did you follow directions? Could your pictures be better or more varied? Do you have an active website? Think of ways to look more serious and professional to the organizers.

(4) *No matter what, don't take it personally and apply again next year.* Circumstances change all the time, and the reason you weren't accepted this year might be irrelevant next year. Organizers are happy to see your name again - it proves you're serious about their show. If at first you don't succeed - apply, apply again.

You got accepted! Awesome! ... Now what?

Oh, the thrill of being accepted to a good show! The joy of knowing someone liked your work! The anticipation of meeting new customers and counting cash in hand! Before getting all wrapped up in daydreams, there's a lot of serious work to do first. Bring out your pencil, paper, and get ready for some planning:

Inventory: How much inventory should you bring? There's no right answer and unfortunately you won't know until you've worked a few shows. Bring a variety of work - different colors, sizes, flavors, and textures. Do you already know what items are most popular? Great, have extras of those. Bring inventory in a wide price range starting at $5 impulse buys. Lots of people attend craft shows and just want a "little something" to remember the day. Set out small items to entice them in your booth, where you can hopefully upsell bigger ticket items.

Signage: We'll discuss the details of signage later in this chapter, but I wanted to mention it first in the planning stage. You'll need price tags on everything, a sign showing which credit cards you accept, business cards, and a banner with your business name and description of what you do.

Price Tags: Yup, every item must be clearly marked with prices. No exceptions. If a customer likes your product, the first thing they'll look for is the price. If the price isn't there, they might be too shy to ask or you might be too busy to answer and BAM - you've lost the sale. Don't just use a price list either - your customer might not see it or know which products link to which prices. Do yourself a favor and buy a $3.99 package of price tags from Staples, write in fine point pen, and put the tags on each product. Trust me.

Packaging: How will you wrap purchases? At the very least you'll probably need some bags. If you sell delicate items, you'll likely need bubble wrap. If you sell small items or jewelry you might need boxes too.

Many people shop for gifts - have tissue paper and ribbon available. I knew a jeweler who packaged each item on a card in a small plastic bag wrapped in festive tissue paper with curling ribbon. Her prices were perfect for gifts and her customers loved that they didn't have to wrap anything. She had people flocking to her table every show, most of them regular customers.

In the beginning, get all your packaging needs at the dollar store - you'll find bags, tissue paper, ribbons, boxes ... everything for cheap. Don't invest in quality stuff until you know you're serious about shows, then buy in bulk from wholesalers. See Chapter 3 for more information about packaging.

Payment: You must accept credit cards. No exceptions. People rarely carry cash and accepting credit cards often means the difference between making a sale and losing it. (Sometimes people even buy more with a credit card.) Nowadays it's absurdly easy to get a credit card reader that attaches to smartphones - I love Square Up (the ubiquitous white square you'll even find at farmers' markets, www.squareup.com), but there's tons of competitors from PayPal, banks, and companies like ProPay (www.propay.com). You can accept personal checks, but know there is some risk the check will bounce. Get the customer's driver license number and telephone number and write it on the check in case there are problems.

Bank: Bring a stack of small bills to make change for cash payments. For most shows, a $100 starting bank is fine - I prefer $40 in singles, $40 in fives and $20 in tens. Don't bother with twenties because everyone pays in twenties and you'll get them easily. I don't accept $100 bills unless I have a pen that identifies counterfeits. (Plus, it really messes with your bank when someone hands you a $100 bill.)

> •PRO TIP• Include the state sales tax in the price of your items to avoid fumbling with coins to make change.

Keep the bank on you at all times: Although craft shows are a generally wholesome place, there are occasional tricksters who try to steal products and cash. Plan where you'll store cash *on your person.* I wear a small eThreads crossbody bag and store the bank, calculator, invoice book, breath mints, and hand sanitizer in it. You'll see a lot of crafters wearing aprons for the same purpose. Never leave your bank in a cash box, even if you think it's tucked safely away. I've heard horror stories about well-hidden cash boxes getting snatched in broad daylight. Plan now to avoid heartache later.

Determine the sales tax requirements for the state: Every state has different tax laws with minimum filing requirements. Determine the sales tax requirements for the state in which you're selling and clear all paperwork ahead of the show, see Chapter 2 for more information.

Marketing: Even though show organizers are advertising the show, build excitement by spreading the word yourself. Did the organizers print postcards or posters? Get some and pass them around town. Do you have a website, Twitter, Facebook page, or mailing list? Blast out messages alerting fans about the show and attach a coupon they can bring to the event. Contact local newspaper editors or bloggers too - they might stop by to cover your booth!

Bring a buddy: If you're not sharing a booth, bring a buddy to the show. You need someone to help unload the car, set up, and watch the booth when you're taking a break. Plus, when you're busy talking with one customer, your friend can help other customers and watch for potential thieves. Bonus - having a buddy nearby is a stress reliever during a long day. You're on your feet talking with strangers for hours, and having a friendly face by your side makes the day much easier.

Bring food and water: You're in for a long day and need refreshments to keep energy up. Don't rely on finding food at the show. There might not be anything available and you might not get a break. I carry snacks in a zippered lunch bag with ice packs that I lovingly refer to as my "feed bag."

Pack a "just in case" bag: Stuff it with extra pens, paper, price tags, tape, markers, stapler, calculator, scissors, and whatever is needed to repair your craft. Consider adding clips, rope, and anything to weigh things down or create a temporary display. Pack personal items too like hand wipes, tissues, lip balm, breath mints, sunscreen, water, camera, and cleaning wipes to clean mirrors or tables. Throw a small plastic bag in there too for trash.

Packing: If you can, pack the car as follows: inventory first, then display items, then tables and chairs. That way, when you're unpacking at the show you can take out items in the order needed. Practice packing the car in advance to ensure everything fits.

HOW TO DISPLAY PRODUCTS TO ATTRACT VISITORS AND DETER THEFT

Your booth is home for the day; it must be functional for you and inviting to visitors. Most importantly, it has to grab attention - shows are filled with people passing by with wandering eyes, and you only have two seconds to get their interest. Make it count.

Do some research

Next time you're shopping, notice what grabs your interest. Take notes on good displays and how to imitate them. Do an online search for "craft show display ideas" or "best craft show display" and find loads of links, a lot of them on Pinterest.

Tents & tables

Tents: Most outdoor shows require a 10'x10' tent. Get a white one because some of the bigger shows require white tents. The tent must come with removable walls for inclement weather. (Some vendors like to have the walls up anyway to make their work "pop.") Get tent weights, around 25 lbs on each leg. Some people use big bags of cat litter, I have velcro canvas bags loaded with $2 bags of gravel from Home Depot.

Tables: You'll likely want a mix of 6' and 8' tables. Some indoor shows allow a 10'x10' space (no tent) and others simply a 6' table and two chairs. I personally use 2x8' and 1x6' tables in my booth, U-shaped around the back with room for me in the corner.

If you have the room in your car - get a pushcart. It's a lot of work hauling your stuff around and those tables get heavy. A simple $40 investment on a decent collapsible pushcart makes a big difference, especially at the end of long day when your car seems so very far away.

•**PRO TIP**• Buy cheap plastic bed risers to lift your tables waist-height instead of hip-height. It's more comfortable for customers and easier for them to see your fine products. This is especially important for jewelers and anyone else selling small goods.

NOTE: Bring a chair. You shouldn't be sitting too much during the day but it's nice to take a break. Get a folding chair because it lies flat in the car and has a rigid bottom - you want to be able to jump up in a flash to make a sale.

6 rules for product display

Display Rule #1: *Vertical is your friend.* Never display items flat on the table because people will walk right past it. Not only that, it just makes products look dull. It's ok to have a few items lying flat, but everything else needs to be nestled in baskets, hanging from display walls, and otherwise shown in varying heights. I've gotten great display items at Goodwill, Marshalls, HomeGoods, and Store Supply Warehouse (www.storesupply.com).

•**PRO TIP**• Hide small storage boxes underneath tablecloths for temporary platforms.

Display Rule #2: *Always have prices clearly displayed.* As we previously discussed, you'll lose sales if you don't have prices marked on each product - everything should have an individual price tag. The exception is small, cheap items which can go in a basket with a sign clearly attached. For example, I always have an "Everything $10 Basket" at shows - then it's ok not having price tags on each item, as long as the sign is clearly visible. Full-priced items should always have price tags however, no exceptions.

Display Rule #3: *Don't crowd the display.* This is a tough rule for some indie artists to follow because we want to put *everything* out because it's all so pretty, right? Wrong. Overcrowding the display limits sales - not only is it harder for customers to view at a glance, but it looks like you're overstocked and thus the product is undesirable.

In fact, limit the display items and even purposefully include a few blank spots. Less items make it easier for customers to see the products and blank spots look like a lot of stuff has already sold - making everything else look more desirable.

Display Rule #4: *Show select products.* Only display the best sellers and one color of each product. For example, if you sell multiple t-shirts in the same color, display just one size in that color. Store the rest under the table and add a sign "More sizes available." If you have a particularly beautiful or expensive piece, display it on its own, away from the "regular" products. Include a variety of products in the display, from cheap impulse buys to expensive lust-worthy items.

Display Rule #5: *Use light whenever possible.* This is especially important for jewelers, glass blowers, and anyone else dealing with tiny, sparkly items. Small clip-on lamps add warmth, character, and a level of professionalism to your display that draws people like moths. Likewise, if you can display your website on a computer or tablet, do so. Not only does it look impressive, but it increases the chances customers go back and visit the site on their own.

Display Rule #6: *Be weatherproof.* As we've already covered, your tent should have walls for rainy days. But what about the wind - are your display items heavy enough to sustain a strong wind? I once had cheap necklace stands that blew across the street on windy days. Not a good look. Invest a few extra dollars in weighted stands to make your display weatherproof.

Signage

Great signs make great salesmen. Display lots of tags, labels, signs, and banners in your booth:

Product information: Create small signs naming your product and describing any features or benefits a customer should know. For example, if you sell wooden bowls, create signs that say "Handmade wooden bowls. Perfect for cereal or salads. Hand wash only." If you sell candles, make signs like "100% soy wax candles. Clean burning and long-lasting scent. Burn time 10-12 hours." For eThreads I have signs like "Custom-made bags. Lined in waterproof nylon. Machine washable." Use details that convince customers of the product quality because you might be too busy to tell them yourself.

> •**PRO TIP**• Put your signs in picture frames from the dollar store for a professional (but affordable) display. If you make signs on a computer, use the same font on every sign to maintain consistency.

Credit card: Your credit card processing company probably provided some credit card signs to display. If not, make a sign listing the credit cards accepted and place prominently in your booth.

Banner: Attract attention from across a crowded hall. Get a large banner listing company name, location, description of products, and pictures of the products. A 4'W x 2'H banner is big enough to be seen from far away yet still fits on the front of a table if you're doing an indoor show and can't hang it up.

You can make your own banner in the beginning, but a decent professionally printed one starts at $20. If you're going to do a few shows, invest in the real deal. Hang the banner high in the back of the booth so potential customers can see it from a distance. If you have a tent, consider a small banner to hang in the front of your booth too - it's a small detail that helps you stand out from the crowd.

> •**PRO TIP**• *Hang large pictures of you making your products too.* This is beneficial in two ways. First, people gravitate towards pictures of artists making their crafts; it helps draw a crowd. Second, people can visualize the labor going into each product and thus justify paying a higher price for your products.

Price tags: Oh my, I'm mentioning price tags again?! Yes I am because they're that important. Price tags are part of your signage, have them everywhere.

Email sign up: Have a clipboard, paper, and some pens available for people to leave their email addresses. Tell them it's for occasional announcements and special deals and you'll never share their info. Print a sheet ahead of time with your logo then lots of blank lines for email addresses. We'll talk about what to do with those email addresses in Chapter 13.

Business cards/postcards: Always have business cards and postcards available on the table. Lots of people will like your stuff, not purchase anything, and ask for a card before walking away. Don't let anyone leave without a business card - see Chapter 13 for more information about creating business cards and postcards.

Decoration

Remember, your booth is home for the day, so create an inviting atmosphere for customers. Small, thoughtful details make a booth welcoming. Visit thrift stores and antique shops for vintage items that add personality like old suitcases or decorative pieces. Look through craft or discount stores for inventive display ideas. Think about baskets, easels, chalkboards, frames ... even peg boards from your hardware store could be great.

Are you selling anything that can be worn? Have several clean mirrors available for customers. If you sell clothing, add a dressing room in the back of your booth with a full-length mirror - it will significantly increase sales. Purchase a portable dressing room ($25-$50) or build your own with fabric or shower curtains (do an internet search for "DIY portable dressing room" for tips).

> **•PRO TIP•** Use colorful tablecloths to attract attention to your booth. Don't use patterned cloths, they're too distracting against products. Use bright, bold, solid colors. I use red; it's the color of our logo and it's distinctive. Be sure the tablecloths hit the floor - you'll be hiding all sorts of stuff under the tables and it looks messy if not well hidden.

Preventing theft

I've only experienced theft once in my 6 years and 100+ craft shows. It was a busy show in downtown Boston, and I was talking with a customer while someone quickly walked by, grabbed the first thing they saw, and kept walking. I didn't notice it happening but another customer in my booth did and I was able to track down the thief and get my stuff back. Other vendors have not been so lucky. Follow these tips to prevent theft in your own booth:

(1) *Say hello and make eye contact with everyone who walks into your booth.* You should do this anyway because it's friendly and good salesmanship, but it also deters potential thieves when they know you've identified them in your space.

(2) *Don't hide behind your display, stay up front and active in the booth.* Keep busy; neaten up the display and interact with customers. Similar to #1 above, not only is it good for sales, but it's also a good theft deterrent.

(3) *Don't make displays so tall you can't see through them.* Avoid creating blind spots, you want to see the entire booth at all times.

(4) *Tie down small items if possible.* Place small hooks around the chains of your necklaces or stash pricey items behind a glass case. Likewise, keep your most expensive items in the back of the booth, far away from passersby with wandering hands.

(5) *Have a friend watch the booth.* Two people are better than one at deterring theft. Plus, you have someone there when you need to take a bathroom break. If you don't have a buddy and need to take a break, ask the event organizers if they can loan a volunteer or in a pinch, ask your neighbors to keep an eye on things for a minute.

(6) *Always wear your cash.* As I mentioned above, not even well-hidden cash boxes are safe because you never know who is watching you use it. Carry your bank at all times, whether in a bag, in an apron, or just your pockets. Never put it down.

Rehearsal

OK, you've got the tent, tables, tablecloths, display items, and signage. Now it's time for a rehearsal. Practice setting up the booth ahead of time because trust me, you do not want to figure this out at your first craft show an hour before it starts. If you're using a tent, set it up with the tables, tablecloths, display, and all your products. If you're just using tables, try this in your living room.

Decide where everything goes ahead of time and get feedback from family and friends. What do they think of the display? It's probably too busy and your friends can help edit it down. Encourage honest feedback because it will increase sales at a show. As you participate in more shows, experiment with the display to see which format brings in the most sales.

Working on your craft

If you can, bring some works-in-progress to the show. People love to see the process and it gives you something to do during downtime. Obviously I can't bring my sewing machine to shows, but I sell hand-sewn hair pins that I purposely work on at craft shows.

If you absolutely can't bring work along, try to bring a sketch pad or some raw materials to help illustrate your process. For example, glassblowers obviously can't bring their torches to shows, but they can bring a few spare glass rod samples to explain how the project starts.

HOW TO SELL LIKE A ROCKSTAR - EVEN IF YOU'RE SHY

Sales used to be my least favorite part of the job. I hated being a salesperson; I didn't like approaching strangers or coming off as "pushy." Does this sound familiar to you?

Have no fear, I'm here. I've shifted from dreading sales to loving it and I'll help you get there too. First, I'm going to explain why you should feel confident about selling. Then, we're going to talk basic sales strategy. Finally, I'll share some super pro tips for increasing booth traffic and sales.

You're not pushy, you're honest

I think a lot of indie artists feel guilty about charging customers or fear they're asking for too much money. Remember the Picasso Principle from Chapter 4: charge for your expertise, not the actual 30 minutes it takes to make the product. Also, when you're selling a product that is high quality and people genuinely enjoy, then frankly you're doing them a favor by selling it to them. You've worked hard to get to this point - enjoy it!

Basic sales strategy

Appearance: Craft shows are casual environments, but don't wear sweatpants. Dress casually enough so you're comfortable moving tables but nice enough to represent yourself professionally. If you're working outside, bring layers - it's often cold in the morning and hot in the afternoon. Finally, keep fingernails trimmed and clean - lots of people will be looking at your hands when you present them products. I once had a guy show me his paintings with long, chipped, yellow fingernails - gross - I couldn't concentrate on his art!

Wearable art: Wear your products if possible. Not only to show pride in your work, but products always look better on a person than sitting on a table. Plus, when you're walking around the show people will see what you're wearing, compliment it, and you can say, "Thanks, I made it! I'm selling these in my booth right down there."

Smile: Smile to show organizers, volunteers, neighbors, and customers. It's exhausting to be upbeat the whole day, but customers pick up on vibes at booths and if you're sitting in the corner scowling (or even innocently reading a book) you're chasing away sales. Have an upbeat attitude no matter how tired, cold, or hungry you are. Always wear a winning smile and your attitude and sales will improve.

Take notes: Keep a small notepad and pen handy to write down what's selling. Not only does it help track sales, but you can reference it later when studying the most popular items of the day.

Be a good neighbor: Since craft fairs are mini cities for the day, good relationships with neighbors are important. The morning is always a little tense - everyone has to unload, set up, they're nervous about making money *and* they're nervous you're selling products similar to theirs. There's definitely a little tension in the air.

After you and the neighbors are finished setting up, break the ice first. Walk over, introduce yourself, and compliment their stuff. This little gesture makes your day so much easier. Your neighbors are now a support system - they'll watch your booth when you have to take a break, they'll loan extra supplies if you forgot anything, and they'll help pass the time when no one has customers. Plus, you might make some great connections for business advice and craft show tips.

Here's some other tips on being a good neighbor:

(1) *Arrive early:* Not only is it less stressful for you but you'll have time to introduce yourself and help others.

(2) *Share supplies:* Since you're prepared and packed extra tape, scissors, rope, etc... offer it to another vendor in need (label it with your name before giving it away). Not only is it neighborly but I guarantee you'll forget something one day and you'll be so grateful when someone else helps you.

(3) *Respect their booth:* If you're talking with a neighbor and a potential customer walks in their booth, stop talking so they can make a sale.

(4) *Don't brag:* Craft show people are very friendly - until you talk sales numbers. No one wants to give up their number for the day, so don't ask. Likewise, if you made a ton of money - believe me, your

neighbors noticed - there's no need to advertise it. Just smile and say, "I had a good day."

(5) *Don't pack up early:* Sometimes you just want to pack up and head home early, especially if you're having a bad day. This is absolutely forbidden. Not only do show organizers hate it, but it's disrespectful to the neighbors. Nothing turns away potential customers more than seeing you pack up your stuff - they'll think there's nothing to see in your neighbor's booth either and keep moving. It's ok to start discreetly packing a few items 20 minutes before the end of the day, but never close shop until the event officially ends.

Sales 101

You're unpacked, set up, and the booth looks gorgeous. Now it's time to greet customers! People show up 15 minutes before the show actually starts, so bring your A-Game for the rest of the day. Here's my top seven sales tips to get started:

(1) *Start a conversation not about your products:* When someone walks in your booth, make eye contact and say hello. Pause for a few seconds. Then start a conversation about anything other than your products: "Is this your first time at the fair?" "Are you local?" "Seen anything good today?" "Love your necklace, did someone make it?" "Great weather, isn't it?" Don't pitch anyone the moment they walk in the booth. Remember, they just walked into your temporary home - let them get settled before you turn on the sales machine. Say "hi" then let them admire your booth unsolicited.

(2) *Provide the elevator speech:* After someone has been in the booth awhile and started poking at items, start your elevator speech. We talked about the elevator speech in Chapter 9; ultimately it's about communicating your business' unique value in a clear and concise statement.

For example, eThreads' elevator speech goes something like this: "We make custom bags. People go on our site, choose the type of bag and fabric, and we sew it in our Boston, MA studio. Everything is super durable, lined in waterproof nylon, and machine washable. I call them 'Emily-proof' because I'm a klutz."

(3) *Don't oversell:* Keep the pitch short - just a few sentences. It's easy to overwhelm with too much information. People need time

to process what you've said, and if you continue to talk they might not get it or just lose interest.

(4) *Observe:* See what people are picking up; observe what they're wearing and doing. Not only is it great market research on your target customers, but it helps focus your sales pitch for each individual.

For example, when moms with strollers enter my booth I point out that small "mommy pouches" fit in diaper bags and I emphasize they're waterproof and machine washable. If a young, fashionable girl enters my booth, I point her towards our clutches and wristlets, find one that matches her outfit, and explain how it's perfect for a night out. If a man walks in looking for a gift, I steer him towards the most popular fabrics and bestsellers, assuring him of their popularity.

(5) *Encourage people to touch the products:* You want potential customers imagining already owning your product, so encourage them to touch and interact with it. Since I sell bags, I invite customers to open the bags and feel the sturdy zippers and waterproof lining. I encourage them to put their own stuff in the bag to "see how everything fits." Sure enough, once people get their personal stuff in a bag, they imagine already owning it and usually purchase it right away.

Find ways for customers to interact with your products and give them a sense of ownership. Can they try things on? Can you give away samples? If you're a visual artist, have pictures of your work placed in homes to help people envision your work in their *own* home.

(6) *Tell stories:* People identify with stories and hold onto them. Especially craft show customers, who love making personal connections with artists. Explain how your product has benefitted other people or even yourself.

If you don't have any stories about the product, tell stories about your process or how you got started. Stories add value and connect customers to your brand in a memorable way. Plus, people love a good story they can repeat to friends whenever they're using the product. Include a story about all the labor that goes into your products, it helps justify the price.

(7) *Give out business cards:* You've pitched, told stories, had them touch the product ... and they still didn't buy anything. Worst yet, you spent 30 minutes with them and they seemed to really like your products! What gives? There are lots of reasons people don't buy things - budget, time, don't want to carry it around all day - so don't

get in a tizzy trying to figure it out. Instead, make the most of every encounter by giving out business cards and getting email addresses.

NOTE: Every interaction with a customer is a success if they have your business card. Allow me tell you two stories about why business cards are so important:

Story #1: In 2008 I worked a five-day music festival. On the second day a lovely couple discovered my booth and stopped by every day after for at least a half hour to say hi and look around. They never bought anything and I was a little frustrated, but at least they had my card. One year later I heard from them with a special request and almost every year since they've come to eThreads with a big order.

Story #2: Years ago my sister visited a craft show and fell in love with one painter's work. Every piece was at least $300 and my sister couldn't afford it at the time. She talked with the artist a long time, learned about her technique, took a card, and kept it in a file. Years later, she saved up enough money to buy a few paintings and will get another one soon.

Remember, as long as you have people walking in your booth, expressing interest, and taking a card, it's a good day. Craft shows are as much about promotion as making sales, so push cards all the time.

> **•PRO TIP•** Try to get email addresses because then *you* have a way to contact *them*. Follow up after the show with a message like, "It was great meeting you last weekend at the Main Street Craft Fair. I appreciate you stopping in the booth, I had such fun talking with you. As promised, here's a link to my website and I look forward to seeing you at the next event!" Follow up any time after that with special deals or information they would like to know. See more about email marketing in Chapter 13.

Super Sales Strategies

We talked about sales strategies a lot in Chapter 9 but I added a few more here that are great for craft shows:

Research the other vendors before the show. Any good show has a website that lists participating vendors. Comb through the vendor list and visit their websites before the show. You'll likely have direct competitors so start there. What makes you different from them? How are their prices? Could you bring pieces to the show that have less competition? Could you hold a contest or special promotion to attract customers to your booth? (See below.)

Hold a contest. This is one of my most effective tricks in the book. A properly planned contest brings valuable sales and promotion.

Here's the deal - people have a tendency to go where the crowd goes. It's because of the psychological phenomenon called *Social Proof* which says that we assume something is good or bad based on other people's behavior, then we follow suit.

For example, people often notice the most crowded booth at a show and head there themselves. Why? Because of *Social Proof.* They're thinking, "Well, something great must be going on there if so many people are in the booth. I gotta check it out for myself." Then they head to the booth, which brings in more people who are thinking the same thing, and the cycle continues. Moral of the story? You want people in the booth at all times, even if they're not buying anything; you attract more customers that way.

So how do you get people in the booth? Hold a contest! I'll give you an example. People design bags on eThreads' website, but I usually can't bring my website to shows. Instead, I bring zipper, lining, and fabric samples and encourage people to design their own bag right on the spot. I host a "Win a free bag" contest and give away a Medium Pouch ($27) to one lucky winner - they just have to design a bag, leave their email, and I randomly choose a winner at the end of the day and ship their bag a few days later. This contest is effective in three ways:

(1) It introduces people to the concept of designing their own bag. They get excited about the process and remember our name.

(2) I get email addresses, which is really valuable for marketing. I follow up with everyone who didn't win and say, "I'm sorry you didn't win, you designed a great bag! Here's a link to it in case you want to see it again." People often visit the site and buy something after that.

(3) It takes a while to design your own bag - some people deliberate for 30 minutes over fabric options. During that time others are attracted to the booth to see what is going on. Though people entering the contest aren't purchasing anything, they're doing a great job of attracting paying customers.

Can you do something similar in your booth, like host a giveaway or special contest? Maybe do something that attracts attention, like a spinning prize wheel or quiz show contest? As you saw from my example, you don't have to give anything expensive away. People are just attracted to winning free things. Use contests to drum up sales, take attention away from competitors, and make your booth the most popular at the show.

Justify with logic. If someone walks in your booth and likes what they see, here's what they're thinking: "Ooh, I like this! I want to have it! What's the price? Oh, that's more than I was expecting. But it is handmade. Still, I can get it cheaper in a store. Yeah, but I'm supporting the artist here. But I'm on a tight budget ..." and back and forth it goes. They want to give you money, they're just having a hard time justifying it. People purchase based on emotion then justify with logic, so provide that logic for them. See Chapter 9 for more about this.

Give something small away. Set out a bowl of candies at the front of your booth for anyone to enjoy. If you're at a dog-friendly show, put out a bowl of water and some treats too. Why? Two reasons:

(1) It's a small gesture of goodwill that increases the overall friendliness and appeal of your booth. It's welcoming, neighborly, and grabs the attention of passersby.

(2) Ever wonder why nonprofit organizations send address labels with your name printed on them? Same reason I'm telling you to give away dog treats. When someone does something for you, you feel guilty and compelled to do something in return. Those organizations give away address labels in the hopes you'll reciprocate by giving them a donation. You're putting out sweets in the hopes people will take one and admire your booth in reciprocity.

At the very least, those dog owners have to look at *something* while their dog is drinking; it might as well be your fabulous booth.

Scents. I really love this tip and no one ever talks about it. You know how pleasant it is to walk into a nice-smelling room? Don't you feel welcomed, calmed, and content? Evoke the same feelings in your booth with a light scent in the air. You could use room spray, unlit candles, car air fresheners, or my favorite, tins filled with scented gel.

Which scent should you choose? Vanilla. Brand experts have been experimenting with scents in marketing and discovered that vanilla is the most well-recognized scent in the world and evokes the most pleasant feelings. When people are happy they are willing to spend money. Associate your booth with homey smells and people will be more comfortable browsing the booth and doing business with you.

NOTE: We've talked about evoking senses like touch, taste, and smell, so how about sound? Should you have music at your booth?

The unequivocal answer is no. I hate to tell you that because I love music, but it's not a good idea. Music (even quiet, mellow sounds) can be distracting to customers. You don't want distractions; all attention should be on your products. Music can really annoy your neighbors too.

Same deal with headphones - don't have them on ever, even when you're setting up in the morning. I used to wear headphones while unloading only, but I realized it alienated my neighbors and started us off on the wrong foot. I'm sorry to say it, but music is not allowed on show day.

More selling tips

Whew! There was a lot of good stuff back there and I hope you're already thinking about how to use some of the tips. Stay with me though because I have a few more selling strategies to share...

(1) *Upsell:* Let's say you sell hair pins and a customer picks up a small pin for $5. Can you show them how to stack four hair pins together for a cooler look (and bigger sale)?

(2) *Cross-sell:* Whenever someone buys a $20 pouch, I suggest they add a $5 wrist strap. Not only does it make the bag easier to use, but it increases the sale 25%. If someone buys your necklace, can you cross-sell them on matching earrings?

(3) *Bundle:* If a customer can't decide between one product or another, offer to bundle them together for a discounted price. Also pre-bundle products in advance for a special gift package. For example, if you sell body products, put together a gift basket with all your items in the same scent for a special price.

(4) *Follow up:* Get people's email addresses and follow up with them after the show. Keep the conversation going long after the craft fair. I'm still talking with some customers from my first shows in 2006!

Two random questions you'll often hear at craft shows

"Do you do custom?" You'll get asked to make custom products. Don't feel pressured to quote on the spot; just get the parameters of the project and respond later with a quote and delivery time. Be thoughtful about this - can you actually deliver on the promise? If you do take on custom projects, get payment in advance.

"Can you hold this?" It happens a lot - someone loves your stuff, asks you to put it on hold, and says they'll "be right back" to pay for it. Should you do it? It's up to you. I've had a 50/50 experience with this - most of the customers never come back, but a lot of vendors do. (Yes, other vendors will buy your stuff, they can be some of your best customers of the day!) I think the best policy is, "I can hold it for one hour but that's it. A lot of people have been looking at this and it's not fair to set aside without payment."

POST-SHOW WRAP UP AND ANALYSIS

Had a bad day? Didn't make the sales you'd hoped? Didn't make any money *at all?* Don't sweat it - sometimes the stars align for a bad day - the show was poorly advertised, the weather was bad, there was another big event at the same time, it's the end of a pay cycle and people have less spending money ... lots of reasons. Shake it off. If you have email addresses, gave out business cards, and got some free market research, you're in great shape.

Take notes. Scribble a few notes about the day while it's fresh in your head. I have a spreadsheet of each craft show, location, sales, and any personal notes about weather or types of customers. Note which items sold best, how much inventory sold, and what you have left. This type of information helps plan future shows.

Follow up with contacts. Did you meet potential customers? Found other vendors with hot tips? Say "hi" after the show to keep the conversation going. Let your customers know the next time you'll be doing a show. Ask your new vendor friends if they'll be at the next show. Indie artists are a tight community - be a part of it.

What's a good show? Obviously if you make a profit you've had a good show, but how much profit makes a *great* show? These numbers are difficult to come by because there isn't much published data and crafters don't like sharing their numbers. Plus, days vary. I was selling at one show in downtown Boston every Friday. The show was a steal - $25 for the booth, $15 for parking - and 100,000 people walked by every day. Some weeks I'd make $800 and some I'd make $50. It happens.

Typical rule of thumb says you want to at least double expenses, but 3-4 times is obviously better. As long as you covered expenses and made a little extra for your troubles that's an ok day. Generally the more expensive a show, the higher your profits. For a $100 show, I've seen artists make $300-$900 "on a good day." For a $700 shows, I've seen artists make $2,000-$5,000 "on a good day." Remember, *expenses* include show fees, travel expenses, any money spent on food or entertainment, and add some extra in there for your preparation, labor, and travel time.

Count your bank. Count all the cash and set aside $100 for the starting bank. Take the remaining cash and total it up with checks and credit card payments received. Note the total number and figure how much is due back to the state for sales tax collected. The remainder is your show profit. Record the numbers in your spreadsheet and deposit the funds in your business bank account.

PACKING CHECKLIST

Preparing for craft shows takes a lot of work. Use the checklist below to help with packing and preparation:

Display: Tent (with walls), tables, folding chair, tablecloths, banner, display items (baskets, shelves, walls, etc…), signage, mirror + cleaning wipes, dressing room (if applicable).

Inventory: All items you have for sale including work-in-progress items (to work on during the show). Anything needed to repair items like glue, thread, tape, etc…

Office Supplies: Pens, paper, invoices, price tags, tape, markers, stapler, calculator, scissors.

Promotional materials: Business cards, postcards, email signup sheet, news clippings.

Sales: Calculator, receipt book, notepad to record sales, credit card processor, cash bank, bag or apron to hold your money (that you're wearing at all times).

Paperwork: Sellers permit, business license, directions, instructions, special permits, parking pass.

Wrapping: Tissue paper, ribbons, boxes, bubble wrap, shopping bags, stickers, stamps, notecards.

Backup: Clips, rope, heavy-duty tape; anything to create a temporary display or weigh things down if it gets windy.

Personal Items: Sunscreen, water, food, tissues, camera, lip balm, aspirin, first aid kit, hand wipes, breath mints, layers of clothing.

Random: If you're holding a contest, do you have everything needed for it? If you're using a scent, did you pack it? What about your bowl of candy and/or dog treats and water bowl?

Chapter 11: **DOMINATE ETSY.**

"It used to be that people needed products to survive. Now products need people to survive." - **Nicholas Johnson**

I'm sure many of you have already heard of Etsy (www.etsy.com), the massive e-commerce site specializing in handmade and vintage items. The website started in 2005 with the mission of helping artists and crafters sell their goods. It has since grown to 500,000+ shops in 150 countries with hundreds of millions in sales of handmade goods, craft supplies, and vintage items.

People have quit their day jobs because of Etsy sales alone. Not only is it a potentially lucrative sales channel, but it's brimming with information and resources for creative people like yourself.

NOTE: This chapter talks exclusively about Etsy, but the same rules apply to other online marketplaces like ArtFire and Zibbet. Check out "Alternatives to Etsy" in Appendix A for more information.

WHY ETSY

People often sell on Etsy before they have their own website and with good reason:

Easy: Setting up an Etsy shop is as easy as loading pictures and writing descriptions.

Cheap: It costs 20¢ for a product listing that expires every 4 months. If an item sells, Etsy takes a percentage of the sale, currently 3.5%. (Note: Most Etsy transactions are processed via PayPal, which also takes 2.9% of the sale and a 30¢ transaction fee.)

Huge: The Etsy audience is huge. How big? According to their October 2013 "Weather Report," there were $109.5 million in goods sold in September 2013 alone. That represents over 5.5 million items sold in one month.[1]

Lucrative: Etsy shops are a part-time gig for most people, but others make their living with it. Some shops sell well over

$10,000/month in products (more about that later.) Granted, most people sell a lot less than that, but the opportunity is there.

Community: The Etsy community is alive and thriving. Everywhere you turn there are people looking to commiserate, support, and provide advice.

Exposure: Magazine editors, stylists, and bloggers are known to use the site for content ideas. You'll regularly see items in magazines that were sourced from Etsy.

Search Engine Optimization (SEO): Remember SEO from Chapter 6? An Etsy shop plays a big part in improving your search engine ranking and getting you to the first page of Google.

Analytics: Get in-depth analysis of your shop and view seasonality of popular items.

Etsy definitely has a lot of potential, but there's a lot of competition too. Your business has to stand out among thousands of others. How? With great photography, accurate titles, unique products, detailed descriptions, clear policies, and excellent customer service. Don't worry, it's easier to do than you think. Keep reading for all the details.

ETSY RESOURCES

The Etsy community is brimming with handy resources. Use these tools to learn how to promote your Etsy shop, file taxes, price products, get press, use social media, and anything else needed to run a successful business:

Teams: Groups of self-organized sellers who provide a sense of support and community for each other. Anyone can start a team about anything, but it's usually based on location or common interest. Go to *"Community"* then *"Teams"* to start your search. Look for teams about your location, medium (printing, knitting, electronics, sewing), or interest (work full-time, candle making, time management). Teams could work together to take out joint advertisements, share photographers, or even sell at craft shows.

Blog: The Etsy blog is filled with success stories, shop features, DIY tips, fun recipes, and loads of interesting content. It's designed for buyers and sellers alike, so it covers a lot of topics.

Seller Handbook: Etsy wants to help you succeed, and their Seller Handbook is crammed with tips for indie artists. It's an invaluable resource for anyone owning a creative business.

Etsy Subscriptions: Sign up for their weekly "Etsy Success" newsletter for tips on running a successful business. The *Etsy Labs* newsletter is really fun for DIY projects too.

Forums: Do you have a question about your indie art business? I guarantee it's been answered on an Etsy forum. This place is loaded with helpful questions and answers from fellow Etsy sellers. You can post questions, participate in discussions, and search the archives to find information about running your store and more.

Treasuries: Treasuries are created by individual Etsians or groups of sellers who curate a small collection of 16 products from Etsy. These treasuries are submitted in the hopes of making it to the front page of Etsy, a valuable place to be.

ETSY SHOP STRATEGIES

I'm not taking you through the step-by-step process of setting up an Etsy shop. It's pretty intuitive and I don't want to waste your time. Also, there's hundreds of resources that talk you through it, and it's better to search online for the most updated information. Instead, I'm highlighting a few things to do to make your shop stand out. Remember, there's 500,000+ sellers on Etsy; you must be strategic about creating and marketing your shop.

Shop dashboard: The dashboard displays everything about your shop's performance. Use this information to guide strategy. For example, the dashboard shows how many items have been viewed by day, month, or year, signaling which are most popular and which to drop. Not only that, but the "Stats" are incredible. Remember Google Analytics from Chapter 6? Etsy's "Stats" are a less complex version of Google Analytics. My favorite features are the *traffic sources* (how people found your shop) and the *keywords* (words people use to find you).

We talked about keywords extensively in Chapter 6. They're very important and kind of difficult to define and Etsy just hands them to you. Use this knowledge when you're writing product descriptions or targeting ads.

Photographs: These are extremely important on Etsy. Great photographs are important in general, but on Etsy they're practically more important than the product itself. Etsy shoppers *love* their photographs, so make 'em count. We talked about photography in Chapter 6, flip back there for detailed tips.

Item title: A good title is everything on Etsy. There's lots of strategy behind it. Let's break it down into four techniques:

(1) *Say what it is:* Don't title your product "The Marjorie Bag." It doesn't help customers or Etsy search engines find you. Be descriptive in your titles: "Blue Tote Bag for Books, Groceries, and Shopping." Try describing it like people would in an Etsy search.

(2) *The first three words are most important:* Etsy SEO ranks the first three words of an item title higher than the rest. Therefore, use the first three words to best describe the product. In the example above, "Blue Tote Bag" works perfectly.

(3) *Keep it short:* The best Etsy titles state what the product is and how to use it in 10 words or less. Do your own search - type in words similar to what you're selling and study how other product titles are written.

(4) *Vary product titles:* Google and Etsy don't like it when the same titles are repeated for different products; it's considered spammy. Try to vary each title slightly to increase your item's ranking. For example, "Blue Tote Bag for Books, Groceries, and Shopping," "Red Shopping Bag for Books and Groceries," and "Green Book Bag for Shopping and Groceries."

Description: We covered effective product descriptions in Chapter 6 and the same rules apply here. Talk about product dimensions in terms of measurements *and* what people can fit into it (i.e., "holds a laptop," "fits your sunglasses," "cell phone pocket.") Help readers imagine already owning your product - what does it feel like? How can they use it? Be descriptive about your materials and product quality. Add a story or memorable product feature.

PLUS, repeat the first three words of the title in your product description for better Etsy SEO. For example, in the product title, "Blue Tote Bag for Books, Groceries, and Shopping" try opening the description with, "This blue tote bag holds your books, groceries, and shopping items like a pro…"

Tags: Tags are keywords associated with your product and shop. They help shoppers find your stuff, so they're really important. Etsy allows you to "tag" any item up to 13 times. The first 3 tags should be the same 3 from your title and description (i.e., "blue" "tote" "bag") then 10 others related to your product. Again, think about the keywords shoppers use; for example, many people find our products by searching for "vegan bags."

Also think about *uses* for the item. We sell pouches that are used for makeup, travel, organization, or a small clutch. Therefore "makeup pouch," "toiletries bag," and "clutch" are all great tags.

Finally, list your materials as tags. A lot of people search for "canvas bags," "silver necklaces," or "soy candles."

Shop section: Etsy allows you to divide products into different shop sections. For example, instead of listing all your products under "Bag," you could break them down in sections like "Messenger Bags," "Diaper Bags," "Makeup Pouches," and "iPad Cases." You can have up to 10 sections in a shop; use them all if you can. Why? Sections make it easier for customers to browse - they much prefer 6 sections with 2 pages of product each then just 1 section with 12 whole pages of product. Even if you sell all the same product (e.g., necklaces), break it down by size or type (gold, silver, short, long, charm, chain).

Materials: Etsy allows listing up to 13 materials for each item. Get a little descriptive with materials. For example, instead of listing "cotton, wool, and thread," try "cotton broadcloth, Merino wool, and waxed thread." Also, get a little funny with the list, like adding "wishful thinking" or "enthusiasm." Etsy shoppers appreciate whimsical details.

Pricing: Etsy shoppers love their bundles; consider packaging some items together as one discounted product. Do you make bridesmaid gifts? Bundle six together for a discount. Do you make cards? Bundle an entire set together. Can you offer a subscription service, like one new headband a month or candle every season?

Coupons: Etsy makes it really easy to apply discounts to your shop. You can offer a percentage discount (20% off), fixed dollar amount ($5 off), or free shipping. I like coupons occasionally as exclusive deals. Otherwise I feel it cheapens your brand; see Chapter 4 for more information.

Policies: Etsy will ask for your shipping, returns, and payment policies. Check out Chapter 7 if you're unsure how to handle this.

Shop banner image: It's the first thing shoppers see so it should look professional. Snappy banners tell shoppers you're a serious business with quality products for sale. Try to showcase your logo, tagline, and sampling of products. If you don't have any graphic design skills, turn to Etsy. Post a question on the Forum or search the Teams for "banner." I just did this and found several teams dedicated to banners, even one called "Free Etsy Banner." Yup, there's fellow Etsians who can make the banner for you; the Etsy community is great like that.

Shop announcement: This is very important for two reasons. First, it's listed at the top of your shop so it's the first thing customers see. Second, this is how your shop page appears in Google search results; Etsy even offers a preview. Only the first 160 characters of your shop announcement are visible without clicking more, so load those first 2 sentences with keywords and important information.

Featured items: You can feature up to four items at the top of your shop. Choose the top four best sellers or those with the best photographs. Click the "star" in your listings to feature them and preview how they look together.

Promote: Etsy makes it easy to buy ads. They let you determine the keywords and budget. I have not purchased an ad before but I've heard they can be very effective. If you have a few extra dollars to spend and feel comfortable with keywords, give it a try to see how it works for you. See Chapter 13 for advice about purchasing ads.

Profile: Etsy allows you to load profile pictures, studio pictures, artist bios, and company background. Be personal. Tell stories. Engage with customers. People love to know exactly who they're doing business with, so include pictures of yourself, your family, your pets, or anything else that's important to you.

Extra Etsy tips

Shipping profiles: If you ship a lot of the same type of product and shipping costs are the same, set up a shipping profile (e.g., "bags" or "necklaces") for easier listing.

Vacation mode: Taking a break and unable to ship products? Put your shop on vacation mode and alert customers when you're back and ready for business.

Shop reviews: Remember that people can leave feedback about your products. Monitor the reviews to ensure happy customers. See Chapter 7 for advice on dealing with irate customers and tips for providing stellar customer service.

Share on social media: Share links to items, sections, or your entire shop on social media. It helps SEO and reminds customers about your Etsy shop.

Etsy Wholesale

Etsy just launched an exciting new venture, *Etsy Wholesale*, which facilitates orders between sellers and wholesale buyers. Etsy's partnerships with independent boutiques and large retailers like Nordstrom, West Elm, and Indigo open doors indie artists couldn't get to themselves.

Because Etsy Wholesale is a private juried marketplace, you must apply to participate. Additionally, Etsy requires sellers to offer the standard 50% wholesale discount to retailers (flip back to Chapter 4 for more information about wholesale pricing). If you're approved, you'll pay a one-time $100 fee and Etsy will keep 3.5% of all transactions. This can be a great opportunity if you can afford to sell in bulk at wholesale prices. Check out www.etsy.com/wholesale/apply/sell for more details.

A final thought

We talked about CraftCount (www.craftcount.com) in Chapter 3. It's the site that lists the top performing Etsy shops by category and it's updated every 24 hours. Now that you've got a good handle on Etsy, take a look at those shops and study what they're doing. Examine their products, photography, pricing, and descriptions. Consider what they do well, and how you can do the same for your business.

---

[1] Traub, Michelle. "Etsy Statistics: September 2013 Weather Report." *Etsy News Blog.* Etsy, 14 Oct. 2013.

Chapter 12: **BREAK INTO RETAIL.**

"The way you position yourself at the beginning of a relationship has profound impact on where you end up." - **Ron Karr**

Stores are a fantastic sales channel for artists, crafters, and makers alike. Independent shops, boutiques, coffee shops, restaurants, art galleries, museums ... anywhere there's a cash register there's a chance to sell your goods. Not only is it great exposure, but it's fun to see your stuff in a store too.

Note to visual artists Though this chapter talks about "products" and "stores," it's very relevant to you too. Just insert "artwork" and "galleries" instead. If you're a visual artist who makes prints or other objects out of your art, then this chapter will be particularly helpful.

HOW TO FIND STORES

If it's your first time selling in stores, start local. It's better to live near shops where you can check in and restock easily. Plus, store owners are more receptive to featuring local artists.

Start an internet search for your area. Look for independent, small shops to start your burgeoning retail career. Think of unique partnerships too. For example, if you make greeting cards, potential stores might be flower shops or hospital gift shops. If you make dog collars, ask local veterinarians to set up a display in their waiting room (and offer them a percentage of the sales).

Once you have a full list, whittle it down with research. Look at a store's website - what type of merchandise is for sale? What's the price range? What type of customer do they cater to? Would your items be a good fit? Also, research the reputation of the shop - does it have good online reviews? Contact other indie artists who sell there and get the inside scoop.

Since you're local, go to the store as well. Don't mention you're an artist looking to sell, just act like a regular shopper. Could you see your products in that store? Note specific details to mention later in your pitch.

Rate your top five choices in each area. Stores don't like when you sell in competing shops, so pitch your top pick first then work your way down the list. If you're in a big city, you could get away with pitching stores across town from each other, but if you're in a small town, don't sell in more than one store in the area.

Museum gift shops: These can be a potentially lucrative sales channel with great exposure. Competition is high at these venues, so get creative to stand out. Try to provide your own display, attractive packaging, and printed materials they can include with purchase. Do you have products that tie into their next exhibit? BONUS.

Most gift shops are juried; your work will be judged by a panel of experts. You'll likely be asked for a portfolio including images, product descriptions, artist bio, and a list of other locations where your products are sold. See Chapter 10 for advice about putting together a winning application.

Just like stores, it's best to start with local museums. When you're ready to expand, check out the massive Museum Retail Conference and Expo, sponsored by the Museum Store Association (www.museumstoreassociation.org).

HOW TO APPROACH STORES

Once you've found your favorite shops, send the owner a package with product photos, item descriptions, and artist bio. You'll want to include something called a "line sheet" too, more on that below. Include a cover letter stating you'd like to sell in their store and why your products are a good fit. Be personal too - indicate somehow that you've visited their website or store recently. Mention you'll follow up in a few days to make an appointment.

You could also send an email with this information, but sometimes that gets lost in spam. If the shop means a lot to you, send the package first.

Follow up a few days later with a phone call. Ask for the owner and tell them you're following up on your letter. Request an appointment to show your products in person. Understand these people are very busy, so be brief.

Appointment day

Be punctual, presentable, and prepared. This is a business meeting, treat it as such. Be on time. Wear clean, tailored clothes. Trim your hair and nails. Know your product line and prices extensively.

Think about your mobile display too. Remember, first impressions are everything, so you don't want shopkeepers seeing your products wrapped in plastic bags and rubber bands. Find something that acts like a mobile store and looks great too. Try old suitcases. Use the bottom for display and product storage and the top for all your business cards, marketing materials, and order forms.

Make it clear you're reliable and easy to work with too. Stores especially love those artists who can provide their own displays, packaging, or printed materials.

"What are your terms?"

If the manager or store owner likes your products, they'll say those four special little words: "What are your terms?" They're asking about your policies, including:

Minimums: The minimum dollar amount for opening a wholesale account and reordering. It's common for the opening amount to be higher than the reorder. For example, some crafters might say $500 minimum to open the account then $250 minimum to reorder.

Some indie artists also have *product minimums* - minimum orders for each type of product. For example, greeting card makers might require retailers to purchase two of each set of cards (birthday, anniversary, thank you) in one order.

Lead time and shipping: How long until the store receives the order. This includes your manufacturing and shipping time, typically 4-6 weeks after trade shows. You'll also have to advise of shipping costs if applicable.

Return policy: It's painful to think about someone returning a $500 order, but you should allow it for a limited time. I allow wholesale returns seven days after receipt and assuming the products are in saleable condition.

Payment Policy: Payment is usually COD (*Cash on Delivery;* you get paid when you deliver the product) or paid in advance. Most stores expect COD, but occasionally you can get an advance deal or deposit. Once your relationship with the store is established, you could consider Net 30 terms, which means the store pays within 30 days (sometimes this encourages the store to order more).

"We sell on consignment"

You're going to hear that a lot, especially in the beginning. Consignment means the product is displayed in the store, but you're not paid until the item sells. You still legally own the item too. This type of deal is really popular because it reduces the risk for shop owners. A lot of indie artists don't mind this arrangement either because it usually means more money. Though some shops require a 50/50 split, many are amenable to 60/40 or even 70/30 in your favor.

Take the consignment deal if it works for you. However, ask the store manager how many items are on consignment and how many are purchased outright. Then find out what it takes to get purchased outright. Also, learn about their policies on damaged goods, duration on shelves, and how unsold merchandise is handled.

Get everything in writing. Create an agreement that outlines how many products you're selling at what price and the sales split. The agreement should also state when you get paid, typically once a month. When you do get a check, confirm the shop owner includes a list of items sold.

If you sell on consignment, start with just a few items until you've developed a relationship with the store. Most shop owners are honest and reliable, but I've heard occasional stories of destroyed merchandise or missed payments. Start small, build trust, and expand from there.

PAPERWORK TO BRING TO STORES

There are two components to selling in stores: product and paperwork. Yes, the *paperwork* you bring to stores is just as important as the *product.* You're trying to convince stores you're professional, organized, and easy to work with. The right printed materials will go a long way with that.

Line Sheet: This is important. A line sheet is basically your catalogue and it tells a store what they need to know to purchase your products. It's usually several pages long and includes everything we discussed above plus a little more:

(1) *Minimums:* Dollar amount and product amount.

(2) *Lead time:* How long it takes to deliver wholesale orders (typically 4-6 weeks).

(3) *Shipping:* Shipping time and cost.

(4) *Returned, cancelled, and damaged goods:* What if items are damaged on arrival?

(5) *Payments:* Advance payment, deposit, COD, or Net 30.

(6) *Contact information:* Your name, business name, address, telephone, email, and website.

(7) *Pricing:* Wholesale prices and MSRP ("Manufacturer's Suggested Retail Price," that is, your suggested retail price).

(8) *Descriptions:* Size, measurements, materials, and mention if it's popular or a bestseller.

(9) *Photographs:* These are essential not only to help sell products but also to help store managers visually track items.

(10) *Product numbers:* Develop a system for numbering your products and label each item with the accompanying number. Product numbers are required for most stores.

When you're first starting out, it's ok to make your own line sheet with Google Docs, Word, or Excel. As your business grows, I urge you to create a professional-looking line sheet with the help of a graphic designer or do it yourself with Line Sheet Maker (www.linesheetmaker.com), similar to what the pros use. The line sheet is often the first impression shop owners have of your products, so it should look great.

Invoice: A proper invoice has the following elements:

(1) *Seller's information:* Your name, business name, address, telephone, email, and website.

(2) *Buyer's information:* Contact's name, store name, address, telephone, email, and website.

(3) *Date and invoice number:* Stores need invoice numbers to track their payments. Develop a system for invoice numbers and be consistent with the store.

(4) *List of items (with product numbers):* Whatever the store has decided to order.

(5) *Prices:* List the wholesale prices.

(6) *Total sum due:* Add up the entire order + shipping costs (if applicable).

(7) *Payment terms:* COD or Net 30 and indicate if a deposit is already paid.

(8) *PO number:* Most stores will give you a PO (Purchase Order) number for their bookkeeping purposes. Include it in the invoice for their convenience.

Resale tax form/resale certificate: Wholesale purchases are not taxed because they're not a final sale (i.e., the store is not the final consumer, the store's *customers* are). However, if you're audited the IRS will want proof the wholesale purchases were nontaxable. Therefore, you'll need a resale tax form (a.k.a. "resale certificate.") It's basically one sheet you can make yourself that includes the store's name, address, permit number (their tax ID), and an itemized list of their wholesale purchase from you. Both of you should sign and date the form. Likewise, if you purchase wholesale from a distributor, show them your tax ID to enjoy tax-free status.

Order form: Pre-print these to easily take orders in stores. Put your logo, business name, and contact information at the top. Leave a blank space to include the store's name and contact information. Make columns for product number, name, price, quantity, and total. Sometimes order forms are included in line sheets.

Once your items are in a store, check in occasionally; especially if you haven't heard from them in a few months. See how products are selling and examine inventory levels. Store owners are really busy, so they appreciate when artists proactively check on their own products.

Also, talk about the store everywhere. List it on your website and mention it in social media. Encourage your customers to go check it out for themselves - store owners will especially love you for that.

When you're ready to expand your retail experience, start looking across the country. Look for stores that have been featured in your favorite magazines. Examine fellow crafters' websites and see where they're selling. Ask friends if they know stores in their own areas. Do an internet search for shops or boutiques in big cities. Selling in long-distance stores poses a unique set of challenges (most notably shipping costs and risk of damage), but the exposure is often worth it.

One final note on selling in stores - you might not get accepted to all your favorite shops. Rejection is common for dozens of reasons: your products could be out of season, they might not fit with the shop's ideal customer, or the store just bought something similar. Perhaps they just stocked up for the season and lack extra cash flow. Whatever it is, don't give up. Either pitch the store again later or move on to your next favorite shop.

> •**PRO TIP•** It's very difficult to pitch stores January through March, the slowest retail season. April, May, and June are great. So are September, October, and (early) November. If any of your products are seasonal (i.e. Christmas ornaments or Valentine's cards) then contact the store 2-3 months in advance.

Chapter 13: **MASTER MARKETING.**

"If we all did the things we are capable of doing, we would literally astound ourselves." - **Thomas Edison**

Marketing is a broad term that encompasses anything done to generate sales. This includes printing business cards, interacting on social media, surveying customers, buying ads on Facebook, creating DIY videos, writing blog posts … *anything you do to promote your business is considered marketing.*

This is a weighty chapter because marketing is critical for artists, crafters, and makers. You can't just put products in an Etsy shop and expect them to fly off the shelves. Oh no, there's a lot more to it than that.

Don't worry, marketing is fun and you really get to know your customers in the process. In fact, great marketing is all about engaging customers and helping them understand why they should buy products from you.

It's not enough to sell a cool product. Today's most successful businesses position themselves in the right market to the right customers. Marketing is about communicating your value, competitive advantage, and unique selling proposition to help customers realize you're their best choice.

SET MARKETING GOALS AND PLAN YOUR MARKETING CALENDAR

Since marketing encompasses so many things, it's important to set goals and commit them to a schedule.

Way back in Chapter 1 we talked about setting short-term and long-term goals that are SMART (**S**pecific, **M**easurable, **A**ttainable,

Realistic, and Timely). Same goes for your marketing plan. First, revisit those business goals - consider where you want to be in six months, one year, and two years from now. What sort of marketing do you need to do to get there?

You may be thinking, "I want more customers and more sales." That's a good overall goal, but you have to be more specific than that. How *many* customers? How *much* in sales? How *long* will it take you to get there? Your answers provide mini-goals and timelines, and this guides your marketing plan.

You might have other goals too like writing articles for popular magazines, improving customer service, breaking into a new field, selling 30 items a month, making $5,000/year in advertising revenue with your blog, attending 5 more craft shows ... this sort of stuff influences marketing strategy too.

Look at your goals for the next six months. I'm sure it's a lengthy list, probably too much to actually do in that time frame. Can you whittle it down to 3-5 specific, measurable, attainable, realistic, and timely goals?

The key here is *realistic and timely*. Don't set yourself up for failure by putting too much on your plate. If time is limited, that's fine. You just have to be extra scrupulous in choosing the next set of goals.

Strategic Marketing

Strategic marketing is like drawing a map for your marketing plan. Look at your 3-5 goals. Break them down into actionable steps and divvy them up over the six months. Then, break down each month into a specific 30-day marketing plan.

For example, say you're just starting out and your goals for the next six months are:

(1) Take better photographs
(2) Open Etsy shop
(3) Create logo and business cards
(4) Open social media accounts and start using them

Now break down each of these bigger goals into smaller tasks:

(1) *Take better photographs:* Organize lighting set up, research how to use camera, learn photo editing software, find model for lifestyle shots.

(2) *Open Etsy shop:* Design banner, write descriptions, price products, create shop info, join an Etsy team.

(3) *Create logo and business cards:* Choose images, write text, contact graphic designers, find printing company.

(4) *Open social media accounts and start using them:* Decide which networks to use, set up accounts, get to know the features, interact with popular groups or forums on the sites.

Pull out your 30 day calendar and determine how much time you have available each day to devote to the marketing agenda. Some days might be impossible and that's ok, just add extra time elsewhere.

Think about efficiency too. It's easier to do tasks in bulk, so try writing all your blog posts in one day then schedule them to publish over the next month. Schedule social media posts ahead of time too. Try Hootsuite (www.hootsuite.com) to schedule Facebook, Twitter, and Instagram feeds. If you have an Etsy shop, try Promotesy (www.promotesy.com) to easily integrate your Etsy shop items into social media feeds.

I manage seven social media accounts. Every Tuesday I spend 2-3 hours on Hootsuite scheduling posts for all those accounts for the next week. Then, I only spend 15 minutes each day searching the social media sites for things to "like," "retweet," or "favorite." You'll read more about this type of stuff in Chapter 14.

TYPES OF MARKETING

Marketing is so huge it can be broken down into different categories like strategic marketing, content marketing, niche marketing, social media marketing, and traditional marketing. We've already discussed strategic marketing so let's talk about some others:

Content Marketing

Nowadays a lot of people are talking about "content marketing." There are even entire companies dedicated to doing it. Simply put, content marketing means creating and sharing quality content that's relevant to your target customer.

Duh. Obviously you want to share quality content with your customers. What exactly *is* quality content though? It's anything that's useful, relevant, authoritative, sharable, interactive, inspirational, personal, or actionable.

Content marketing includes many things. It can be personal with behind-the-scenes pictures. It can be authoritative with a how-to DIY craft video. It's often shareable with jokes or contests. How about a call to action with sales or email signups? Consider your target market and things they'd like to know. Then design content that's important to them. We'll talk about this a lot in Chapter 14.

Blogging is one of the best tools for content marketing. Now that you're familiar with content marketing, reread the section in Chapter 6 that talks about blogging. Brainstorm blog posts to write that appeal to your target audience and fulfill content marketing goals.

Niche Marketing

Niche marketing focuses on your niche customers and hyper-targeting them. It combines a lot of skills we've already discussed in this book. Go ahead and reread these sections if you need a refresher:

Chapter 2: *Customers: Who are they and what do they want?*
Chapter 3: *Find your niche*
Chapter 5: *Appealing to customers*
Chapter 6: *Keywords*

First, identify your niche. Then, create a customer persona around that niche. Next, find popular keywords related to your niche and customer persona. Finally, appeal to the niche with marketing content built around those keywords.

For example, let's say you make stationery. You've identified a niche and created a customer persona named Sarah who is a young bride-to-be looking for wedding invitations. Your niche marketing goals would be all about targeting Sarah: advertising where she shops, sharing content that's important to her, and publishing articles that inform her. Then you might advertise on popular wedding blogs, share tips for choosing wedding stationery on your social media networks, and publish a "how to" article about wedding invitation etiquette on a popular website (then link it back to your own website).

Search your keywords for niche ideas and ask your own customers what's important to them, where they like to shop, or how they get information. Build a niche marketing plan around that.

Social Media Marketing

This is so important I've dedicated the next chapter to it. I'll just say here that social media marketing involves sites like Facebook, Twitter, Pinterest, and Instagram and it's a valuable tool for executing marketing strategies. Not only is it handy with content and niche marketing, but marketing on social media is a skill unto itself. There's hundreds of resources dedicated to doing it right, but I've broken down the most vital information (and some secret tips) in the next chapter.

Traditional Marketing

This is "old school" marketing, the kind that was around before the internet. Traditional marketing includes printing business cards, advertising in magazines, and teaching classes. This is all still relevant today and helpful for supplementing other marketing strategies.

Networking: Attending events, hosting home sales, teaching classes, and sponsoring industry events. A lot of networking is now done online in blogs and forums too. Revisit Chapter 1 under "Resources" - Meetups and Etsy forums are great places to start.

Advertising: Paying for ad space in magazines, newspapers, radio, and TV. Traditional advertising is really expensive for indie artists, it's better to advertise on Google, Facebook, or popular websites. More on that later in this chapter.

Printing: Business cards, postcards, catalogues, banners, flyers. Printed materials are still very important today, especially line sheets like we discussed in Chapter 12.

Newsletters: Once printed on paper and mailed monthly, today's newsletters are sent mostly by email. Newsletters are a very effective marketing tool, I'll talk about this later in the chapter.

PRINTED MATERIALS

Because printed materials are so important, let's take a moment to discuss the big ones:

Business cards: Think of business cards like handheld ads. They should be attention-grabbing, visually appealing, and packed with relevant information. You want someone to hold on to your business card, not just throw it out. Here's some business card tips:

(1) *Include all relevant contact information:* Your name, telephone, email, website, and social media accounts. If it feels like you're cramming too much information on a small space, stick with just name, telephone, email, and website.

(2) *Include the business name and logo:* Keep it consistent with the rest of your branding - use the same colors and fonts.

(3) *Use the other side of the card for pictures of your product:* People collect business cards; help yours stand out with pictures of the products they love. This is especially important if you sell at craft shows. People pick up a lot of business cards that day, and those without pictures get lost in the shuffle.

(4) *Hire a professional to design your cards:* Unless you have sufficient design skills, leave this one to the pros. Remember, business cards are your first impression and they must be memorable. Professional graphic designers have years of business card design experience and know what works best. See Appendix A at the end of this book for tips about finding and hiring graphic designers.

(5) *Use a professional printing service:* Avoid the sites that give you free business cards. Not only will they put their website's name or advertisement on the back, but the paper quality is poor - it's not a great way to make a first impression. Besides, professional printing services are really affordable nowadays. Moo (www.moo.com) is pretty cool because you can print different product photographs on the back of each card. For example, if you're printing 100 cards, you can upload 4 different photographs and have them printed in groups of 25. I like Green Printer (www.greenprinteronline.com) because they use recycled paper and vegetable-based inks that are high quality and affordable. Overnight Prints (www.overnightprints.com) is also a quality printer with paper sourced from sustainable forests. Wherever you go, request samples from the printer first to decide paper weight (80-pound cardstock is ideal) and finishes.

(6) *Start small:* Order a minimum amount of cards to start, try 100. This is important for two reasons. First, to confirm you like the printing company and design job. Second, it will probably take a while to give away 100 cards and you might want to update the design with new information soon. Start small until you're sure what works for you.

Postcards: Postcards are great because they're larger versions of your business cards - they act like advertisements, but they hold a lot more information. The same rules that apply to business cards apply to postcards too - use a professional printer, a professional designer, include contact information, logo, and product pictures.

What additional information can you include in the space? Try customer testimonials, press mentions, or pictures of you at work. Give people a reason to hang on to your postcards ... put a "Top 10" list or "How to" information on the back.

If you can't afford postcards at the moment, consider teaming up with another artist and split it. Each of you could "own" a side and divide the printing costs. Plus, when the postcard goes out you're both helping each other reach new audiences.

Catalogue: This is just like those clothing and gift catalogues you get in the mail, except nowadays it's usually shared in an email attachment. Catalogues have lots of photographs, concise product descriptions, retail prices, options like colors and sizes, and item numbers for easy identification and ordering. Catalogues also include the business name and contact information. This type of "printed" material is usually available in electronic format on your website for press or store buyers to access. See Chapter 12 for more details.

Banner: This is used at craft shows and special events, so I've included more details about it in Chapter 10.

Invoices: If you wholesale or sell in stores, you'll need invoices. The full invoice checklist is in Chapter 12, but I wanted to mention it here as a piece of marketing material.

At the bottom of an invoice, add a personal touch for marketing benefits. Say something like, "Thank you for your business! I look forward to working with you again. I'll tell all my customers about your store. Follow us on Facebook, Twitter, and Instagram to stay up to date on our latest products."

VIDEO

Hardly anyone uses video as a marketing tool, which is a shame because it's effective for many reasons. First of all, the video site YouTube (www.youtube.com) is the second most popular search engine. It's listed right behind Google, which purchased YouTube in

2006 and has heavily promoted the site since. Second, videos are great for SEO (we talked about SEO in Chapter 6). Videos help get you to the front page of search engines (because Google and YouTube are very good friends). Third, videos make excellent sharable content and we're all about content marketing here. Finally, videos establish your expertise and authority, which we talked about in Chapter 8.

Before making a video, there are three questions to ask:

(1) *What are your goals?* What do you want to accomplish with this video? You might want to increase sales, promote brand awareness, create valuable content, improve SEO, attract a new audience, target a niche, or highlight new products.

(2) *Who is your target audience?* Are you creating content for your everyday customers or for a niche customer? Consider the target audience when creating content - it helps focus the material.

(3) *What action do you want the audience to take?* Think about your "call to action." Do you want the viewers to give you their email address, go to your website, visit your Etsy page, or view other videos? You can choose more than one call to action, but don't make it so overwhelming people do nothing instead. (Remember K.I.S.S. - Keep it Simple, Stupid from Chapter 5.)

Guidelines for making a video

First, keep it short. Promotional videos should be 30 seconds or less. Informational videos should range 1-2 minutes and DIY or "how to" videos are usually 3-5 minutes. Don't go over five minutes on a video because most people won't even bother watching it.

Film several segments in one day then schedule them to publish later. You want to publish content consistently so always have several videos queued up.

Study other popular videos about your topic on YouTube. Find ones with high viewings and positive ratings. What are they doing well? Can you learn anything from them?

If you post videos to YouTube, create a "channel." Why? Channels collect all your videos in one spot, making it easy for others to see all the videos you've created. Anyone can "subscribe" to your channel and be alerted when you post new videos. Name the channel and choose a username that describes the business and what you do (e.g., "GreenRibbonDesigns.") You could even say, "GreenRibbonDesignsdotcom" to lead people directly to your website.

148

Types of video content

Your videos don't have to be slick and filled with graphics. The most powerful, sharable videos are often the simplest ones. Just be your authentic, creative self and make content that's valuable to your audience.

Not all videos have to be about your products either. Entertain people with funny messages, cute animals, beautiful quotes, delicious recipes, and compelling stories. Remember - these are short videos, surely you can come up with something!

Think about the potential purposes of your video. Can you make one for your *About* page so people get to know you and why you create products? How about videos that feature your stuff in a "lifestyle" setting, like worn on a model or displayed in a living room?

"How-to" or DIY videos are really popular. Can you create a video showing off how to make one of your own products? If you're not comfortable with that, try making a "how-to" video about something else not related to your products, like sharing a delicious recipe or easy car detailing tips. Remember, the video doesn't have to be about your business, it just has to be relevant or interesting to your audience.

Interview other artists or people who inspire you. Film it if you can, or just make a video with audio and some pictures.

Finally, take your frequently asked questions and answer them in videos. eThreads' customers frequently ask about the features of our bags, the durability of our materials, and if our bags are machine washable. Each of these questions can be answered in a short video for easy and compelling marketing content.

Video making tools

First, you'll want a decent video recorder and a good audio source. Audio quality is just as important as video quality, so think about the microphone. Lots of digital cameras have perfectly adequate video recorders and microphones. You could also record on your computer with a webcam and microphone, most laptops have these built in. Test a short video first to see how you like it. I bought a lapel (a.k.a. "lavalier") microphone for $60 and it's been a great investment for quality audio.

If you're making informational videos, you could just talk over a PowerPoint. Try CamStudio (www.camstudio.org) or Jing (www.techsmith.com/download/jing) for free screen capture software.

If you're making DIY videos, film at an angle that's useful for your viewers, like over your shoulder or in front of your hands.

Edit content with free video editing software. Try Windows Movie Maker or the very easy Kate's Video Toolkit (search online for "Windows Movie Maker" or "Kate's Video Toolkit" to find a free download button, they're everywhere).

When the video is finished, upload it to YouTube (www.youtube.com) and/or the other popular video site Vimeo (www.vimeo.com).

Video SEO

Videos make effective SEO tools. Here's some tips:

(1) *Put keywords in your description.* Ideally have a set of keywords in mind while making the video. Also think about the words or phrases people would use to find your video.

(2) *Embed the video on your blog, website, and anywhere else that will accept your content.* For example, if you make a "How to" video, turn it into an article for a popular website.

(3) *Make a transcript of your video.* This is awesome for SEO and not a lot of people know about it. Create a transcript of your video and post it on your blog - not only for quality content, but Google will read it and rank your site higher in search results.

MAILING LISTS AND NEWSLETTERS

Email marketing is one of the most effective forms of marketing with high returns on investment. Collect email addresses whenever you're working craft shows or public events. Gather the emails of people who have purchased from you. Create an email sign up form with WuFoo (www.wufoo.com) and post it everywhere, including your Facebook page and website. Whenever you're producing marketing materials, include a call to action like, "Sign up for special announcements and exclusive deals."

Once you have more than 100 people on the mailing list, consider enrolling with a CRM (Customer Relationship Management) service like Constant Contact (www.constantcontact.com), MailChimp (www.mailchimp.com), or AWeber (www.aweber.com); they all start at about $15/month. These companies make creating, sending, and managing emails easy. They also make it possible to connect mailings with your social media networks. You can get all sorts of analytics too about the number of emails opened and how many emails bounce back.

Mailing list content

Now that you've collected email addresses, what should you send and how often?

Create simple one-page emails or put together entire newsletters - as long as it's content that's interesting to your audience. Your message can't be all about promotion, there has to be something else interesting, compelling, touching, entertaining, or noteworthy too.

For example, let's say you're sending a quick email about an upcoming craft show. In addition to mentioning the details of the show, offer a 20% discount if they bring that email to the show. Include a picture of items you're selling and a customer testimonial. Always include a link back to your website too. This message is really effective because it has pictures, a coupon, a testimonial, and a call to action.

Add other compelling content like an inspiring quote, cute picture, product origin story, your favorite recipe, DIY tip, a peek behind the scenes, a story from your everyday life, or a new craft project. See "What to say on social media" in Chapter 14 for more content suggestions.

Finally, how often should you send emails or newsletters? They take a lot of work, so try sending one every 6-8 weeks to start. As you get more comfortable with the process and have more things to say, consider sending an email every 3-4 weeks. This is the perfect amount of time to stay relevant to your audience without being overwhelming.

> •PRO TIP• Whenever you're sending a mass email or newsletter, tell people they are receiving it because they signed up or made a purchase with you. Always have an "unsubscribe" link so people can opt out too. Include a privacy policy on your website that says something like, "Your privacy is important to me. I never sell or exchange email addresses." Because you don't - right?!

ADVERTISING

I don't advertise too much myself. I'm all about free marketing and advertising is not free. I'd rather run a contest or special promotion than buy ads.

That said, I know a lot of business owners who have had great success with advertising, so it's important to talk about in this book. For small business owners like yourself, forget about print advertising - that's way too expensive. If you have a budget for advertising, spend it on ads for Facebook (www.facebook.com/advertising) and Google (www.google.com/adwords).

Those two websites are particularly effective for advertising because they're affordable and targeted. Facebook and Google are all about gathering data. Therefore you can hyper-target ads for certain ages, genders, locations, interests, and so much more. Try running ads on both sites at once, then over time determine which is more effective for your business.

Before we get into that, take a step back and consider your advertising goals. You probably want people to visit your website or buy products. That means your ad has to:

(1) Relay critical selling points - get to the heart of what's important to the audience.

(2) Include a link to your website, Etsy shop, or even better - link directly to the product that you're advertising.

(3) Include a call to action like "Buy now," "Click here," "Sign up," or "Like this page."

The key to successful Facebook and Google advertising is hyper-targeted ads. Go back and revisit your niche and target customers we discussed at the beginning of this chapter - who are you trying to reach with this ad and what do you want them to do? Tailor your ad accordingly with the ad copy, call to action, and keywords.

For example, let's say you're that stationery maker targeting young brides-to-be. In this case you'd write an ad like "Quality Wedding Invitations, Affordable and Made in the USA" using keywords like "bridal," "wedding," and "invitations" and including a link to the "Bridal" section of your website. This is more effective than, "Quality Stationery, Wedding Invitations, Birth Announcements" using keywords like "bridal," "parent," and "baby" and including a link to your homepage - that ad is all over the place. Spend your money wisely; hyper-targeted ads are lucrative ads.

Experiment with different versions of your ad. Try different combinations of titles, pictures, and words to see what performs better. This is known as A/B testing, and professionals do it to craft the most effective ad. Experiment with different niches too, notice which groups respond best to your ads. Both Facebook and Google offer data on your ad campaigns to track performance.

Craigslist: "Hey Emily, Craigslist is free, how about advertising on there?" I have not tried it yet but I know some people who have with good results. If you make custom orders, wedding gifts, or otherwise solve people's problems write an ad for it - see Chapter 17 for Craigslist tips. Use attention-grabbing headlines on Craigslist too; learn how to write them in Chapter 16.

Set an advertising budget

Both Facebook Ads and Google Adwords offer several ways to budget ads. For example, you can set $7 as an advertising budget, and when that runs out, the ad stops running. This is great when you're testing ads; you don't have to spend a lot of money to get data. Not only that, but your ad can be charged in several ways including:

CPM (Cost Per Thousand): Also known as "impression advertising," you're charged every 1,000 times your ad appears, regardless if anyone clicks it. This typically costs $3-$5 per 1,000 impressions. If you choose this option, pay attention to the CTR (Click Through Rate) - this tells you the percentage of time people actually click the ad. Low CTR tells you the ad is not compelling or attracting customers - time to edit and update it.

CPC (Cost Per Click): Also known as PPC or "Pay Per Click," you only pay when people click the ad. This can cost anywhere from $0.25 to $3.00+ per click; the rate depends on the popularity of the keywords you've chosen.

Another advertising option besides Google Adwords and Facebook Ads is popular blogs and websites. Do you know a site that is adored by your target market? Consider buying ad space there. Ask for a rate card and determine if it's within your budget.

I've never advertised on blogs myself. Instead, I like to partner with them and run giveaways or special promotions. This is an effective way to reach the same audience and it doesn't cost anything other than some products. Read more about it below.

PARTNER UP

There's so many advantages to partnering with other businesses. First, it's free marketing. Also, you're exposed to a whole new audience and it builds credibility. Finally, popular websites bring an instant boost in recognition and revenue for your business.

Find other blogs, websites, and businesses that cater to your target demographic. Who sells different types of products to your ideal customer? For example, crafters who make bridal headwear would do well partnering with bridal gown designers, stylists, and wedding photographers. Why not partner with top wedding planners and offer 20% off to their customers? Partners love getting exclusive deals for their customers and you'll love getting their business.

Here's an easy way to find potential partners: start an online search with your keywords. Get more leads by adding "blog" or "forum." You might also find leads with Google Alerts; you'll learn more about that below.

Once you've got a list of potential partners, research them. Check out their social media accounts - are they active? Do they have a lot of followers? Are there comments on their blog posts?

> •**PRO TIP**• Check out potential partners' website stats with Alexa (www.alexa.com) or Compete (www.compete.com). Enter any domain name and see how it ranks in terms of popularity and number of visits. Yes, this information is easily available and it helps tremendously with strategic marketing.

What to do with marketing partners

Do things that benefit your partner as much as you:

Offer to be a guest contributor: If you're familiar with the website and its audience, offer to write an article or publish a video. People are always looking for content, and if you offer something useful they'll likely take it.

Propose an exclusive discount: Offer 20% off to your partner's readers or customers. Use a coupon code with your partner's name and it will feel ultra-exclusive.

Suggest a giveaway: Recommend ways to bundle your products together or host a giveaway. For example, a lot of women use our Medium Pouch as a makeup bag. I've partnered with a popular makeup retailer and several beauty blogs to give away one Medium Pouch or "makeup bag" to a lucky winner. To enter the contest, people had to "like" eThreads on Facebook, "follow" on Twitter, or visit the website and leave a link to their favorite bag. These giveaways are always successful and benefit both eThreads and our partners.

GOOGLE ALERTS

Have you heard of Google Alerts? It's an amazing service from Google that sends regular email alerts about any topic you want. Most people monitor their names and business, but did you know Google Alerts is quite possibly *the* most powerful marketing tool in your arsenal ... and it's free?!

Why is Google Alerts such a great resource? First, it's a convenient way to track your name in the news and monitor VIPs. Also, it's easy to study the competition and learn what they're up to. It's also useful for generating content to share with your audience. Finally, it's really handy when you're shopping for bargains or new equipment for your business.

Head over to www.google.com/alerts to get started. You'll see several boxes: *Search query* (what you're looking for), *Result type* ("everything" is a great place to start), *How often* ("once a day" is fine), *How many* (start with "all results" then edit later if you need to), and *Deliver to* (your email address). You can set up to 1,000 alerts, so ... it's basically limitless.

Now that you're familiar with Google Alerts, flip the page to learn search query tips to optimize your alerts.

Google Alert Search Query Tips:

"exact search query"	Use quotation marks (" ") around your search query to improve accuracy. Especially important with names. **Ex:** *"Emily Worden"* (If I didn't have quotes around my name, I'd get alerts with Emily AND Worden.)
- exclude items	Use a minus sign (-) to exclude irrelevant terms from your search query. **Ex:** *"Emily Worden" -runner* (There is an Emily Worden who runs and I don't want alerts about her.)
link:yourdomainname.com	Use (link:) to see who is talking about your site. **Ex:** *link:emilyworden.com* (This shows everyone who is linking to my site.)
site:anydomainname.com	Use (site:) to search a site for specific content or mentions. **Ex:** *"Emily Worden" site:sheownsit.com* (This tells me every time my name is mentioned on the site.)
related:sites you like	Use (related:) to find other sites similar to the one you like. An excellent marketing tip for finding prospects. **Ex:** *related:sheownsit.com*
location:your neighborhood	Use (location:) to keep up to date with local industry info or news anywhere else in the world. *Tip: Change the "Everything" tab to "News" for best results.* **Ex:** *"marketing" location:Boston, MA*

Critical Google Alerts to set up:

Since Google Alerts is such a valuable marketing tool, use it to its full advantage. Remember, you have up to 1,000 alerts, so go nuts.

(1) *Set up alerts on you and your business:* Set up alerts with your name, business name, and domain name. It's a handy way to discover press mentions.

(2) *Set up alerts on keywords relevant to your industry:* A great way to stay on top of the trends in your industry. Also, set up alerts on keywords relevant or interesting to your customers; it's a useful resource when you're writing content.

Bonus tip Change your "Result type" from "Everything" to "Discussion" to find forums where your topic is being discussed. This is an excellent way to assess the market and even join the conversation.

156

(3) *Set up alerts on your top clients:* This is an advanced tip, but if you have major clients like stores, wholesalers, or top customers, set up alerts about them. Not only their name, but also topics that might interest them. When you find an article of interest, email a link or better yet, print it out and send with a personalized card. It's a great way to demonstrate expertise.

(4) *Set up alerts on your dream customers, VIPs, and influential people in your industry:* Stay up to date about their activities and then you're perfectly prepped when you're ready to pitch them. It's also a great opportunity to reach out with personal emails and cards, see #3.

(5) *Set up alerts on your competition:* Not only their name, but also domain name and names of their top team members. Do exactly as we discussed in #1, but for your top competitors instead. Pay attention to what their customers are saying - how you can serve them better?

(6) *Set up alerts for fun stuff like sales and Craigslist:* Oh yeah, Google Alerts are fun too! Get sweet deals with your favorite retailers, just set up alerts for *"sales" site:nameofyourfavoritestore.com.* When I'm in the market for a sewing machine on Craigslist, my search query is *"sewing machine" site:craigslist.com* and I'm notified when they become available.

*Bonus Tip** Set a budget with (..). Ex: *"Sewing Machine" site:craigslist $300..$500.*

MARKETING IDEAS

Is your mind bursting with marketing ideas yet? Hang on, I've got a few more:

Blog: Update your blog regularly with relevant content. It's useful marketing because it engages your audience and improves SEO. See the "blogging" section of Chapter 6 for more information.

Contests: Host a contest to generate excitement. For example, post a picture of your newest product and ask people to nickname it. Choose your favorite and the winner gets the product or a gift certificate to your online store.

Comment on forums: Be active in the craft communities on Etsy (www.etsy.com), Craftster (www.craftster.org), Get Crafty (www.getcrafty.com), or any other websites dedicated to your skill and target audience.

Etsy: Besides commenting on the forums, Etsy Treasuries and Communities are both great marketing opportunities. Check out Chapter 11 for more information.

SEO: Continually focus on improving your SEO to rank higher in web searches. See Chapter 6 for more information.

Email signature block: Include your name, title, business name, website, and links to social media. Also include something small like a coupon code, picture of your latest work, special announcement, link to an exclusive deal, customer testimonial ... just something extra for a little marketing boost.

Social Media: Share pictures of your work on Flickr, pin Etsy items on Pinterest, offer design advice on Twitter ... there's so many ways to market on social media - and it's absolutely free. Check out Chapter 14 for more information.

Follow the trends: Associate yourself with something that's trending or popular. For example, can you make Super Bowl-themed products? How about a video sharing your favorite Christmas cookie recipe? This kind of stuff is picked up by bigger press outlets all the time. If you make wearable art, can you make something that's trendy? For example, owls are huge right now. Smart crafters should make owl pins, jewelry, hats, gloves, bags, and notebook covers. See Chapter 3 for more about working with trends.

Partner with charities and nonprofits: These groups are always looking for fun ways to raise money. Offer your products at 50% off and allow the group to resell the products and keep the profits. Donate products to their silent auctions or fundraising events. Create products exclusively for their fundraising purposes, like limited-edition prints or bags with their name sewn on it. I've partnered with charities by giving them their own discount code - anyone can use the discount code (say for 20% off) then I donate a portion of that sale to the charity. Other times I've just donated a portion of all sales to charity. Partnering with charities is a win-win situation: the organization raises money and you enjoy free (or relatively low-cost) marketing, a great press opportunity, exposure to a whole new audience, and the happiness of knowing your business is helping other people. Write a press release and contact your local newspaper about the collaboration for extra press mileage.

HOW TO GET PRESS

Press is important for brand awareness, social proof, credibility, authority, and bragging rights. Press mentions are a stamp of approval for your business and a big boost for sales. Getting press is so important that I've dedicated Chapter 16 to it. It's a critical part of the marketing plan though, so I have to mention a few things in this chapter.

Just like you did for marketing partners, look for blogs, magazines, and popular websites that would be interested in featuring your product. Remember, your product has to appeal to their target audience. If your stuff is seasonal (e.g., Christmas ornaments), note that print magazines usually have a five month lead time - that means you should be pitching Christmas ornaments in the summer.

It's easier to get press locally; start pitching close to home. Local press like to feature local stories. Plus, smaller press outlets are followed by larger press outlets, and they are always looking for interesting regional stories.

Before pitching anyone, come up with a unique story angle. What makes your product different or feature-worthy? What's the story behind it? Why should anyone care about your business? Press outlets love anything that's interesting or inspirational for their audience. It helps to write a press release first; see Chapter 16 for advice.

Just like you did for marketing partners and VIPs, find the contact names for your local, regional, and national press possibilities. Find the proper editors, writers, or contact names. Develop a relationship with them like you would marketing partners – follow on social media, send interesting articles, and maintain regular contact.

Publications prefer exclusivity, so start with your first pick and move down from there. Call the press outlet to verify your contact's title, address, phone number, and email address. Send contacts press kits specifically tailored to them. Use their name, location, and say something about their newspaper or blog. Mention why their readers would care about your product. Send the press kit and follow up a month later if you don't hear anything.

Never made a press kit before? No sweat, it's pretty easy; you'll read all about it in Chapter 16. For now understand that a good press kit is necessary for any journalist or blogger to take your seriously. Have a downloadable version of a press kit on your website too. Include fact sheets, press releases, and high-resolution photographs available for download. The press love it when you're organized and easy to work with; it often makes the difference if you're published or not.

If you do get press, congratulations! Share it on social media, publish it on your website, blog about it, and advertise it in the next postcard. Also, keep the momentum going - how can you get press like this consistently?

Hiring a publicist

Publicists are professionals at getting press - they do it every day. You can pay someone to get you into national magazines and possibly on TV. They're expensive though, think $1,000-$5,000/month. They add a lot of pressure to the business too - can you handle the attention that comes with getting national press, including an overnight onslaught of orders? Publicists also want you updating products often - they need to introduce fresh material to keep you relevant in the media scene. If you're unable to commit to a full-time publicist right now, consider hiring one temporarily to help develop a marketing plan or train you on media etiquette.

When you're ready to hire a publicist, start by asking other artists, crafters, and small business owners for referrals. It's better to get suggestions from people just like you. Ask Etsy or another crafter forum. Understand though that many publicists are selective with their clients; they want to work with people who deliver products and results. They'll likely want you to sign a contract for at least six months too. That's because good press takes time; usually a few months pass before there's some serious traction.

On that note, I'll say one final thing about marketing - there's nothing short-term about it. Getting press and developing relationships is a long-term, ongoing process. When you're planning the marketing calendar, include time for press outreach. Don't be frustrated if you don't see results right away. Stick with it. Like all good things in life, getting great press takes time.

Chapter 14:
NAVIGATE SOCIAL MEDIA.

"If people like you, they'll listen to you, but if they trust you, they'll do business with you." - **Zig Ziglar**

Whenever I mention social media people start to groan. I get it, I really do. I run several accounts myself and it's the least exciting part of my day. You know what is exciting though? Getting new customers, free market research, and insider access to VIPs. Yup, social media can do that and so much more.

SOCIAL MEDIA IS HUGE AND INFLUENTIAL

Exactly how big is social media? Well, there's over 1.2 billion users on Facebook alone. Allow me put it this way - if Facebook were a country it'd be the second most populated on the planet, just behind China. According to an August 2013 report released by Facebook, 128 million Americans visit the site everyday - that's 40% of the US population![1] And that's just Facebook - let's also consider Twitter, Pinterest, Instagram, Tumblr, Reddit, and all the new social media sites that seem to pop up every day.

Not only is social media big, but it's influential. People trust recommendations from others they know, and they're willing to spend more money on something that's recommended by friends. In fact, consumers are 70% more likely to make a purchase based on social media referrals.[2] Not only that, 43% of social media users purchase a product after sharing or favoriting it on Facebook, Twitter, and Pinterest.[3]

The point is, everyone is already on social media, it's an influential tool, and conversations are happening with or without you. Get behind social media and use it for competitive advantage. Research your industry and competition. Interact with customers and get valuable feedback about products. Make connections with influential editors, bloggers, and VIPs too.

THE MAJOR SOCIAL MEDIA SITES

Facebook: I'm betting you're already familiar with the site that virtually started social media. You're probably already on Facebook and connecting with old friends. Did you know Facebook also connects you with customers? Create a business page and use it as your business hub.

There are already hundreds of excellent resources that explain how to set up a Facebook business page step-by-step so I'm not covering that here (do an internet search for "How to start a Facebook Business Page" to get started), but I am telling you why you need to do it *now*.

Consider your Facebook business page a mini-website. It has all your business information plus pictures, links to blog posts, and interesting articles. Your Facebook page is a community-building website that is easily sharable among friends and fans. Not only that, but *Facebook Insight* provides powerful statistics about your business page such as traffic, popular posts, and keywords. It's useful and it's *free.*

Twitter: It's really popular - as of February 2014, there were over 243 million active visitors a month. Like Facebook, Twitter is great for networking and connecting, but messages are limited to 140 characters. It's a micro-blogging site - it's meant for quick updates, not long posts. I recommend leaving 20 characters free for people to reply, so really you're working with 120 characters. If you're also including a link or picture, there's even less characters available. It's a little tricky at first, but you'll get the hang of it and the site does have its advantages.

Go to www.twitter.com to open an account, all you need is an email address. There are thousands of great resources that explain Twitter in depth, but I want to mention a few things here:

Twitter Tip #1: Have conversations with other users using @reply. Anytime you want to start a public conversation with someone, "reply" to one of their tweets. Your message will start with @theirname. This way anyone can follow the conversation and chime in themselves.

Twitter Tip #2: Use Direct Messages (DM) for private conversations. Direct messages are sent only between you and the follower, as long as you both are following each other. No one else can see DMs but they are also limited to 140 characters.

Twitter Tip #3: Give credit to others with Retweet (RT) and "via." If you like someone's message and want everyone else to see it, click "Retweet" and the original message will appear with "RT" in front of it. If you want to change the original message and add your personal spin on it, add "via @theirname" to give the original writer credit.

Twitter Tip #4: Share the love on Follow Fridays. Social Media is all about building relationships and Follow Fridays are a great way to do it. Every Friday, send a message with the Twitter names of some people you like to follow and add #FF or #FollowFriday (those are hashtags, more about them later).

Twitter Tip #5: Create Twitter Lists. Create public or private lists of people you follow to stay up to date at a glance. For example, I made private lists for my competitors and VIPs. Then I quickly scan those lists without wading through my whole Twitter feed. You can create public lists such as "People I Admire" for everyone to see - it's a great way to build relationships with VIPs because they'll see they're on your list.

Twitter Tip #6: Thank followers and follow them back. If someone starts following you, send them a direct message and tell them how much you appreciate it. Include a call to action in your message like, "Thanks for the follow! Check out my site ethreads.com to design your own bag - let me know what you think!" (Warning – some of the "followers" are robots or spam. Confirm the follower is a real person before you interact with and/or follow them back.)

Instagram: 150 million people use this photo- and video-sharing app to turn snapshots into creative pieces of art. Thanks to a multitude of filter options, photos can look sun-kissed and cheery, pixelated and mysterious, or bright and bold. The app is available on smartphones and tablets and photos or videos can be shared instantly on Twitter, Facebook, and Tumblr. Your gallery can be public or private, and you can follow friends, businesses, and public figures just like Twitter or Facebook. You and your followers interact by liking and commenting on each other's photos.

Instagram Tip #1: Don't use too many filters. Even better, don't use any at all. Filters are distracting. Take beautiful shots and just crop them instead.

Instagram Tip #2: There's at least a dozen handy smartphone apps that take professional-looking photos. Start an internet search for "best smartphone camera apps for Instagram" to see the latest.

Instagram Tip #3: Add the location to your pictures. People like knowing where pictures are taken and some people search Instagram pictures by location.

Instagram Tip #4: Create text-only pictures announcing contests or special offers. Make it easy to read. Outline the contest terms and any important information. Search Instagram for #contest, #sale, or #coupon to get ideas (those are hashtags, we'll talk about them later).

Instagram Tip #5: Ask lots of questions. We'll talk more about social media content later, but for now understand that people love interacting on Instagram, so posting questions or asking for opinions goes a long way. For example, put two designs next to each other and ask people which they like better, A or B. I post pictures with two fabrics side-by-side and ask for opinions. These types of posts always have the highest engagement.

Instagram Tip #6: Don't fill the entire Instagram feed with products. Post pictures and videos of things you enjoy or inspire you. Post photos of your studio, materials, beautiful videos of sunsets or adorable animals, inspirational quotes, favorite recipes (with pictures of the food) ... people love to see the personal side of a business.

Pinterest: Pinterest is a photo-only site. Think of it like your virtual pinboard. (Get it? Pin-board? Pin-terest?) Lots of Etsy sellers are already on there and most of Pinterests' 70 million users are female. Just like Instagram, share pictures of your work, behind the scenes, and things that inspire you. Unlike Instagram, catalogue these items onto different "pinboards" and people can follow you or your individual pinboards. For example, I have pinboards like "Fashion," "Bags," "Food," and "DIY." "Food" is overwhelmingly the most popular board and that's ok, because every time someone sees one of eThreads' pins, even if it's about food, our name is attached to it.

Here's another way Instagram and Pinterest are different - Instagram is about taking pictures and posting them, Pinterest is about finding original content and "pinning" it. The trick with Pinterest is that you have to share content that is already on the web. That is, if you're publishing your own pictures, they have to be from your website, blog, Etsy page, or anywhere else your images are on the web.

Pinterest Tip #1: Try pinning original content. It's great to "re-pin" other stuff, but your followers overwhelmingly want to see original content, like items from your blog, Etsy page, or website.

Pinterest Tip #2: Give credit where it's due. Too often people re-pin a re-pin and the original source doesn't get credit. If people click on your pin they want to go right to the source material, not someone else's pinboard. Likewise, don't ever pin something from a Tumblr post because it's often impossible for others to find the source material.

Pinterest Tip #3: Try to share larger images; users prefer it.

Pinterest Tip #4: Put a watermark on your images; Pinterest doesn't mind and it helps protect your work. (Watermark images easily with any of the photo editing tools suggested in Chapter 6.)

Pinterest Tip #5: Share the love by creating boards like "Artists Who Inspire Me" or "Crafting Geniuses." It's a great way to get attention from people you admire.

Flickr: Also a photo-sharing site, Flickr is less about marketing and more about sharing great images. That said, don't be shy about posting beautiful pictures of your work for 87 million users to see.

Flickr Tip #1: Fill out the profile information with your business information. Link to your website, Etsy shop, blog, and social media accounts.

Flickr Tip #2: Put a link to your blog in the description. It's against Flickr's terms of service to post a link to your store in a photo description, but you can link to a blog.

Flickr Tip #3: Join groups of other people involved in your craft. Participate in groups your target audience would join too. Consider joining groups outside your craft as well. For example, if you love kayaking, join other groups about kayaking or outdoor sports. Those people will see your profile and get to know your work as an indie artist.

Flickr *Tip #4:* "Heart" or "favorite" other people's pictures. It's great for networking and marketing. Plus, it's good karma.

Tumblr: There are 216+ million monthly users on this blogging/photo-sharing/networking site. People start Tumblr pages about anything. Create one about your business, your products, and your journey as a working indie artist. Post long text, add images, link to other social media accounts … just like you would with any of the sites above.

Google+: This site is handy for connecting and conversing with 300+ million members including other business owners, makers, and creators. Some businesses also create Google+ "Hangouts" in order to interact directly with their customers.

LinkedIn: Use LinkedIn to connect with 300 million professionals all over the world. It's a valuable networking site even for indie artists; it's worth setting up a profile. Be active in groups and make connections with others in your field. Ask your followers for feedback just like you would other social networks.

THAT'S TOO MUCH! WHERE DO I START?

With two websites. Just two. If you try to do them all you'll do it poorly and lose your mind in the process. Two websites are a manageable, perhaps even fun, way to start.

Start with a Facebook business page for four reasons:

(1) You're likely already on Facebook or know someone who is, so you can get comfortable fast.

(2) Invite all your friends to "like" your page; it's a great start.

(3) Facebook reaches a large target audience.

(4) Once your Facebook page is up and running, check out *Facebook Insights* too. It ranks your popular posts and provides valuable demographic information like age, gender, and location. This helps identify your target customer.

For the second site, go where your audience is. For artists and crafters, I'd say it's Pinterest. That audience is largely female, and as we know women make 80% of the household purchasing decisions. Plus, women are more likely to share content and tell their friends.

If you're feeling up to the task, get into Twitter next. Though it's not a very visual site, it *is* awesome for networking and connecting.

Find new customers and interact with VIPs, editors, and favorite bloggers.

OK, one more recommendation. Open up a LinkedIn account. You don't have to use it too often, but it's handy for networking and making connections.

No matter where you go, here's a few social media tips that apply everywhere:

(1) Whichever sites you choose, reserve your name on all the sites right now. Even if you never use the account, prohibit someone else from taking it and pretending to be you.

(2) Be consistent on all your sites: use the same name, picture, logo, and voice. Keep the brand consistent so customers can recognize you anywhere.

(3) Before diving into social media, define your goals. This is just like we talked about in Chapter 1 - decide what you want to accomplish and how you're going to do it. Consider your metrics too - are you trying to increase followers on Facebook or going for more retweets on Twitter? These kind of questions help develop your social media strategy.

NOTE: *How to choose a profile name and picture:* Your profile name and picture should be consistent across all social media sites. Here's some things to consider:

Name: Different sites have different length requirements; keep your profile name under 12 characters to be safe. Also, incorporate your name and what you do. For example, "eThreadsBags" is better than "eThreads." Why? Because few people know the eThreads brand name, but adding "bags" piques interest; people want to learn more.

Picture: Some people recommend using a picture of yourself because customers like to identify the person behind the brand. Others recommend using a picture of your best product so people get a sense of what you do. I'm going to cheat and say do both - the best profile picture is of you holding one of your products or working at your studio. This way people see you, your product, and a story. Remember, this image is going to be tiny so don't put too much detail into it - keep it simple and easy to see.

WHAT TO SAY ON SOCIAL MEDIA

People engage with brands on social media to learn about new products, keep up with daily activities, participate in coupons and contests, and provide feedback. Social media is *not* about advertising or pushing your message. Social media is about having conversations and building relationships. It's all about communication - talk with people, not at them.

Social media is not an overnight fix for short-term sales. Instead social media nurtures long-term relationships with customers to keep them engaged with your business.

The Social Media Formula: There's a magical formula for social media marketing and it goes something like this:

80% Entertainment + 20% Advertising = 100% Social Media Formula

According to the Social Media Formula, *only 1 in 5 messages should be business related.* The rest should be something *sharable or interactive.*

Shareable: Post things that you like and others will like too: quotes, inspirational messages, jokes, beautiful images, or funny pictures. Include images of behind-the-scenes at your studio or pictures from a day in your life (your neighborhood, pet, hobbies, favorite dinner, etc...) People like personal posts - it's highly sharable content. Ask for pictures of customers using your product; that's highly sharable content too.

Be educational - share a tip or interesting story your readers will enjoy. If you make travel bags, share an article about the next great vacation spot. If you make ceramics, share popular recipes that can be baked in your casserole dish.

Interactive: Ask questions; your audience loves responding and interacting to inquiries. I ask for fabric and design advice all the time - they're some of our most popular posts and our customers have really insightful suggestions.

Ask questions about current events: "What are your Memorial Day plans?" "Happy New Year! What's your resolution?" "It's going to be beautiful weather this weekend - are you doing anything fun?"

Join conversations. Jump into chats that are happening online and ask your readers for their opinions too.

Hold a contest, something like "50% off when we reach 1,000 Likes" or "Caption this photo and win a free pin." You could even use a contest to solicit testimonials. For example, "Tell us about all the stuff you carry in your eThreads bag," or "Share pictures of your favorite meal served in our ceramic dishes."

Finally, partner up with other websites and host a contest like we talked about in Chapter 13.

After you've entertained 80% of the time, use the last 20% to advertise. Offer a special discount to social media followers or tell them about new products launched on your site. Talk about a big order you just scored or the deadlines for special holiday delivery.

Whatever you say, be authentic. People love to know they're talking with a live person and they're doing business with honest people. Be personal, tell stories, share pictures - help customers get to know you better and feel more comfortable doing business with you.

Social media checklist: Keep your social media formula on track with a social media checklist. Here is the weekly checklist I created when I started social media marketing. You see it includes sharable, entertaining, and interactive content. You are allowed to advertise or promote only after these objectives have been achieved. Use this checklist with a social media scheduler like Hootsuite (www.hootsuite.com, more on that below) for effective and efficient social media marketing:

Week of 3/11 Twitter	Week of 3/11 Facebook
Picture	Picture
Retweet	Question
Quote	News Article
Favorite	Quote
News Article	Funny
Trending Topic	Testimonial
Random	Random
Thematic	
Thank followers	
Funny	
#FollowFriday	

DIRTY LITTLE SECRETS ABOUT SOCIAL MEDIA

Here are my time-tested tips for increasing engagement and snagging more followers on social media:

The power of hashtags: What is a hashtag? It's most popular on Twitter, Instagram, and Facebook and technically it's just a word with a "#" in front of it. Really though, it's the key to social media success. Use hashtags to direct conversations, track trends, monitor your competition, and so much more.

People use hashtags to track topics (#marketing), monitor breaking news (#Cairo), and follow special events (#election). Sometimes hashtags are funny (#ThingsKidsSay) or part of a trending topic (#SuperBowl).

There are well-known hashtags too like #ThrowbackThursday (#TT) or #FollowFriday (#FF, we discussed this above). See what's popular right now with What the Trend (www.whatthetrend.com). Use Trendsmap (www.trendsmap.com) to view popular trends by location.

Why should you care about all this? It's important to use trending hashtags; a lot more people see posts that include popular hashtags. Use hashtags to keep track of your industry too. I use hashtags in eThreads posts like #custom, #bag, #fabric, or #fashion. Other like-minded people who are searching those hashtags will see my message and hopefully continue to eThreads' site.

Six hashtag rules

(1) *Use a limited number of hashtags.* Include hashtags in every post on Twitter, Facebook, and Instagram, but never more than 1-3 per post. Instagram is an exception, you can use up to 10 there. Everywhere else, keep it short or it looks obnoxious.

(2) *Use appropriate hashtags.* Don't just pick a popular but irrelevant hashtag and attach it to your post; it's considered spammy and turns people off. Scan the trends for what's popular and only choose hashtags that are relevant to your business.

(3) *Search for hashtags related to your niche and "favorite" or retweet stuff people say.* For example, if you sell soy candles, search social media sites for #candles, #soy, or #ecofriendly and get involved in the conversation.

(4) *Track hashtags the competitors use.* For example, I like to search #Longchamp or #Coach to see what people are saying about those bags. Then I study Longchamp and Coach's social media sites and note the hashtags they use.

(5) *Study other hashtags your target audience uses.* I had never heard of *#ootd* before starting social media. It means *Outfit of the Day* and I discovered that lots of people who love fashion use that hashtag. Study the hashtags your target audience uses and include them in posts.

(6) *Use Hashtagify (www.hashtagify.me) to find popular hashtags in your industry.* For example, type in "jewelry" and you'll see #Etsy, #handmade, #fashion, and #vintage are popular. Use these hashtags in your posts to boost engagement.

The power of pictures: Social media posts with pictures are viewed and shared more than posts without. Pictures tell stories and people love stories. Attach pictures to your social media posts to increase sharability and popularity.

Shorten links: Long URL links look sloppy and you don't have a lot of characters to spare. Use URL shorteners to cut the length of links in half and save valuable characters. My favorite site is Bit.ly (www.bit.ly) but there are lots of other options. Social media schedulers like Hootsuite (www.hootsuite.com) or Tweetdeck (www.tweetdeck.com) have built-in link shorteners too.

Interact and like: Get involved in the communities on your social media sites. "Like" other people's posts, retweet their messages, comment or answer their questions, and share their pictures. The more involved and interactive you are with others, the more they'll reciprocate by sharing and interacting with you.

"Like" the same amount of people who "like" you. It's social media courtesy to follow most of the people who follow you. Keep the number of "follows" and "followers" relatively equal. People are turned off if you have 1,000 followers but only follow 100 people; it violates unspoken social media rules.

> •**PRO TIP**• Interact with your VIPs and build relationships with them on social media. See Chapter 15 for more information.

Go where your customers go: Hang out in the communities where your customers are. If you sell furniture, spend time in home design and decor communities. If you knit, find the popular Facebook pages and Instagram accounts of other knitters and get involved in the conversation. We sell bags so I'm active in the fashion and accessory communities.

Post regularly: Don't post five days in a row then disappear for two weeks; you can't build a loyal following that way. Try posting something and interacting with people on each social media site every day. If you're not able to post regularly, space out the messages over time, like every two or three days.

Schedule posts to save time: It's a lot of effort to post and interact every day; save time and plan posts in advance. As we discussed in Chapter 13, use a social media scheduler like (my favorite) Hootsuite (www.hootsuite.com), or Tweetdeck (www.tweetdeck.com). Write all the posts at once (remember the 80/20 rule - 80% entertaining and 20% advertising) and schedule one or two posts every day. Then, spend just 15 minutes a day on social media sites to "like," comment, or retweet other people's stuff.

Post during popular days and times: There is no perfect science to the ideal date and time for social media, but there are some general guidelines:

(1) *People are on social media a lot during the weekend* - you might not be working on the weekend, but your social media should be. If you can only post one night a week, make it Sunday night when everyone is home and on their computers.

(2) *People are on social media during work*, particularly 1-3 pm (after lunch). Besides Sunday night, this is the second best time to post. Mondays are popular as people ease themselves back into the workweek. Thursdays and Fridays are good too because it's the end of the week and people are more relaxed at work and checking social media more often.

(3) *Don't forget about time zones* - I'm on the east coast, so when I post at 7:30 pm EST it's only 4:30 pm PST, which is commuting time on the west coast.

(4) *Experiment with different dates and times.* Facebook *Insights* gives you great statistics about how many people have viewed or shared your posts. Use that data to experiment with different dates and times to determine the most popular time to post.

(5) *Don't overdo it.* Facebook is a *personal* social media site; don't post more than once a day or you'll overcrowd followers' walls with "advertisements."

Post a lot (2-4 times a day) on Pinterest, Tumblr, Flickr, and Instagram but space out the posts so you don't overwhelm followers' feeds all at once.

Twitter is a free-for-all; everyone knows it's just about fast updates. Tweet up to a dozen times a day, people won't hate you for it.

Engage your VIPs: Set aside social media time to interact with your VIPs. I've interacted with TV personalities, magazine editors, and personal idols all through social media. You can also engage the assistants, interns, and associate editors at your VIP spots for a greater chance of personal interaction and name recognition. See Chapter 15 for more information.

How to get more followers: Engage everyday - "like" other people's stuff, ask questions, and post sharable content. Use popular hashtags in your posts so more people see them. Team up with popular people and blogs for special events and promotions. Host your own contest and offer a special discount when you reach 1,000 followers.

If you want more likes, retweets, or followers, *just ask for it.* Studies have increasingly proven that posts that say "we're trying to get to 1,000 likes" or "please retweet" are more effective - people will often "like" or retweet things if you ask nicely.

ADVERTISING ON SOCIAL MEDIA

All the social media tips we've covered so far don't cost a thing, and that's how I like it. The best advertising is word-of-mouth - I've never had to pay for advertising and I don't think you should either. However, some people do want to know about advertising on social media so I'd be remiss to not address it here.

The biggest and best social media advertising option is Facebook Ads. Facebook makes money by selling advertisements and they offer targeted ads to your ideal audience. Because Facebook collects and mines personal data, they can define users by all sorts of demographics and interests. You could write an ad specifically for 18-25 year old females living in the Boston area who like crafts. Or target single people over 40 who like movies. Or furniture enthusiasts who enjoy eco-friendly products. Facebook's super-targeted ads are usually effective. Plus, Facebook helps you track ad response and target results.

You determine the cost of your Facebook ads. Choose between a daily or lifetime budget and Cost-per-Thousand impressions (CPM) or Cost-per-Click (CPC). In both cases you pay for the clicks or impressions received and the ad stops running when you've reached the top of your budget. Ads that include popular keywords are more expensive; you can get cheaper ads by being more specific. For example, "custom cotton handbags" is cheaper than "custom bags" because the latter is a very popular keyword.

The same rules that apply to Facebook Ads apply to most online advertising including Google Ads. I don't think you need to pay for ads, especially when you're starting out and the budget is tight, but don't completely rule them out for future use. See Chapter 13 for more details about online advertising.

You've just finished a crash course on social media! Is your head spinning? Go back and reread the chapter and jot down ideas to use right away. Gather up lots of content and spread it out over time.

Set your social media marketing goals too. Perhaps you could start joining groups this week, then try hosting a contest next week, then find potential marketing partners the week after that. Get into a social media scheduler like Hootsuite and try scheduling posts 1-2 weeks in advance. Experiment with different times on different sites to see what works best for your business. Most importantly, be personal, professional, and have fun.

---

[1] Saba, Jennifer. "Facebook Reveals Daily Users for U.S. and UK, Data Aimed at Advertisers." *Reuters*. N.p., 13 Aug. 2013.

[2] "New Data on How Social Media Drives Purchasing." *Vision Critical*. N.p., 26 June 2013.

[3] Ewing, Mike. "71% More Likely to Purchase Based on Social Media Referrals [Infographic]." *71% More Likely to Purchase Based on Social Media Referrals [Infographic]*. HubSpot, 9 Jan. 2012.

Chapter 15: **WOO VIPS.**

"If opportunity doesn't knock, build a door." - **Milton Berle**

VIPs are normally known as Very Important People, but I like to think of VIPs as Very *Influential* People. They are editors, bloggers, mentors, celebrities, and others who can skyrocket your business if they talk about it. Building relationships with the top influencers in your field is a highly effective, fun, and free marketing strategy.

TYPES OF VIPS

Everyone's VIPs are different, but they generally include popular bloggers, celebrities, personal heroes, and even organizations you admire.

Think about your field and the most influential people in it. For example, eThreads is in the fashion category so one of my VIPs is *Lucky Magazine*, a very popular shopping magazine. Rather than targeting *Lucky* directly, I identified the editors, associate editors, interns, and assistants at the magazine. In fact, if your VIP is an editor or CEO, follow their assistant, interns, and everyone working in their office. Why? Editors are extremely busy and probably won't notice you, but their assistants and interns are usually young, socially-savvy people who enjoy interacting with others online.

You want Mavens. In his insightful book *The Tipping Point*, Malcolm Gladwell talks about the importance of *Mavens* - those who have large groups of followers who look to the Maven for information and spread the word about what the Maven likes. Mavens run in wide circles and know a variety of influential people. Mavens could be editors. They might be bloggers. Many Mavens are famous personalities or popular authors. Other Mavens are the heads of organizations and groups. For example, if your product is largely targeted towards women, find Mavens who head organizations also targeted towards women like sororities, parenting groups, women's magazines, female-owned businesses, and support organizations.

VIPs could also be someone you admire. For example, I adore Barbara Corcoran, the business mogul who appears on ABC's television show *Shark Tank*. I've read her books, watched her lectures, and interacted with her on social media. I respect her strength of character, sense of humor, and savvy business knowledge. Is there anyone you admire and you'd like to know better? Keep reading to find out how.

HOW TO IDENTIFY VIPS

You might be able to list some VIPs off the top of your head. It's a great start, but here's some strategies to build a longer list:

(1) *Start an internet search with the best keywords associated with your product*. Target the results and get more leads by adding "blog" or "forum" to your search. Now you'll find websites that are discussing your exact field and the important people in it.

(2) *Identify the most popular magazines and websites in your field and the people behind it*. Research the staff behind your VIP magazines or websites. Review their social media accounts, blogs, and personal websites. Find the most influential people and build a relationship with them.

(3) *Good old-fashioned research*. Next time you identify a person or organization who might be a VIP, check out their website and social media. How many followers do they have? Are they active on their blog and social media accounts? How many people leave comments on their site? Get even more information with Alexa (www.alexa.com) and Compete (www.compete.com). Both sites give you basic website analytics, like number of visitors each month, for free. Paid subscriptions to these sites get you detailed information like number of unique visitors, time on site, pagerank, competitive sites, and so much more.

(4) *Determine their influencer score*. Influencer score?! Yup, it's a real thing. Check out these tools to evaluate your VIPs and their level of influence:

(a) *Social Inbox* (www.hubspot.com/products/social-inbox): This paid service from Hubspot allows you to create "smart lists" based on user data like influencer score and types of customers. Then choose which keywords you'd like to follow. The result - a highly targeted list of influential people who are talking about the topics in your field.

(b) *Twitalyzer* (www.twitalyzer.com): Get helpful insight for free on their homepage. Type in the name of any Twitter user and get their Klout score, number of followers, popular hashtags, and people who influence them the most. Free, fast, and valuable info at your fingertips.

(c) *Klout.com:* You'll see "Klout" scores listed everywhere, so let's talk about what it is and what it means. A Klout score is basically an influencer score. It's measured from 1-100; the higher the score, the higher your Klout. For example, President Obama's Klout score is 99 - unbelievably high - because he's on Twitter, Facebook, has a popular Wikipedia page and hundreds of thousands of people interact with him on social media. For someone who barely uses social media, their Klout score will likely be 20 or below. The average person's Klout score - someone who uses social media casually - is usually 40 or below. If someone's Klout score is over 63, they're in the top 5% of influencers and you want to work with them.

You automatically have a Klout score if you have a public Twitter account. How can you improve your Klout score? First, figure out your score by signing up at www.klout.com. Then, tell Klout what other social media sites you're on so they can include those in your score. Then, create highly shareable and interactive content that is informative, entertaining, and engaging (see Chapter 14 for more information). Also, start discussions on social media or jump into popular conversations. Finally, connect with people with high Klout scores and interact with them. The more you're discussed, mentioned, or interacted with on social media, the higher your Klout score.

WHAT TO DO WITH VIPS

Follow: Follow your VIPs on social media. They're most likely to recognize you if you're actively involved on all their networks.

Engage and entertain: Remember, the purpose of social media is to *communicate*, not sell. Don't be pushy with your VIPs, just engage with them.

For example, find things you have in common and strike up a conversation. Whenever you see stories they might find interesting, forward it with a short note. Find their office address and send cards on birthdays or during special events. Share, retweet, and comment on their posts regularly. Make them laugh or feel inspired with a great quote. Talk about how they influence you. Congratulate them when something great happens. Be memorable and stand out from the crowd.

Target with incentives: You want VIPs talking about your products, so get your products in their hands. Send samples or create special offers. Ask for their opinion on your product or website. Suggest a contest where one of their followers wins one of your products. Get your VIP thinking about how your business can benefit *them*.

Set up Google Alerts: We talked about Google Alerts in Chapter 13 and it's the easiest way to track VIPs. Set up alerts on your VIP, their organization, and their industry. Then send timely messages to your VIPs anytime they (or something they care about) are in the news.

Defend them: If you receive a Google Alert with something negative about your VIP, go online and defend them from attackers. Believe me, your VIP will notice.

Follow who they follow: Find out who your VIPs follow and follow those people too. It's so simple but so effective. You know why?

Let's say your VIP is a magazine editor who has hundreds of thousands of followers; they likely don't really care about most of those followers. But they DO care about the people they're following - probably just a few hundred people who are likely other magazine editors, celebrities, and VIPs. Become active on those people's accounts too (with your business name as the profile name, of course) and there's a greater chance your VIP will notice your posts.

BEHOLD THE POWER OF THE BLOGGER

Bloggers are people who operate their own web log. There are millions of bloggers who write about anything imaginable, and some make handsome careers doing it.

Top bloggers have lots of readers, an active social media presence, high advertising fees, and receive perks from companies all the time. Not only that, but the most popular blogs like Huffington Post, Drudge Report, and Politico are often the source for today's headlines. You'll regularly find CNN, *The New York Times*, and Fox News using these types of sites as sources.

Top bloggers are influential, but they're also under immense pressure. There are millions of blogs; it's a competitive field. Popular bloggers have to post constantly (sometimes up to 10 times a day) to satiate their readers. They must write about topics that are important to readers and engage with highly sharable content. Popular bloggers have to keep readership numbers high so advertising revenue is steady.

What does this mean to you? Everything! Your job is to identify the most influential bloggers in your field and get them to write about you. Remember - bloggers are under immense pressure and tight deadlines, so make their job easy.

How? *Write the story for them.* Pitch bloggers a compelling story or unique perspective their readers would love. Forward a press release that essentially has the article written for them. Explain how their readers would benefit from knowing about you. We'll talk about this more in Chapter 16.

Send bloggers free stuff to review too. Suggest a contest for their readers - I've done dozens of contests with popular blogs where we give away one Medium Pouch to a lucky reader. The blog readers enter the contest by "liking" eThreads on Facebook, Twitter, etc... and the blogger randomly selects one winning entry. Bloggers love contests because it provides something of value to their readers; you love contests for the free advertising (and new fans).

•Super Pro Tip• Here's a top-secret strategy about using blogs to your advantage. Oftentimes you'll see the big sites like Huffington Post or Gawker pull stories from smaller sites. Define your top-level blogger VIPs then write down their source sites (you'll always find sources in the body or at the bottom of articles). Then try to get your stuff published in those sources, which are often smaller and easier to get into. This is similar to the "follow who your VIPs follow" social media strategy I talked about earlier - it's easier to get the attention of your VIPs if you go where they go. Before you know it, you could turn a brief mention in a small blog to a front page blurb on Gawker.com.

Remember to follow the blogs and the people behind them on social media too. Engage with them regularly so you'll have a better chance of getting recognized and accepted onto the blog.

A NOTE ON CELEBRITIES

Do you dream of your favorite celebrity using your products? You could make it happen. First, follow the VIP steps I've outlined above - follow the celebrity, their assistants, their agent, their stylist, their hairdresser or makeup artist ... anyone who works for them. Then, engage with those people and build relationships with them.

Can't find that info easily and have a little cash to spare? Try Contact Any Celebrity (www.contactanycelebrity.com). For a $197 annual membership fee, you have access to celebrities, their agents and publicists, and their contact information. CAC offers a 14 day free trial before signing up. I have not tried the service myself but I know several people who like it.

NOTE: You can contact a celebrity and send a sample product, but there's a very good chance the sample will go home with someone else and the celebrity will never see it. Instead, try participating in celebrity gifting suites. These events usually happen in Los Angeles. They're most popular from September through March and particularly during award season in January and February. Celebrities attend gifting suites to get free stuff in exchange for taking pictures with the product. See Chapter 17 for more information.

Chapter 16: **GET PRESS.**

"Nothing BIG will happen in your life, until you build off of the many SMALL things" - **John Paul Aguiar**

Press mentions are the holy grail of marketing. Magazine articles, TV spots, blog posts - this kind of stuff is really valuable for business. Not only do press mentions mean high-value (and free) advertising, but they validate your business and introduce your product to an entirely new audience.

It's not too difficult to get press because most journalists, editors, and bloggers are under immense pressure to continually deliver valuable content. They welcome fresh ideas that appeal to their audience, especially if the story is essentially written for them.

That's what this chapter is all about. Whether you're writing a press release, assembling a press kit, or developing a story pitch, make it easy for the press to work with you. Provide the story, the media, and the background and you've got yourself a successful press pitch.

WHAT IS A PRESS RELEASE?

A press release is a 1-2 page document announcing something exciting about you or your business. Essentially all content in blogs, magazines, newspapers, and talk shows are created from press releases. Unless it's breaking news, the story you're reading in your favorite magazine was likely pitched via a press release that was picked up by an editor.

Thousands of press releases are sent every day by businesses looking to get free press. There's a different angle each time - new store opening, new product line, new management team - but the goal is always the same: to get the attention of writers and editors.

WHY WRITE A PRESS RELEASE

I know press releases are not as sexy or exciting as social media and other marketing tools, but they're reliably effective at accomplishing three things:

(1) *Free press:* Great press builds credibility and saves money on advertising fees.

(2) *Improved SEO:* Search engines read published press releases and this helps land you on the first page of Google. (Some sites like www.PRWeb.com even optimize their press releases before publishing to be extra Google-friendly.) Include keywords and links to your website in the press release to maximize exposure.

(3) *Build relationships:* Regularly send quality content to story-hungry editors and build relationships with VIPs.

Of all my free marketing tricks, the press release is the most immediately effective. While social media and VIPs are all about building long-term relationships, press releases are about one thing - getting press immediately.

HOW TO WRITE A PRESS RELEASE

Pick a subject: The press release will likely be about something new in your business - you opened an Etsy shop, collaborated with a new retailer, introduced a new product - but for goodness sakes, no one else wants to read that! Editors will definitely pass over a story that's all about you.

Press releases should be news stories, not sales pitches. Tie your press release to a current trend. It could be a national holiday, special event, or something in the news. For example, if you sell backpacks and back-to-school time is coming up, talk about great products for kids and list your bags. If you sell cat toys, write a press release about how much pet owners are spending on toys and quote yourself in the article.

Choose the unique story angle: Editors will be reading your press release and thinking, "So what?" They're always scanning with their readers in mind, so make your press release appealing to editors with an engaging story or newsworthy topic. Tell a story about overcoming adversity or achieving something amazing for your customers. Solve a popular problem or tie your business to a current trend. Link your business to a national holiday or special event. NYC-based PR pro Alix Abbamonte says:

> You have to get creative. Editors see the same thing over and over. Get their attention by equating your business to something happening in the news. Tie your business to a holiday. I did a Valentine's Day press release for an allergist titled *Allergic to Love* and she talked about romantic things people might be allergic to like perfume or chocolate. The story was picked up everywhere.

•**PRO TIP**• *Think local.* Write a press release just for your local news and bloggers. Why? Newspaper editors love local angles on national stories. Also, it's easier to get into your local paper than a national one. Finally, local news leads to national news. Interesting local stories are always picked up by major news outlets - you see it every day on the national news.

Answer the 5 Ws first: Remember, your press release is a *news story*, not a sales pitch. A good press release answers the who, what, when, where, why, and how in the first 250 words. Not only does this help busy editors, but your press release will often be published verbatim and cut short somewhere in the middle. Get your vital facts up front to ensure basic information is listed in the article. Spend the rest of your press release backing up facts and claims made in the first 250 words.

The headline is everything: I could write an entire chapter about why the headline is so important. It's the first thing your reader sees and it determines if they keep reading or move on. *A good headline offers a benefit to the reader and an incentive to keep reading.* Here's some tips to get you going:

(1) *Write the headline last:* This sounds counterintuitive because it's the first thing you see, but headlines are so short and so important it really should be the last thing you do. Wait until the entire press release is written then sum it up with the perfect headline.

(2) *Use attention-getting words:* Use words like: *how to, why, quick, easy, guarantee, results, sale, save, last chance.* Remember, people want to know what's in it for them.

(3) *Arouse curiosity:* Ask a question, make a provocative statement, or promise something outrageous. Use mystery and intrigue to get attention.

(4) *Use lists:* Try "Top 10 Ways to Decorate Your Home" (if you sell art or home furnishings) or "7 Reasons Why Buying Handmade Helps the Economy" (and mention your website in the article).

Writing tips: There isn't a standard press release format, but they all basically look the same. They all have a headline, location, company bio, and contact information. Do an internet search for "press release format" and choose which you like best. Here's some more tips:

(1) *Keep your press release under 1 page, ideally 400 words or less.* You can go to two pages if you want, but most people won't read that far. Aim for 3-5 short paragraphs.

(2) *Attach pictures and videos whenever possible.* Attaching media like pictures and videos to press releases increases engagement. Include captions that are descriptive and keyword-rich, these will get picked up by search engines.

(3) *Try to send press releases once a month* to remain relevant and build relationships with your contacts. Press releases are a lot of work, don't beat yourself up if you can't do one a month. Just try to do at least one press release a quarter (four times a year).

(4) *Don't include a date at the beginning of the press release,* say "FOR IMMEDIATE RELEASE" instead. Type it just like that - in all caps, often you'll see it in bold. Why? Because if you include a date, people will ignore the release a week after it's published. Instead, "FOR IMMEDIATE RELEASE" lives on in eternity.

(5) *Quote yourself in the press release.* Editors love quotes because it adds a personal touch to the piece and they don't have to fact-check it. Plus, it's a great way to get your name in the press release without sounding like a sales pitch.

(6) *Make the press release keyword-rich.* Mention your name, business name, and website once, then include all relevant keywords. Google likes keywords and this helps get your website closer to the first page for relevant search terms.

WHAT TO DO WITH YOUR PRESS RELEASE

Distribute! If you wrote a press release specifically for editors or bloggers, send the press release directly (email *and* snail mail) with a note that says something like, "I thought you might find this interesting." Follow up with a phone call 2-3 later.

Next, send the press release to your VIPs, the 10 or 20 people whom you admire and/or are influential in your industry (see Chapter 15 for more information). Send it via post with a personal note. It's a great excuse to stay in contact without sounding like a sales pitch.

Then, think about any journalists, editors, or bloggers who are in a similar industry or share a target demographic who might be interested in your press release. Send the press release via email and regular mail and follow up (with a phone call if possible) 2-3 days later.

Next, distribute among the press release sites. There are a lot of free press release publishing websites, I like www.PRNewsWire.com. (Also check out www.BusinessWire.com, www.GlobeNewsWire.com, www.MarketWire.com, and dozens of other sites.) Paid sites offer wider distribution and greater access to quality VIPs; I like PRWeb (www.PRWeb.com) starting at $99/year.

> •PRO TIP• Press releases are generally published Monday and Tuesday mornings from 8-9 am EST, so try sending a different date and time to stand apart from the crowd. Send your press releases at odd times like 10:12 am to avoid getting buried in the releases at the top of the hour.

Finally, publish the press release on your website. Put it in your "News" section to increase credibility and authenticity. This also helps SEO - since you included keywords in the press release, it will help get you to the front page of Google for your category.

THE PITCH LETTER

When you're pitching specific journalists include a "pitch letter" in your correspondence. A pitch letter is a brief introduction in email or letter form that covers the following:

(1) *Personal introduction:* Never say "Dear editor" - use their names! Also, if you're pitching a magazine, don't write to the editor-in-

chief directly. Instead, contact the editor in charge of the department you're pitching, like fashion, design, editorial, art, or creative directors. Look for these names on the masthead of the magazine or with an internet search.

(2) *Something personal about their media:* Mention something you like about their website or magazine. Make it personal so they know you've done your homework.

(3) *Link your product to their readers:* Journalists and editors will be reading the letter thinking, "So what?" Answer that question by explaining how their readers will benefit knowing about your product. Give them a unique angle; make it really easy for them to write a story.

(4) *Be brief:* Use short sentences, bullet points, and short paragraphs. Editors are very busy and usually receive thousands of pitches a week. The more you type, the less likely they are to read it.

(5) *Attach images:* Choose well-lit, high-quality images they can publish. (See Chapter 6 for more information about taking good pictures.) If you're emailing the pictures, keep it under 800 pixels and offer high-resolution downloads on your website.

(6) *Include your contact info:* Name, email, address, phone number, LinkedIn, Twitter. Make it easy for them to follow up.

(7) *Be timely:* Print magazines have a 4-5 month lead time. Pitch Christmas sweaters in July and beach bags in January.

•**Super Pro Tip**• Get in contact directly with top journalists and writers with HARO - Help a Reporter Out (www.helpareporter.com). You'll get daily emails filled with inquiries from journalists, writers, authors, bloggers, and TV producers. I've gotten loads of great opportunities from HARO - even a mention in *The New York Times*. Here's some HARO tips to get started:

(1) *Check the emails as soon as they go out and reply ASAP.* The journalist will receive dozens of responses to their inquiry (some get over 50) and the person who gets there first is often quoted first.

(2) *Answer the journalist's question in an intriguing, thoughtful, or unique way.* Say something they've never heard before to stand apart from the crowd.

(3) *Don't be pitchy - be informative.* The journalist doesn't care about you, they care about getting a good quote. Give them something

that relates to their story and not just a sales pitch about your business. Trust me, if they like your response, your business will be mentioned.

(4) *Use an interesting subject line.* A reporter will see the subject line before they see your response, so make it something they'll notice and want to click. Use their name and specifically mention the story. For example, "Bill, here's a great tip on firing bad customers."

(5) *You'll likely not get a response.* I've had lots of reporters use my quote and not tell me. Never ask the reporter if they got your response and if they liked it. They're on tight deadlines so they've likely written the piece, used your quote or not, then moved on with their lives. The best way to find out if you've been mentioned is to set up a Google Alert on your name, see Chapter 13 for more information.

CREATING PRESS KITS

Also called "publicity kits" or "media kits," they can be physical or electronic. Most professional media outlets want to see a press kit on your website or they won't take you seriously and move on to someone else. Remember, your reporter is working on a deadline, so make it really easy for them to work with you.

Press kit checklist

(1) *Basic biography of you (and any other key people involved in your business):* Your background, experience, where you're located, and special interests or skills.

(2) *Summary of your business:* What you do, what you make (including price points), who you serve, why you're in business, why you're unique, etc... Anything noteworthy that helps explain your business. Tell your story here - editors love stories.

(3) *Timeline:* The date you started the business, anything notable that has happened since (new product design, new website, new member of the team ...).

(4) *Testimonials:* A list of your best testimonials. Include name (first name and last initial, ex: Emily W.), location, and a picture of their order if possible; it increases credibility and believability.

(5) *Press:* Copies of press features or special awards.

(6) *Media:* Downloadable files of high-resolution pictures or videos of you and your products. If you have a catalogue (as discussed in Chapter 13), include it here too.

(7) *Contact info:* Your email, telephone, website, LinkedIn, Twitter, etc.

(8) *Consistency:* Ensure every piece of the press kit is in the same font, has your logo, and any other identifying characteristics are consistent. *Remember your branding.* The materials in your press kit should match the overall look and feel of the business. Include your logo and contact information on everything. If one of your inserts were to separate from the kit and someone picked it up, they should easily know where it goes.

(9) *Make everything flat and don't include anything small:* Your physical press kit will hopefully go in an editor's file drawer and not the trash. Make it easy for them. Ensure it stores flat and there aren't loose bits that could fall out.

> •**PRO TIP**• *Send product samples to your press VIPs.* If you want a better chance at getting published, send a small sample of your work with your press kit and pitch letter. Include a self-addressed stamped envelope or UPS account where they can charge the return of the sample. Sometimes samples aren't returned however, so don't send your favorite products.

Whew! We covered a lot of marketing strategies in the last four chapters. Marketing is a huge topic - remember, it covers anything done to generate sales. As you've seen, there's a lot of marketing strategies that don't cost money. My most effective marketing tactics are free, and yours can be too.

However, great marketing takes time. Whether you're on social media, contacting VIPS, or going after press, great marketing takes practice and patience. It's hard work; if it were easy everyone would be doing it and running million-dollar businesses. Marketing is necessary though because it's the primary way people learn about your products. Follow my tips and devotedly stick to it - you'll see a payoff, I promise.

Chapter 17: **GROW.**

"Never get so busy making a living that you forget to make a life." - **Rev Run**

If you've been running your business for a while, this chapter is for you. It's packed with ideas for improving your business and opening up new sales channels.

If you're just starting a business, don't worry about too much of this stuff yet; you already have a lot on your plate! Please just read the chapter with an eye towards the future.

Hire employees and interns

Hiring people is a lot of responsibility. Depending on the laws in your state, if a person works more than 20 hours a week they're considered a part-time employee and you're likely responsible for their workers' comp, payroll taxes, health insurance, and a host of other issues. Ask a local accountant and attorney about the employer responsibilities for your state. (We talked about hiring accountants and attorneys way back in Chapter 2 - flip back there for advice.)

You will likely need a payroll company to handle the legal and financial intricacies of paying employees, ask your accountant for suggestions. You'll also need employees to sign an NDA (non-disclosure agreement) or non-compete agreement. You can draft your own from a template, but it's safer to ask an attorney for help. Check out *The Craft Artist's Legal Guide* by Attorney Richard Stim for sample paperwork and excellent advice on hiring employees.

As we discussed in Chapter 3, find employees through Craigslist, posting in stores, or ads in your local paper - don't hire friends, it often doesn't work out well.

There are loads of employee opportunities through academic internship programs too. I've worked with several interns and it's always been a great experience. Interns are enthusiastic, smart, have lots of energy, and they're ok working in unconventional work environments. You might get better applicants if you offer a paid internship, but I've met excellent interns in unpaid positions too. If you want to offer course credit, it will have to be approved through the school. Talk to the university's career services department for information about listing your business as an internship opportunity.

Whether you're hiring employees or interns, the rules for being a good employer are the same:

(1) Listen to your employees, especially if they have concerns or complaints. Be patient too, particularly with new recruits. Allow mistakes and use them as teaching opportunities.

(2) Be very clear with instructions, timelines, and expectations; leave no room for ambiguity. Your employees should know exactly what they're doing and why it's important for the business.

(3) Delegate tasks and don't micromanage. Be explicit about the goals and deadlines, then let people work independently.

(4) Pitch in and be part of the team. Everyone loves to see the "boss" empty the trash can. Likewise, provide tools and support when employees ask for it.

(5) Keep your personal and business lives separate - don't try to be a best friend and a boss.

(6) Coach employees and encourage them; think of yourself like an instructor and a cheerleader.

(7) Schedule periodic reviews, ideally every three months. Ask them to review *you* as well - there are always things you can do better and their insight is helpful.

(8) Show your gratitude with praise and parties. Say "thank you," "good job," and host occasional pizza parties. Happy people are more productive; they work harder when their work is appreciated.

Apply the Pareto Principle

Remember way back in Chapter 2 we talked about the Pareto Principle? It dictates that *80% of outcomes result from 20% of the effort.* You're a busy person; you don't have time to waste. I urge you to think about the Pareto Principle and how to apply it to your life:

What's the most profitable thing in your business?

Who are your top customers?

What is your most effective marketing tool?

What makes you happiest in life?

The key here is to identify the 20% in your business and life that is the most *effective, beneficial, and rewarding* then focus exclusively on that. For example, take an honest look at your product line - are you investing time and energy into something that simply isn't selling? If so, it's time to drop that product, I don't care how much you love it.

Don't be busy, be productive. Only work on important activities with high-value clients. How would you rather make $500 - with 50 clients handing you $10 or with 10 clients handing you $50? Better yet, how about one client handing you $500? It's possible if you focus on the Pareto Principle.

Look bigger than you really are

It's easy to look like there's 10 people running your business rather than lonely ol' you. Here's how:

(1) Don't call yourself "CEO" - it screams startup. Call yourself "Founder," "Owner," or "Proprietor" instead.

(2) Don't list your home address or PO Box. Instead, rent a PO Box and list the physical address of your post office and "suite" number. For example, "1523 Main Street, Suite 410" sounds much better than "PO Box 410" and they both get to the same place.

(3) Set up a toll-free 800 number. You can do this for as little as $2/month with www.kall8.com. There's loads of other telephone options, see Chapter 2 for a review.

(4) Create multiple email addresses like "sales@mybusiness.com," "customerservice@mybusiness.com," and "contact@mybusiness.com." Use Google Apps for business (www.google.com/enterprise/apps/business) for $5/month to set up all these accounts and forward to just one email address.

Get your own studio

Having your own studio is great, but there are lots of drawbacks too. First, it's expensive. Besides paying rent every month, you likely have to deal with first month's rent, last month's rent, and security deposit. Plus you'll inevitably spend money setting up the studio - I spent hundreds of dollars alone on raw materials to make work benches. Consider getting insurance too - what if the building burned down or was broken into? Definitely have insurance if there's any customers visiting your studio or employees working there. Remember also internet fees, electricity, water, gas … there's all sorts of extras to build into the budget.

Plus, traveling to a studio takes time. If you're going to be there all day, you have to pack food and materials. Sometimes you'll bring work home with you and realize you forgot something critical back at the studio. You might end up with two sets of working materials too, and sometimes it's hard to keep track of what you've brought home and what's left at the studio.

If you do look for studio space, go where other artists go. Try to find buildings that specifically cater to artists - it's great for camaraderie, connections, and sharing ideas. Plus, artist buildings often have regular "open studio" events for the public, which is valuable promotion. Try looking on Craigslist too, many artists with studios to share advertise there.

Join an artist co-op

Is there an artist co-op in your town? In my Boston neighborhood I'm lucky enough to have three near me. Artist co-ops are usually members-only organizations that also operate a brick-and-mortar store. You usually have to apply for membership, be accepted, and pay a fee to join. Additionally, most co-ops expect you to donate a few hours a month to the store or organization. Co-ops offer great benefits - not only as a community resource, but they often buy advertising and host regular events. Plus, you get to sell in a store and be a part of the local artist community.

Collaborate with other artists

Stuck on product ideas? Want to reach different markets? Interested in learning something new? Identify artists who interest you or might complement your work and figure out ways to collaborate on a project. For example, I've partnered with visual artists on fabric designs for limited-edition bags.

Work for hire

Many people are looking for creative-types to make a lawn sculpture, paint a family portrait, design a custom engagement ring, photograph pets, sew a custom skirt, or create a dining room table from reclaimed wood. Advertise your unique skills and project capabilities on the following websites:

CustomMade (www.custommade.com): This fantastic website connects thousands of artists with consumers who are looking for one-of-a-kind custom projects. Apply to CustomMade to be a Maker. Once you're approved, you're instantly connected with customers looking for custom projects. List your own project ideas in your gallery and accept custom orders too. CustomMade takes 10% of the sale and provides attentive support along the way. I have not tried CustomMade myself, but I've heard from several creative entrepreneurs who have and they loved the experience.

Craigslist (www.craigslist.org): List your skills under "Services" or "For sale" and make a list of projects you're capable of doing. For example, as a seamstress I'd list: custom clothing (skirts, dresses), custom accessories (scarves, bags), and custom home furnishings (pillows, blankets). Be descriptive, suggest jobs, you just might put project ideas into someone's head! Scan the "Gigs" section of Craigslist too - creative projects pop up there all the time.

Spread the word locally too. Ask shops if you can put ads in their window. Tell your family, friends, neighbors, and colleagues you're available for hire; you never know where a job might pop up.

Visual artists - sell your work on CafePress and Zazzle

Sites like CafePress (www.cafepress.com) and Zazzle (www.zazzle.com) allow artists to print images on stuff like mugs, t-shirts, and greeting cards. What does this mean to you? Take your coolest designs, print them on an iPhone case or set of stamps, and rake in some dough.

People can make a lot of money doing this - we're talking tens of thousands of dollars. Zazzle in particular loves helping indie artists make money. In fact, their goal is to employ "a million people a year" - that is, they want to help a million people a year make money selling items on Zazzle.

The best part? *This doesn't cost you a thing.* You don't have to print or ship anything, Zazzle and CafePress do it all for you. You just have to upload your design, determine the types of products for sale, and the price. When an item sells, they'll print it, ship it, and pay you directly. Now how easy is that?

Visual artists - join Behance

Post your portfolio on Behance (www.behance.net) to share your work with the world. Not only is it great for networking, but it's fantastic exposure - companies search Behance for potential employees plus there are thousands of creative jobs posted too.

Visual artists - license your work

I am not an authority on this subject, so if this interests you, speak with a licensing attorney to learn more about it. Licensing your work can be a lucrative way to make cash from your art. Lots of companies are constantly searching for art to feature on their next skateboard, t-shirt, greeting card, or toy.

There are two ways to get paid: an upfront flat fee (they pay you once to use your image forever) or a royalty agreement, in which you get a small percentage of each item sold. There are a lot of legal considerations to consider such as copyrights, reproduction rights, ownership, and terms of agreement. Try an online search for "How to license your art" or "Companies interested in licensing art" to get this journey started. Hello Craft's book *Handmade to Sell* has a great story about one couple's experience licensing to Urban Outfitters and other outlets. *The Craft Artist's Legal Guide* by Attorney Richard Stim has excellent advice about licensing too.

Visual artists - sell in galleries

It's tough to break into professional galleries, so start your career at unconventional locations like coffee shops, restaurants, bars, and retail stores. Try your luck at smaller galleries too, particularly those who support burgeoning local artists. Make a list of potential venues and contact them for submission guidelines. Look for group shows, they're easier to get into than persuading someone to give you a solo show.

Include high-resolution pictures of your work on a clean, white background. Photograph straight on and include close-ups. Be consistent with picture orientation (horizontal vs. vertical), image color, and overall composition for the most pleasing "flipbook" effect. Revisit Chapter 6 for more photography advice and Chapter 10 for tips on writing a winning application.

If a gallery accepts your work, examine the contract carefully. Who is responsible for shipping costs? Does the gallery accept responsibility if any damages occur during display? How long will your work be exhibited? Check out the commission fees too - galleries usually take 50% of each sale. Understand the full terms of the deal before signing a contract or turning over your work.

Craft artists - become a craft designer

Craft designers are paid to create new craft ideas. Most manufacturers love hearing about new ways to use their products. Have you designed a new craft project using their materials? Let the company know and they might feature you in their next catalogue. Similarly, contact craft companies and popular craft blogs too - they're always hunting for new craft talent.

Crafters and Makers - apply to The Grommet

If you make an especially unique or useful product, apply to be a Grommet. The Grommet (www.thegrommet.com) is based in Somerville, MA and they're a product launch platform – they find undiscovered products and help them succeed. The Grommet is all about supporting Makers and they have a large pool of customers at their fingertips. Plus, in the summer of 2014 they launched a wholesale initiative to "connect independent Makers with Main Street retailers." Check out their curated collection of products to see all the neat inventions your fellow Makers are selling on The Grommet. If you think your products would be a good fit for the website, apply to be a Grommet yourself.

Teach a class

This is a great way to make extra income with your skills. People have probably asked how you do what you do; teach a class and show them!

Don't be afraid to show people your creative secrets. Remember in Chapter 8 we talked about Martha Stewart? She built an empire by giving away secrets. *Sharing secrets is good for business* - you'll make more money in the long run, trust me.

It takes a lot of work to get a class together. You have to think about projects, instructions, supplies, location, fee, and marketing strategy. Create projects that are easy to understand and make. Find locations that might support your event like a community center, craft store, workshop, or even a library or local church. You could also try to teach at community colleges (apply four months in advance) or conventions (apply six months in advance). List the items used in the class to warn potential students who might be allergic or sensitive to the materials (like solvents, paints, and glue).

If you teach at a store, incorporate products that are sold in that shop. People will inevitably want to purchase something they used in the project, and store owners appreciate you promoting their products.

Sell your patterns

Think of this like a mini-version of teaching a class. Create tutorials about making some of your products, package them up in a pdf, and sell them on your website or Etsy shop. Even better - sell kits that include the pattern and materials. There are loads of indie artists making big bucks like this - you should get in on the fun too.

If you sell patterns and kits, start with something easy to make. Write down step-by-step instructions and take lots of pictures. Remember to label the tutorials "Easy," "Medium," and "Expert."

•PRO TIP• Make a video of some of the steps and include links in the tutorial. Not only does this help your students, but it's great for marketing too. Check out the *Video* section of Chapter 13 for advice on making videos.

Still not comfortable sharing your trade secrets? That's fine - create something totally new that complements your product line and make a tutorial about that.

Host a trunk show

Trunk shows are special events usually held at a retail store. You and the shop owner agree on a date, time, and commission if you're splitting the sales. Coordinate your marketing efforts to attract a larger group. Send out emails, create postcards, announce on social media, tell the local press, have a crazy promotion ... do whatever you can to get people in the door.

Participate in house parties

You know the drill - someone hosts a party, people come over and buy things, the host gets free stuff. Tupperware, Mary Kay, and many other companies built their name on this sales channel.

Can you bring your fabulous products and sales pitch to someone's house? If so, advertise those services on your website, Craigslist, and local venues. The parties can even have a theme – eThreads has participated in design-your-own-bag bridal showers, bachelorette parties, and birthdays parties.

Pump up your house parties by partnering with multiple artists. Maybe you can even host your own party together and attract five times the amount of customers. Invite shop owners or local media to these events for extra marketing opportunities.

Affiliate marketing

Affiliates are people who work on commission to sell your product. They typically charge 50% commission, but you can find affiliates who charge less. Affiliates work day and night attracting customers to your business and they're incentivized because they get paid when you do. Create your own affiliate marketing relationships (like working with popular blogs) or hire professionals like ClickBank (www.clickbank.com) and Commission Junction (www.cj.com) to find affiliates for you.

Sell at trade shows

Also known as "wholesale shows," these massive events are usually held at convention centers or large hotels. Each show caters to a specific market like crafts, jewelry, gift, art, accessories, fabric, pets, etc... The attendees are usually wholesalers or professional buyers from small boutiques and large chain stores.

It's expensive and time-consuming to do a trade show. The tiniest booth will likely cost at least $1,000. Add in display and travel expenses and you're spending thousands of dollars for a 3-5 day show. It takes months to prepare a display, make the product, design printed materials, and promote the event.

Trade shows have a lot of advantages too. The buyers are serious and the sales can be huge. If you work a trade show, here's a few things to keep in mind:

(1) Keep the display simple - let your products be the star. Focus on a clean presentation, good lighting, and descriptive signage. See Chapter 10 for more display ideas.

(2) If it's your first show, bring prototypes to see what the buyers respond to. Don't waste your time making lots of product that no one eventually wants.

(3) Bring your line sheet (from Chapter 12), product catalogue, press kit (from Chapter 16), order forms, product/material samples, and mailing list.

(4) Be clear on lead time and terms. If a wholesaler likes your product, don't get so excited that you agree to unrealistic terms. Give yourself enough time and money to complete the order (the average wholesale delivery time is 4-6 weeks).

(5) Promote the show ahead of time. Make a list of potential buyers, influential bloggers, and members of the press and tell them you'll be at the show. Host a contest or offer an incentive for visiting the booth, like free samples.

The largest and most well-attended trade shows for arts and crafts are *ACRE* (American Craft Retailers Expo), *The American Made Show* (from the Buyers Market of American Craft), Craft and Hobby Association's *Mega Show*, and the *Pool Trade Show* put on by MAGIC. Designers and visual artists should also check out *SOFA* (Sculptural Objects and Functional Art) and *Surtex* in New York City.

There are trade shows for everything, like the *National Stationery Show* in New York City and the *JCK* jewelry show in Las Vegas, NV. Start an internet search for your medium + "trade show" to find one for you.

New York International Gift Fair (NYIGF)

This is the trade show to end all trade shows. Held twice a year in New York City, the NYIGF has been known to turn indie artists into household names overnight. NYIGF jurists are looking for eye-catching product lines with a wide price range to appeal to the largest market. This show is competitive, expensive, and lucrative if you can get in. Any sales representative worth their salt has a booth at the NYIGF, so if you've got a good sales rep you're probably already in the show.

Hire a sales representative

Is it too overwhelming to work a trade show yourself? Hire a sales rep to do it for you. Sales reps are like affiliate marketers in the real world. They usually have a showroom, participate in all the major trade shows, and approach stores on your behalf. Some sales reps travel the country, others only represent certain regions.

Sales reps are great - if you can afford it. First, they usually take 15-20% of each sale - and remember, these are wholesale prices which are usually 50% less than retail prices. Then, they'll charge for displaying your products in their showroom. They might charge additional commission fees or ask you to reimburse travel expenses. You'll often have to provide free samples too.

I don't want to sound foreboding because sales reps are great for business, just understand they come with a lot of responsibility. Check out Attorney Richard Stim's book *The Craft Artist's Legal Guide* for excellent advice about finding and hiring sales reps.

Travel to craft shows

A lot of indie artists make their living traveling to the best shows in the country. If that sounds like the life for you, start an internet search for "best craft shows in the United States." Here's some big ones to get started:

American Craft Council Shows (www.craftcouncil.org/shows) are annual juried events in Baltimore, Atlanta, St. Paul, and San Francisco featuring over 1,500 artisans from around the country.

American Made Show (www.americanmadeshow.com, from *Buyers Market of American Craft*) is now operating out of Washington, D.C. and continues their 30-year tradition of showcasing the finest in arts and crafts.

Bazaar Bizarre (www.bazaarbizarre.org) started in Boston in 2001 and has since expanded to Cleveland and San Francisco. This is "not your Granny's craft fair" - it's offbeat, unusual, and a lot of fun.

BUST Craftacular (www.bust.com/craftacular/bust-craftacular-home.html) is sponsored by *BUST* magazine and their NYC Craftacular is the city's oldest semi-annual juried craft fair and indie shopping event. You'll also find Craftaculars in Boston, Los Angeles, and London.

CraftBoston (www.societyofcrafts.org) was founded by the Society of Arts and Crafts, a national non-profit and the country's oldest craft organization. CraftBoston is held twice a year and is considered one of New England's premier craft shows.

Philadelphia Craft Show (www.pmacraftshow.org) is held once a year to benefit the Philadelphia Museum of Art and to support local exhibitions and educational programs.

Renegade Craft Fair (www.renegadecraft.com) originally started in Chicago in 2003. There are now Renegade shows in London, Brooklyn, Chicago, Austin, San Francisco, and Los Angeles attended by over 250,000 people a year.

Smithsonian Craft Show (www.smithsoniancraftshow.org) is held annually in Washington, D.C. This prestigious juried show features fine arts and crafts.

There are hundreds of other excellent shows including *Maker Faire* (Washington, D.C.), *American Craft Exposition* (Evanston, IL), *Crafty Wonderland* (Portland, OR), *One of a Kind* (Chicago, IL), *Crafty Bastards* (Washington, D.C.), *Art Star Craft Bazaar* (Philadelphia, PA), *Indie Craft Experience* (Atlanta, GA), *Urban Craft Uprising* (Seattle, WA), *Craftin' Outlaws* (Columbus, OH), *Crafty Supermarket* (Cincinnati, OH), *Coconut Grove Arts Festival* (Coconut Grove, FL), *Scottsdale Arts Festival* (Scottsdale, AZ), *La Quinta Arts Festival* (La Quinta, CA), *Bayou City Art Festival* (Houston, TX), *Best of the Northwest* (Seattle, WA), *Festival of Arts* (Laguna Beach, CA), *Little*

Falls Arts and Crafts Fair (Little Falls, MN), and *Wausau Festival of Arts* (Wausau, WI). Ask your fellow crafters on forums too. They'll tell you the inside scoop on all the big shows.

Celebrity gifting suites

Want to get your product in the hands of celebrities? Unless you have an inside contact, don't send anything directly to them - it'll never get past their agent's mailroom. Instead, contact celebrities by participating in a gifting suite.

These events usually happen in Los Angeles from September through March and they're particularly popular during award season in January and February. Celebrities attend gifting suites to get free stuff in exchange for taking pictures with the product. PR firms put these events together - they find the location, hire photographers, attract celebrities, court magazine editors to mention the gift bags, and coordinate the actual gifts.

The first time I was approached to do a Hollywood gifting suite, I told my friend and she said, "How much are they paying you?" I laughed so hard I almost cried. No, no, no, *you pay* to participate in a gifting suite, and you pay *big time.*

Just how much? Well, it's usually about $2,500 to have your name mentioned in the program. To get a table at the event you'll have to pony up at least $5,000, but it's usually closer to $10,000. You can pay up to $25,000 to have your name all over the event - but let's be serious, none of us are doing that. Oh yeah, and you'll have to pay to get there and figure out a display.

On top of paying fees, you have to supply product - and lots of it. At minimum you'll have to give away 100 items, but it could be up to 400. These goodies go in gift bags and are sent to VIPs, celebrities, and magazine editors.

If you're approached by a PR firm or find one on your own, ask for a list of celebrities who have attended past events and a list of invited media contacts. Also strategize about how to leverage the event for more press - these kinds of things can turn into priceless publicity if you spin it right.

Continuously improve your sales process

Review your Google and Etsy analytics - which products or pages are most popular? Where are people leaving your website? Why are people abandoning their shopping carts?

Study the stats and see if there are ways to improve your sales process. Can you cut out sales steps? Write better descriptions? Provide more photographs? Change your store policies? Always look for ways to improve your products and sales process.

Survey your customers

People are scared about soliciting customer feedback because they don't want to hear anything negative. I understand, but I have to state the obvious here: *you're in business to serve your customers and if they're unhappy, you're out of business.* Also, people are more likely to share negative experiences than positive ones, so don't you want to stop negative talk before it starts? Truth is, negative feedback is great because it helps pinpoint exactly where your business can improve.

Get regular feedback from customers. It makes them feel valuable and builds loyalty. Also, customer insight is vital – learn what they love, what they hate, and what they'd like to see next. Social media is a powerful tool for product research, but so is a simple survey. There are many types of surveys:

(1) *Customer satisfaction:* What did your customer expect and did you deliver on it? Send this survey just after they've received the product – you'll get a fresh reaction.

(2) *Customer dissatisfaction:* You have lots of one-time customers who never returned. What did you do to let them down? This survey gives valuable feedback – you'll win old customers back and prevent losing more in the future.

(3) *New product design:* You're developing a prototype and need feedback on the design. Who better to ask than the people who buy your products? Send this survey during the development process and create a product your customers will love.

(4) *Regular check in:* Send this every six months to take a temperature on your business and get key market insight. Discover your customers – who they are, where they shop, and how they found you. Properly-worded questions produce very insightful results.

It's easy to send surveys. We use SurveyMonkey (www.survey monkey.com), but there are dozens of options out there. Create an account, write your first survey, and send it to your customers via social media and email. Here's some tips for survey writing:

(1) *Be direct and specific about the purpose of your survey.* "The purpose of this survey is to understand your recent experience designing a bag on eThreads.com."

(2) *Keep your questions short and specific.* Don't be vague. "How long did it take for your bag to arrive?" is better than, "Did your bag arrive in a timely manner?"

(3) *Keep the survey short and manageable.* Make it 10 questions or less. The longer the survey, the less feedback you'll receive.

(4) *Be objective and unbiased.* Ask neutral questions. "Were you satisfied with your experience?" is better than "Tell us how satisfied you were with your experience."

(5) *Offer an incentive.* You want a large pool of feedback, so offer an incentive like a coupon, free gift, or entry into a drawing to boost survey participation.

(6) *Limit open-ended questions.* People don't respond well to blank boxes. Use multiple choice or "On a scale of 1 to 10" formats instead.

> **•PRO TIP•** Ask your customers what search terms they'd use to find you. This is excellent insight for branding and marketing. Here's how I phrase it on my surveys, "Imagine your friend just told you about eThreads. You go home to check it out but forgot the name. Oh no! What words do you type into a search engine?"

Once your survey is sent, compile the data and analyze it. Develop a plan of action based on feedback. Use it to guide short- and long-term decision making.

Surveys make your products more effective and ad campaigns more productive. They help uncover new target markets. Your customers are telling you how to make money – listen to them!

CONCLUSION

"Discipline is choosing between what you want now and what you want most."
> **- Augusta F. Kantra**

Well hello again! You made it to the end of the book! Quite a journey, wasn't it?

Listen, I spared no expense here - you have now learned everything you need to know about starting a creative business and making it thrive. As you see, it isn't pretty. It takes a lot of work, perseverance, and grit.

Let me tell you though, there's no greater feeling than making a sale. Sharing your talent with the world, getting appreciation for it, and making money to boot … well, it just makes you feel like sunshine. I want all of you to have that experience a thousand times over, so I'm here to help you get there.

Contact me anytime with questions or for a swift kick in the pants. I have coached many creative entrepreneurs and I love to help; I'm known as the "the Maker Maker" for a reason. If you're on Twitter, follow me for daily business tips (www.twitter.com/eMakeitHappen) and check out my website for more business resources. Finally, if you have a special story, resource, or tip that you'd like to share, tell me about it and it might be included in the next edition!

Thank you for reading this book and being an intrepid entrepreneur. I can't wait to hear your success stories.

Emily Worden
emily@emilyworden.com
Twitter: @eMakeitHappen
www.emilyworden.com
www.makesellrepeat.com

ACKNOWLEDGEMENTS

This book would not be possible without the support of my family:

To my husband Case: Thank you for editing, designing, and overall being so darn smart and handsome. You are the perfect partner in crime and I'm a lucky lady to know you.

To my sister Jessica: Thank you for your endless hours of editing, cheerleading, and belief in the impossible. We always do things the hard way and we're so much better for it.

To my mom Barbara: Thank you for teaching me strength, tenacity, and a love of creativity. You taught me how to sew and my world has not been the same since.

To my dad Mark: Thank you for teaching me to think, imagine, and "Make it happen." You circuitously helped me write this book and I carry your spirit with me every day.

Appendix A: **RESOURCES**

There are over 100 resources listed in this book. Here is a collection of the most important resources, alphabetized by category with their accompanying chapters. To learn more about using each resource, read the corresponding chapter.

2D and 3D printing (from Ch. 1)

One of my favorite sites is Ponoko (www.ponoko.com), which can cut any shape out of nearly any material. You can buy the materials through Ponoko then sell the finished items right on their site. Similarly, Thingiverse (www.thingiverse.com) by MakerBot prints an unbelievable array of 3D objects designed by people like you and sold directly on their site.

Accounting and bookkeeping (from Ch. 2)

Track all your sales and expenses with a simple Excel sheet, Google Docs spreadsheet, www.mint.com, or use professional accounting software like Quickbooks. Attend a bookkeeping, Quickbooks, or accounting class at your local community college or adult learning center. Also talk to an accountant or professional bookkeeper who specializes in small business, especially your first year in business. For more information from a tax expert, read *Etsy-preneurship* by Jason Malinak. He is a CPA and Certified Treasury Professional who specializes in taxes for creative types like yourself.

Alternatives to Etsy (from Ch. 11)

aftcra (www.aftcra.com) is focused exclusively on American-made handcrafted products. The family-owned Milwaukee-based site prides itself on customer service, responsiveness, and listening to their buyers and sellers. There are no listing fees, instead aftcra keeps 7% of each transaction.

ArtFire (www.artfire.com) attracts artisans and buyers from all over the world looking for handmade, vintage, art, or craft supplies. They have a great *Setup for Success* guide plus an active forum and blog. Instead of charging listing and commission fees, Artfire charges $12.95/month to be a seller on their site.

Bonanza (www.bonanza.com) was formerly known as Bonanzle, then it acquired 1000 Markets in 2010 and changed its name to Bonanza. Sellers say the site is easier to use than eBay, Amazon, and Etsy and Bonanza lets you easily import your listings from those sites. There are no listing fees, instead Bonanza collects a commission fee of 3.5% for items under $500 or 1.5% + $17.50 for items over $500.

DaWanda (www.dawanda.com) is based in Germany but many American sellers use it too. With detailed search options and a great "Gift Ideas" section, DaWanda makes selling fun and easy. There are no listing fees and DaWanda keeps 10% of each transaction.

Storenvy (www.storenvy.com) offers great analytics and every listed item gets included in the Storenvy marketplace. There are no charges to sell items on Storeenvy. Once you open a shop you can choose to add $5 options like a custom domain name or super discount codes.

Supermarket (www.supermarkethq.com) is bursting with beautiful products. Because the site is curated, you'll have to apply to open a shop. There are no listing fees and Supermarket keeps 10% of each transaction.

Zibbet (www.zibbet.com) If you already have an Etsy shop, Zibbet makes it easy to copy those listings onto your Zibbet shop. There are no listing or commission fees. Instead, you pay $0/month for up to 10 items (1 photograph/item), $4/month for up to 50 items (4 photographs/item), and $8/month for unlimited items, 8 pictures/item, plus important features like coupons and gift certificates.

Blogs (from Ch. 6)

Blogs are usually published through Wordpress (www.wordpress.com), Tumblr (www.tumblr.com), Typepad (www.typepad.com), or Blogger (www.blogger.com/features), among others. Many of the DIY website services listed at the end of this appendix have blog capabilities too.

Children's products (from Ch. 3)

The Consumer Products Safety Improvement Act of 2013 imposes strict guidelines for producing children's products ("children" is defined as anyone 12 years old or younger). There are also new requirements for manufacturers of apparel, shoes, personal care products, jewelry, accessories, toys, and probably anything else you'd want to make. It's worth checking out, especially if you're making products for children: (www.cpsc.gov/en/Regulations-Laws--Standards/Statutes/The-Consumer-Product-Safety-Improvement-Act/)

Email marketing (from Ch. 13)

Create multiple email addresses for your business like "sales@mybusiness.com," "customerservice@mybusiness.com," and "contact@mybusiness.com." Use Google Apps for business (www.google.com/enterprise/apps/business) for $5/month to set up all these accounts and forward to just one email address. Create an email sign up form with WuFoo (www.wufoo.com) to include on your website. Once you have more than 100 people on your mailing list, consider enrolling with a CRM (customer relationship management) service like MailChimp (www.mailchimp.com), Constant Contact (www.constantcontact.com), or AWeber (www.aweber.com). They all start at about $15/month.

Health insurance (from Ch. 2)

Yes, you can get affordable health insurance as a freelance indie artist - it's possible through an artist guild or similar association. Check out membership organizations like the American Craft Council (www.craftcouncil.org/membership/join), the Craft and Hobby Association (www.craftandhobby.org), and the Freelancers Union (www.freelancersunion.org). The Artists' Health Insurance Resource Center (www.ahirc.org) is filled with helpful advice too.

Hiring graphic designers and programmers (from Ch. 5)

If you need help on your website, logo design, business card design, or other similar issues, search freelance sites like Elance (www.elance.com), 99 Designs (www.99designs.com), Crowdspring (www.crowdspring.com), oDesk (www.odesk.com), Craigslist (www.craigslist.org), or inquire on Etsy forums and groups. Ask for their portfolio and check references.

Legal help (from Ch. 2)

Communities usually have a law library at the local university that offers free legal days or legal aid clinics. Local law schools often offer free legal clinics to the community too. You might find an attorney for free through SCORE (www.score.org); there are over 1,500 business experts providing free advice, including lawyers. Finally, check out Volunteer Lawyers for the Arts (www.vlany.org); they specialize in pro bono legal advice for artists and crafters.

Niche (from Ch. 3)

You can't be everything to everyone, so don't even try. Find your niche group(s) and develop products to satisfy their wants, needs, and desires. Study these resources to get product ideas for your niche:

eBay Popular (popular.ebay.com): View the most popular items selling on eBay. This gives you an idea of what people really want - find a way for your products to fit in there.

Amazon Best Sellers (www.amazon.com/Best-Sellers/zgbs): Just like eBay, you can view the most popular items on Amazon to get a good idea of what people are really buying.

CraftCount (www.craftcount.com): This site lists the top performing Etsy shops by category and it's updated every 24 hours.

Etsy search (www.Etsy.com): Search your category (e.g., crochet) and examine different shops' statistics like items sold and customer reviews. Study the most popular items, including photographs, descriptions, prices, and product feedback.

Google Trends (www.google.com/trends): Search any word, term, or phrase (up to 5 per search) and see how popular it's been over 30 days or several years. Add words to narrow your search or see how they compete with each other (e.g., crochet vs. knitting).

Google Analytics (www.google.com/analytics): This free service gives you in-depth analysis of your website's performance. This type of information may help define your niche. See Chapter 6 for more details about Google Analytics.

Organization (from Ch. 1)

Use Evernote and Google Docs for online organization. Evernote (www.evernote.com) gathers all your pictures, files, notes, and web pages in one easily accessible place from a computer, tablet, or smartphone. Google Docs (www.docs.google.com) is Google's version of Microsoft Office and it's free with a Gmail account. Create documents, spreadsheets, forms, and slide presentations that are easily searchable and automatically saved to the cloud.

Photo editing (from Ch. 6)

Free online tools to make your product photographs professional and appealing:

PicMonkey (www.picmonkey.com): They make photo editing really easy and intuitive and there's tons of great editing features.

Photoscape (www.photoscape.org): It has cool features like combining photographs, splitting images, and batch processing.

Photoshop Online (www.photoshop.com/tools): Not only is this version free, but it's easier to use than the real Photoshop software.

Press (from Ch. 16)

Press release distribution: There are lots of free websites to publish your press releases, like www.prnewswire.com, www.businesswire.com, www.globenewswire.com, and www.marketwire.com. Paid sites offer wider distribution and access to quality VIPs, I like PRWeb (www.prweb.com) starting at $99/year.

Help a Reporter Out (HARO) (www.helpareporter.com): Get in contact directly with top journalists and writers. Sign up for HARO and get daily emails filled with inquiries from reporters, authors, bloggers, and TV producers.

Printing services (from Ch. 13)

Avoid the sites that give you free business cards. The paper quality is poor and they might advertise on the back side. Use Moo (www.moo.com) to print different product photographs on the back of each card. I like Green Printer (www.greenprinteronline.com) because they use recycled paper and vegetable-based inks that are high-quality and affordable. Overnight Prints (www.overnightprints.com) is also a quality printer with paper sourced from sustainable forests.

Researching and registering a domain name (from Ch. 5)

Search available domain names with WhoIs (www.whois.net) or Network Solutions (www.networksolutions.com). If you want a website, you'll also need a web host. Most domain name registrars also provide hosting services. If you use one of the DIY website resources listed at the end of this appendix, the hosting is done for you.

For those hosting on their own, Media Temple (www.mediatemple.com) is very reliable but a little more expensive than others. When you're starting out you can go with cheaper options. Do an internet search for "Top 10 cheapest web hosts" and read the customer reviews. You'll find something for $7-$10/month.

Shipping (from Ch.3)

It's easy to ship from home - you just need a postage scale ($30) and shipping labels. Get shipping labels from Online Labels (www.onlinelabels.com), they're half the cost of anything at office supply stores. Ship online with the United States Postal Service (www.USPS.com), Stamps.com (www.stamps.com), or Endicia (www.endicia.com).

Social media (from Ch. 14)

Schedulers: Hootsuite (www.hootsuite.com) is a free and useful resource to schedule Facebook, Twitter, and Instagram feeds. If you have an Etsy shop, try Promotesy (www.promotesy.com/home) for $5/month to easily integrate your Etsy shop items into your social media feeds.

Hashtags: See what's popular right now with What the Trend (www.whatthetrend.com). Use Trendsmap (www.trendsmap.com) to view popular hashtags by location, which is great for local businesses and special events. Use Hashtagify (www.hashtagify.me) to find popular hashtags in your industry.

Shorten links: Use URL shorteners to cut the length of links in half and save valuable characters. My favorite site is Bit.ly (www.bit.ly)

but there are lots of other options. Social media schedulers like Hootsuite (www.hootsuite.com) or Tweetdeck (www.tweetdeck.com) have built-in link shorteners too.

Support services (from Ch. 1)

Are you stuck on a business problem? Need help with your business plan? Looking for advice on manufacturing tips or craft shows? There are loads of resources for business advice from professionals and fellow crafters:

The Society of Arts and Crafts (www.societyofcrafts.org): Founded in 1897 in Boston, The SAC is a national non-profit and the country's oldest craft organization.

The Craft Mafia (www.craftmafia.com): Founded in 2003 by nine women in Austin, TX who formed a group around the shared love of craft. It has since grown into an active forum with networks all over the country.

Meetups (www.meetup.com): An awesome website allowing local people with all sorts of interests to meet and socialize together. It's a great place to find fellow creative people in your area.

Etsy Forums (www.etsy.com/forums): If you have a question about running an indie business, it has probably already been asked and answered in an Etsy forum.

Hello Craft (www.hellocraft.com): The fine folks behind Hello Craft are dedicated to empowering indie artists and advancing the handmade movement.

Handmadeology (www.handmadeology.com): A valuable resource that teaches artists how to successfully sell their handmade goods.

Ravelry (www.ravelry.com): A massive online support community focused entirely on fiber arts.

Indiemade (www.indiemade.com): An excellent resource for building your artist website cheaply and easily, Indiemade is also packed with tips for indie artists.

Craft and Hobby Association (www.craftandhobby.org): An excellent resource for networking and business advice.

SCORE (www.score.org): Free business mentoring advice provided by over 1,500 volunteers in the United States.

U.S. Small Business Administration (www.sba.gov): The SBA has advice on starting and managing your business plus information on loans and grants.

Women- and minority-owned businesses. Check out www.MWBE.com to start, it's packed with tips about starting a business and special grants. There are lots of blogs and networking sites for women business owners too, like www.indiebizchicks.com, www.theswitchboards.com, and www.sheownsit.com.

Craftster (www.craftster.com): This is a HUGE online community for DIY and crafts.

Makezine (www.makezine.com): From the publishers of *Make: Magazine* and pioneers of the Maker Movement.

Telephone (from Ch. 2)

Your cell phone number is fine for business, but it's better (and more professional) to have a dedicated phone line. Try Kall8 (www.kall8.com), where toll-free numbers start at $2/month. Thousands of businesses rely on MagicJack (www.magicjack.com), after you buy their $50 adapter plans start at $3/month. If you use Gmail you can get a free phone number from Google Voice (www.google.com/voice) and make calls with their cell phone app. Of course there's always Skype (www.skype.com) and Vonage (www.vonage.com) too.

Video making tools (from Ch. 13)

If you're making informational videos, you could just talk over a PowerPoint. Try CamStudio (www.camstudio.org) or Jing (www.techsmith.com/download/jing) for free screen capture software. Edit your content with free video editing software. Try Windows Movie Maker or Kate's Video Toolkit (search online for "Windows Movie Maker" or "Kate's Video Toolkit" to find a free download button, they're everywhere). When the video is finished, upload it to YouTube (www.youtube.com) and/or the other popular video site Vimeo (www.vimeo.com).

Website DIY (from Ch. 13)

Here's a list of businesses that make creating your own website really easy:

(1) *Squarespace* (www.squarespace.com): If you're selling more than 1 item, you'll want the "Professional" plan ($16/month for 20 items) or the "Business" plan ($24/month for unlimited items).

(2) *IndieMade* (www.indiemade.com): Starts at $4.95/month to sell 10 items. These fine folks really support indie artists, there's tons of great resources on their site too.

(3) *Big Cartel* (www.bigcartel.com): You'll likely want the "Platinum" ($9.99/month for 25 products) or "Diamond" plan ($19.99/month for 100 products).

(4) *Storenvy* (www.storenvy.com): Build an online store and sell in the Storenvy marketplace at the same time. There are no monthly costs, however once you open a shop you can choose to add $5/month options like a custom domain name or super discount codes.

(5) *Weebly* (www.weebly.com): You'll want the "Business" plan for $25/month, it's the only plan that services e-commerce.

(6) *Wix* (www.wix.com): It's free to create a website with Wix. However, if you want a shopping cart, you'll have to choose the "eCommerce" plan starting at $16.17/month.

(7) *Goodsie* (www.goodsie.com): Prices change depending if you're a monthly, bi-annual, or annual subscriber, between $25-$30/month for the cheapest option.

(8) *Carbonmade* (www.carbonmade.com): Strictly a portfolio site for visual artists, no shopping cart support. It's free to join up to 35 images. Then it's $12/month for 500 images and 10 videos.

Appendix B: **SUGGESTED READING**

Books about Sales and Persuasion

Influence: The Psychology of Persuasion by Robert B. Cialdini, Ph.D: If you only read one book about persuasion, influence, or sales, it has to be this book. Robert B. Cialdini explains the psychology of why people say "yes" - and how to use this knowledge in your daily life. It's the classic persuasion book that will leave you astounded and empowered.

Yes! 50 Scientifically Proven Ways to Be Persuasive by Noah J. Goldstein, Steve J. Martin, and Robert B. Cialdini: This short, easy-to-read book is packed with useful advice to get anyone to say "Yes!" It's surprisingly easy to persuade people - this books shows you how.

Win the Crowd: Unlock the Secrets of Influence, Charisma and Showmanship by Steve Cohen, The Millionaire's Magician: Are you nervous about making sales? This book is for you. Steve Cohen is a master magician and shares his showman secrets to persuade, influence, and charm a crowd. He will show you how to shed insecurities and take charge of a situation, whether you're in a job interview or attending a cocktail party.

Predictably Irrational: The Hidden Forces That Shape Our Decisions by Dan Ariely: This *New York Times* bestseller helps us understand why we do things and the decision-making process behind it. Dan Ariely refutes the common assumption that we behave in fundamentally rational ways and instead proves that we consistently make irrational decisions. A must-read for anyone interested in marketing, selling, or learning about human behavior.

Million Dollar Habits: Proven Power Practices to Double and Triple Your Income by Brian Tracy: Successful business owners are efficient, effective, and productive. Anyone can be this way by building the right habits. Brian Tracy outlines easy-to-follow steps to build habits that increase your income and improve overall well-being.

Books about Starting and Growing a Creative Business

The Right-Brain Business Plan by Jennifer Lee: An excellent book that demystifies business planning and dare I say ... makes it fun. Lee speaks in a language creative people understand; this is an enjoyable and useful resource for planning a business.

The Craft Artist's Legal Guide: Protect Your Work, Save on Taxes, Maximize Profits by Attorney Richard Stim: This book should be on your shelf next to the *Right-Brain Business Plan*. It's loaded with easy-to-understand legal tips for creative entrepreneurs including advice on hiring employees, getting paid, and what to do if your work is copied without permission. There's dozens of useful sample forms too, including consignment, non-disclosure, and partnership agreements.

Etsy-preneurship: Everything You Need to Know to Turn Your Handmade Hobby into a Thriving Business by Jason Malinak: This is a great resource from a CPA and Certified Treasury Professional who specializes in tax issues for creative entrepreneurs. Jason Malinak shares insightful bookkeeping, tax, and financial advice plus downloadable tools to get your business finances in order.

Shark Tales: How I Turned $1,000 into a Billion Dollar Business by Barbara Corcoran: For those of you looking to be inspired, entertained, and schooled, this book is for you. Barbara Corcoran is a real estate mogul, an investor on ABC's *Shark Tank*, and partner in many successful businesses. Learn how this self-made millionaire built her empire through humor, determination, and a lot of creative thinking.

How to Start a Creative Business: The Jargon-Free Guide for Creative Entrepreneurs by Doug Richard: This book is packed with Richard's insightful advice as a successful entrepreneur, investor, and founder of the UK-based *School for Creative Startups*.

The Crafty Superstar Ultimate Craft Business Guide by Grace Dobush: This book is filled with handy guides and worksheets for starting your business plus insider advice from successful creative entrepreneurs. I especially like the *Customer Profiling Worksheet* and *Sales Tax Cheat Sheet*.

216

Grow Your Handmade Business: How to Envision, Develop, and Sustain a Successful Creative Business by Kari Chapin: A practical business guide for creative people looking to grow their business, from the author of *The Handmade Marketplace*. Kari Chapin and her "creative collective" provide useful advice in a friendly, accessible way.

Handmade to Sell: Hello Craft's Guide to Owning, Running, and Growing Your Crafty Biz by Kelly Rand with Christine Ernest, Sara Dick, and Kimberly Dorn: *Hello Craft* is a fantastic nonprofit trade association dedicated to helping crafty entrepreneurs succeed. This book is written by the directors of *Hello Craft* based on their annual business conference, *The Summit of Awesome* in Washington, DC.

Craft Inc: The Ultimate Guide to Turning Your Creative Hobby into a Successful Business by Meg Mateo Ilasco: This book has great tips for starting and running a business including dozens of stories from successful creative entrepreneurs. Meg Mateo Ilasco is a creative freelancer, entrepreneur, and author of several books including *Creative, Inc.* and *Mom, Inc.*

The Boss of You: Everything a Woman Needs to Know to Start, Run, and Maintain Her Own Business by Lauren Bacon and Emira Mears: This book is written for any woman who wants to start her own business, but men can enjoy it too. This easy-to-understand guide breaks down the process of starting and running a business including an in-depth look at financial concerns and employment needs.

Handmade Nation: The Rise of DIY, Art, Craft, and Design by Faythe Levine and Cortney Heimerl: Faythe Levine traveled 19,000 miles across the United States to document the DIY movement. She made a documentary film about the journey and wrote the book together with Cortney Heimerl (both the film and book are the same name). The book highlights the stories of dozens of artisans and provides inspirational tips for today's creative entrepreneur.

GLOSSARY

Asset: Anything you own that has value. For your business, it's likely your computer, printer, phone, camera, raw inventory, machines, tools, and available cash. Assets and liabilities are listed on your balance sheet.

Balance Sheet: A financial document listing your total assets and liabilities. It's a snapshot of your business; banks or investors will ask for your balance sheet to determine the financial health of your business.

Bootstrapping: The best way to fund the business is with your own finances, otherwise known as "bootstrapping."

Bounce Rate: The percentage of visitors who leave your website without clicking anything. A high bounce rate indicates your website is not "sticky" or engaging.

Capital: Capital is an asset and broadly includes money, machinery, equipment, and anything else needed to operate your business.

Cost of Goods Sold (COGS): The direct cost to make your product including materials, supplies, and labor. COGS does *not* include overhead costs like studio rental, telephone, or a sales team.

Elevator Speech: The summary of your business delivered in the time span of an elevator ride. An elevator speech is short, direct, includes your unique selling proposition, and the benefits your product provides.

Equity: The value of your business after liabilities and debts are paid. Equity includes profits, assets, and anything else of value.

Keywords: Words or phrases that describe your product or business. Keywords include those words people type into search engines. Keywords are important because they're used to help potential customers find you.

Liability: The opposite of asset, a liability is something you owe. It is an obligation, like credit card debt, advertising bills, or a pending wholesale order. Assets and liabilities are listed on your balance sheet.

Markup: The difference between the cost of making a product and the price charged for that product; often expressed as a percentage. For example, if your small soy candle costs $5 to produce and you charge $10, that is a 100% markup.

Niche: A niche is a specifically defined group of people who would benefit from using your product. In niche marketing, products are marketed differently for various niche groups.

Overhead Cost: The cost of running your business (not including the Cost of Goods Sold). For example, studio costs and promotional expenses are included in overhead costs while the cost for materials and labor are not (those are COGS).

Profit (also known as "income"): Profit is the difference between your revenue and costs. Profit may be "gross" (before expenses) or "net" (after expenses). You want to know the net income - it's the money your business made after all expenses are paid (including overhead costs and cost of goods sold).

Profit and Loss Statement: (Also known as a "P&L," "earnings statement," or "income statement.") This is a condensed version of your monthly income and expenditures. It has a running total of your income on one side and expenditures on another for information at a glance. P&Ls are usually categorized monthly or quarterly.

Quarter: A business fiscal year divided into four. Quarters end 3/31, 6/30, 9/30, and 12/31. This schedule is essential for filing quarterly taxes. For small businesses, it's easier to follow the calendar year and therefore start your fiscal year on 1/1. (Larger businesses sometimes start their fiscal year 7/1 while the federal government starts theirs 10/1, though they all follow the same quarterly schedule.)

Revenue (also known as "sales"): The money made from selling products or services. Revenue does not include expenses like overhead and cost of goods sold (that is called profit).

Sales Channel: An opportunity to sell to your customer. Sales channels are revenue streams and include website, Etsy, craft shows, wholesale orders, and retail stores.

Sales Tax License: (Also known as a "certificate of resale," "sellers permit," or "certificate of authority.") This certificate allows you to charge and collect sales tax for the state in which you're selling. In some states it's a criminal offense to operate without a sellers permit. *If you sell taxable goods, you need a sales tax license.*

Target Market: A group of customers who share a common need or desire that would be satisfied by your product or service. Well-defined target markets are critical for marketing strategy.

Unique Selling Proposition (USP): Also known as the Unique Value Proposition (UVP), this is what sets you apart from the competition. It's something you do that is different from everyone else and it should be part of your elevator speech. Whatever problem you're solving or niche you're serving, *that's* your USP.

INDEX

Search Engine Optimization (SEO),
  75-76, 80, 128, 150, 182
sellers permit, *See* sales tax license
shipping, 45-46, 88, 133, 136, 211
Skype, 28, 213
Small Business Association (SBA), 11,
  213
SMART goals, 8-9, 141-42
social media, 62, 84-85, 133, 143, 145,
  161-74, 211-12
social media formula, 168, 169
Social Proof, 100, 121, 159
Society of Arts and Crafts, 11,
  199, 212
Square Up, 88, 108
Squarespace, 68, 214
Stamps.com, 46, 211
Store Supply Warehouse, 111
Storenvy, 68, 207, 214
studio, 14, 191-92
Sunshine Artists, 104
Supermarket, 207
suppliers, 42, 50
surveys, 202-03
Switchboards, 11, 36, 213

T

Taxes, 22-23, 26, 28, 206, 219
  Federal Tax ID, 26
  sales tax, *See* sales tax license
teaching, 95, 145, 196
Thingiverse, 35, 206
Thomas Register of American
  Manufacturers, 42
trade name, *See* Doing Business As
  (DBA)
Trade Show News Network
  (TSNN), 42
trade shows, 42, 102, 136, 197-199
trademark, 39, 40-41, 62
Trendsmap, 170, 211
Tumblr, 79, 166, 173, 207
Tweetdeck, 171, 172, 212
Twitalyzer, 177
Twitter, 145, 161-63, 166, 170, 177,
  211
Typepad, 79, 207
224

U

United Parcel Service (UPS), 45-46, 88
United States Postal Service (USPS),
  45-46, 88, 211
Unique Selling Proposition (USP), 58,
  220
US Patent and Trademark Office
  (USPTO), 41, 62

V

videos, 94, 147-50, 184, 213
Vimeo, 150, 213
VIPs, 155, 173, 175-180, 182,
Volunteer Lawyers for the Arts
  (VLANY), 29, 209
Vonage, 28, 213

W

Walton, Sam, 83
website, 62, 67-81, 151, 187, 214
Weebly, 68, 214
What the Trend, 170, 211
WhoIs, 61, 211
wholesale, 42, 49-51, 133, 136, 138,
  139, 197-98
Windows Movie Maker, 150, 213
Wix, 68, 214
wordmark, *See* logotype
Wordpress, 79, 207
work/life balance, 12-13
workspace, *See* studio
Wufoo, 150, 208

Y

YouTube, 94, 147-50, 213

Z

Zazzle, 193-94
Zibbet, 127, 207

TRY A FREE COACHING SESSION

Do you want to make more money doing what you love? Sign up for a free coaching session with Emily Worden.

Emily helps business owners and creative entrepreneurs build thriving, profitable businesses. She is an expert at product design, pricing strategy, branding, marketing, sales, and social media. When you're ready to start a business or take it to the next level, Emily can coach you through it – she's called "the Maker Maker" for a reason.

Sign up for a free coaching session with Emily. Yes, it's really free, and there are no strings attached. You won't even hear a sales pitch. Instead, you'll have 30 minutes of Emily's undivided attention to ask her anything about your business. Do you feel stumped about sales, stuck on time management, or stalled over product design? Tell her about your business problem and she'll help you find a solution.

Sign up for a free 30-minute telephone coaching session with Emily at www.makesellrepeat.com or www.emilyworden.com. Bring a pen and paper – you'll finish the session with a list of practical advice for your business. For those who prefer a personal trainer to stay on track, Emily is available for regular coaching sessions. Meet with Emily through email, telephone, or Skype, and become a more efficient, effective, and profitable business owner. Contact emily@emilyworden.com for more information.

Here's to your success!

MAKE
SELL
REPEAT

The Ultimate Business Guide for
Artists, **Crafters**, and **Makers**

Do you know another **artist**, **crafter**, **maker**, or **entrepreneur** who would benefit from reading this book? Order them at copy at www.makesellrepeat.com, www.amazon.com, your local bookstore, or by contacting us below. eBook also available.

Universities, colleges, corporations, and **organizations**:
Discounts available on bulk purchases for educational, gifting, or fundraising purposes. Special books or book excerpts can be created to fit your specific needs. For more information, please contact Filament Press:

(617) 433-8882
contact@filamentpress.com
Filament Press
PO Box 400451
Cambridge, MA 02140

Emily Worden is available for speaking, coaching, and teaching opportunities. Potential topics include communication, leadership, sales, marketing, and customer psychology.
Contact Alix Abbamonte at Alix Abbamonte Public Relations:
(203) 613-5642, Alix@alixabbapr.com

St. Louis Community College
at Meramec
LIBRARY

CPSIA information can be obtained at www.ICGtesting.com
Printed in the USA
LVOW08s0207080815

449342LV00008B/196/P